Code Clone Analysis

Katsuro Inoue · Chanchal K. Roy
Editors

Code Clone Analysis

Research, Tools, and Practices

 Springer

Editors
Katsuro Inoue
Graduate School of Information Science
and Technology
Osaka University
Suita, Osaka, Japan

Chanchal K. Roy
Department of Computer Science
University of Saskatchewan
Saskatoon, SK, Canada

ISBN 978-981-16-1929-8   ISBN 978-981-16-1927-4   (eBook)
https://doi.org/10.1007/978-981-16-1927-4

This Springer imprint is published by the registered company Springer Nature Singapore Pte Ltd.
The registered company address is: 152 Beach Road, #21-01/04 Gateway East, Singapore 189721,
Singapore

Preface

Copy-and-paste is inevitable for any software development project. Code clones are generated by the copy-and-paste process and are one of the factors that make program maintenance difficult. Since the 1990s, numerous studies on code clones have been published, and many tools for code clone analysis have been developed. Code clone analysis has been applied not only to software development but also to other areas such as plagiarism detection and software evolution analysis. However, even with the expansion of these researches and applications, there has been no comprehensive book that summarizes the results. This book is the first attempt to make a collection of research, tools, and applications on code clone analysis.

Purpose

One of the important purposes of this book is to archive important results on the research, tools, and practices related to the code clone analysis. As shown in chapter "Introduction to Code Clone Analysis", there has been a great deal of interest in code clones, but there was no book to collect the results. This book contains the achievement of important tools and researches. Also, some of the practical applications of the code clone technologies are included. This book provides the reader with the basis of the code clone analysis, as well as the pointers to the various publications for the research and applications.

Code clone analysis is a very good topic to teach in university software engineering courses. It relies heavily on computer science theories such as pattern matching, source code analysis, and software metrics. On the other hand, the code clone analysis can be applied to a variety of tasks related to real-world software development and maintenance such as bug finding and program refactoring. It is possible to design an effective course that combines theory and application. We hope that this book will help to do so.

Organization

The study of code clones is very broad, and categorizing and organizing it all into a book is similar to organizing a book on computer science as a whole. We have therefore chosen to include in this book a selection of papers that have been published in the past and that are important to the progress of this field. Although a great many results related on code clone have been published so far, it was impossible to include them all in one book. This book presents only a part of them, and many other results are shown as references of each chapter.

The selected papers have been roughly categorized into three categories; tool, research, and practice. Each of the selected papers has been made into a single chapter with new results and future directions. In addition to these chapters, we have included an introductory chapter as chapter "Introduction to Code Clone Analysis" for beginners in code clone analysis. It defines "clones" and related terms, and discusses the type classification of clones. It also describes the process of code clone analysis and introduces possible applications.

Chapters from "CCFinderX: An Interactive Code Clone Analysis Environment" to "CCLearner: Clone Detection via Deep Learning" are mainly about code clone analysis tools. CCFinderX, NiCad, and SourcererCC are popularly used tools in researches and practices. Oreo and CCLearner are relatively new tools and have been developed with new objectives and analysis methods.

Chapters from "BigCloneBench" to "A Summary on the Stability of Code Clones and Current Research Trends" discuss the foundations and development of important research results; BigCloneBench is an important database that has been used to evaluate a number of tools. Clone visualization, code clone search, and code similarity are important research topics. Also, Late propagation and code clone stability are critical issues for program maintenance.

Chapters from "Identifying Refactoring-Oriented Clones and Inferring How They Can Be Merged" to "IWSC(D): From Research to Practice: A Personal Historical Retelling" discuss applications to actual problems. Refactoring cloned code is a problem that is often faced in practice. Projects need an efficient way to manage clone evolution. An important discussion on the design of software and clones is also presented. In addition, the experiences of a company actually providing the clone analysis technology are shown.

Target Audience

As described above, this book is a collection of important results of code clone analysis. Therefore, this book is a very good starting point for new research on code clones. Important results and findings can be found in this book. Various approaches to code clone analysis are described so that developers of new clone detectors can easily recognize and compare their advantages and disadvantages.

For practitioners who maintain old code and its consistency, code clone analysis is one of the useful engineering methods. This book presents some valuable use cases of code clone analysis.

This book is a good textbook for graduate-level software engineering courses, especially program analysis and software maintenance. In one lecture, each chapter is presented by a teacher or student, followed by a discussion of features and limitations. Most tools are provided as free software, and then experimenting with them is a good exercise for getting a deeper understanding of code clone analysis.

Acknowledgments

This book was planned by Inoue and Roy. Inoue had been concerned about the lack of books on code clone for many years, and after discussing it with Roy, we decided to create this book.

We are deeply grateful to all the authors, who, during the COVID-19 pandemic, carefully wrote their manuscripts and completed them on time.

We would also like to express our deepest gratitude to the pioneers of code clone technology. While we could not have included all of them in this book, this would not have been possible without their efforts. Their achievements can be seen in the bibliography of each chapter.

Osaka, Japan   Katsuro Inoue
Saskatoon, Canada   Chanchal K. Roy

Contents

Introduction to Code Clone

Introduction to Code Clone Analysis

Katsuro Inoue

Abstract Code Clone is a code snippet that has the same or similar code snippet in the same or different software system. The existence of code clones is an issue on software maintenance and a clue to understanding the structure and evolution of software systems. A large number of researches on code clones have been performed, and many tools for code clone analysis have been developed. In this chapter, we will explain some of the terms that are important for understanding code clones, such as definition, type, analysis granularity, and analysis domain. We will also outline the approaches and applications of code clone analysis.

1 What Is Code Clone?

Code snippet is a part of the program code in a source code file of a software system. Sometimes we duplicate a code snippet by a copy-and-paste action, modify the pasted snippet by changing the variable names, and execute both snippets inside the same or different software systems.

An intuitive definition of *code clone* is a code snippet having the same or similar code in the same or different software systems. Figure 1 is a part of the code generation program of a simple compiler written in Python. The code snippet from line 1211 to 1217 is similar to one from line 1219 to 1225, and they are code clones. Both snippets were probably made by a copy-and-paste action from one to another or from a different original snippet to those, with small modifications made to some identifiers and strings.

A pair of two code snippets that are the same or similar is called a *code clone pair* or simply *clone pair*, and it is an element of a *clone relation* over a set of all code snippets in the target software systems. Clone relation is reflexive and symmetric, but the transitivity does not always hold. It depends on the similarity policy we choose for the code snippet pair. When the transitivity of a clone relation holds, it is

K. Inoue (✉)
Osaka University, 1-5 Yamadaoka, Suita, Osaka, Japan
e-mail: inoue@ist.osaka-u.ac.jp

© The Author(s), under exclusive license to Springer Nature Singapore Pte Ltd. 2021   3
K. Inoue and C. K. Roy (eds.), *Code Clone Analysis*,
https://doi.org/10.1007/978-981-16-1927-4_1

```
                    ...
1211            elif t_id1==SNOTEQUAL:
1212                obj("\tJNZ\t")
1213                obj(lb1)
1214                obj("\t; jump NONEQUAL\n")
1215                obj("\tXOR\tGR1,GR1\t; set GR1 as 0\n")
1216                obj(lb1)
1217                obj("\tNOP\n")
1218
1219            elif t_id1==SLESS:
1220                obj("\tJMI\t")
1221                obj(lb1)
1222                obj("\t; jump LESS\n")
1223                obj("\tXOR\tGR1,GR1\t; set GR1 as 0\n")
1224                obj(lb1)
1225                obj("\tNOP\n")
                    ...
```

Fig. 1 An example of code clone

an equivalence relation and its equivalence class is called *clone set, clone class*, or *clone group*. Any two code snippets in a clone set are in the clone relation.

The copy-and-paste practice is not only the reason for code clones. Frequently used code patterns or idioms would make code clones unintentionally. Invocation (call) to an Application Program Interface (API) might require a specific code pattern, and the repeated invocation would create similar code snippets that are code clone pairs each other. Also, machine-generated code from an automatic source-code generator can generate a lot of the same or similar code snippets that are code clones.

A partial snippet (substring) X' of a code clone X of a clone pair (X, Y) can be also a code clone element of clone pair (X', Y') where Y' is a substring of Y. Since there are many substrings from a code clone, we usually deal with the *maximal* code clone pair (X, Y) that has no surrounding code clone pair (X'', Y'') where X'' and Y'' are superstrings of X and Y, respectively. In the example of Fig. 1, we mostly focus on the maximal clone pair (1211–1217, 1219–1225), but we do not deal with smaller pairs such as (1216–1217, 1224–1225). Also, we generally set the *minimum* cutoff threshold for the length of the clones generated by the code clone detector and investigated by the clone analyst. A lower threshold such as one line might generate a lot of clones to handle, and a higher one such as 1000 lines might lose important clues to make further investigation. We will discuss the issues on the granularity and threshold of the analysis in Sect. 3.

Code clones composed of simple code structures such as repeated assignments or repeated table initialization might be unimportant or sometimes might hinder a further investigation. Some code clone detectors have a feature to identify and remove such simple code structures. In such a sense, the output of the detectors might be different from the set of all code clones in the original clone definition. Furthermore, some repeated code patterns such as machine-generated code snippets could be code clones by definition, but they might be deleted by the clone analyst as *meaningless clones*. It is important to note that some papers mention code clones as the ones after the deletion, which might be a smaller part of the original definition of code clone. We will discuss it in Sect. 3.

Code clone is sometimes called simply *clone*, or referred to *software clone, duplicated code, code duplication, copy-and-paste code*, and so on. As we have mentioned above, code clones X and Y of a code clone pair (X, Y) are identical or similar. Based on the similarity policy, we will classify code clones into four types, type-1 to type-4 as described in Sect. 2. Finding code clones in software systems is called *(code) clone analysis* or *(code) clone detection*, the tool for code clone analysis is referred to *(code) clone analyzer, (code) clone detector*, or simply *detector* here, and the engineer for the clone analysis is named *clone analyst* or simply *analyst* here.

The notion of code clone can be seen as duplicated code in an early publication in 1992 by Baker [2], where important ideas in clone detection such as parameterized matching, suffix tree algorithm, and dot plot visualization were already presented. It is not well known who had really started to use the term "clone" for similar code snippets, but we can see that "clone detection" was used by Carter et al. in their paper in 1993 [6]. In this paper, they have proposed the classification of clones into four types, which is very similar to the currently-used classification presented in Sect. 2.

From the mid 90s, important papers on the clone detection and visualization methods have been published by Davey et al. [7], Lague et al. [19], Baxter et al. [5], and Duccase et al. [9]. From '00s, practically available clone detectors have been developed by Kamiya et al. [14] and Jiang et al. [13], and a large number of clone-related publications on the new detection methods, tools, applications, survey, and so on have been published. As shown in Fig. 2, the number of academic publications including the terms "code clone", "duplicated code", or "software clone" increases very rapidly these days, showing the growth of interest in the code clone.

Along with the growth of interest, a meeting for discussing code clones had been held as the First International Conference on Software Clones (IWSC) in Montreal in October 2002, in conjunction with the International Conference on Software Maintenance (ICSM) 2002. The first research paper with "clone" in its title in the International Conference on Software Engineering (ICSE), which is the most influential leading conference in software engineering, was by Basit et al. in [3]. At ICSE 2007, four research papers and one tool paper were presented with the titles of clone, and a research session entitled "Clone Detection and Removal" was settled for three of those research papers. Several papers entitled with clone have been presented annually as research papers in the ICSE series, which would indicate strong and continuous interest in code clone research by academia.

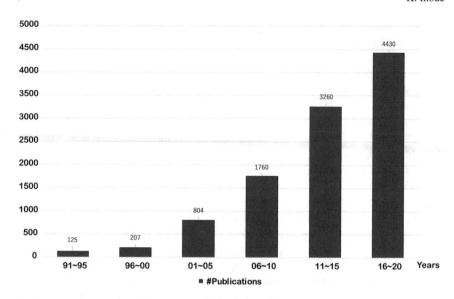

Fig. 2 Growth of publications with terms "code clone", "duplicated code", or "software clone" associated with "software", or "program" by Google Scholar

2 Classification of Code Clone Types

Here, we show a classification of a code clone pair (X, Y) into four types as follows. This classification is well recognized and acknowledged by many code clone researchers.

Type-1 X and Y are syntactically identical code snippets, with possible differences of non-executable elements such as white spaces, tabs, comments, and so on.

Type-2 X and Y are structurally identical code snippets, with possible differences of identifier names, literals, and type names, in addition to the differences of type-1.

Type-3 X and Y are similar code snippets, with possible differences of several statements added, removed, or modified to another snippet, in addition to the differences of type-2. The similarity structure and threshold θ are predetermined by the clone analyst.

Type-4 X and Y are syntactically different code snippets, but their functionalities are the same.

We may call a snippet X *type-k (code) clone*, without clearly specifying another element Y of a clone pair (X, Y).

2.1 Type-1 Clones

Figure 3 is a part of an editor program, and it contains similar `while` clauses. Inside these, there are the same `if-else` clauses annotated by *, which form a type-1 code clone pair. The computation of these `if-else` clauses are the same with differently set variable $p1$ at lines 2789 and 2811, respectively. The author of this code would intentionally duplicate the same computation. These clauses would be potential targets of refactoring, and so they might disappear in a future revision of this system.

```
     ...
2788 while (true) {
2789   p1=U.indexOf(page.pageData.roLines.getline(fy),
                                 ignoreCase,s,p1);
2790     if (p1 >= 0) {                                    *
2791       cnt++;                                          *
2792       editRec.deleteInLine(fy, p1, p1 + s.length()); *
2793       editRec.insertInLine(fy, p1, s2);              *
2794       if (!all) {                                     *
2795         return new Point(p1 + s2.length(), fy);      *
2796       }                                               *
2797       p1 = p1 + s2.length();                          *
2798     } else{                                           *
2799       break;                                          *
2800     }                                                 *
2801 }                                                     *
     ...
2810 while (true) {
2811   p1=U.indexOf(sb.subSequence(0,x),
                                 ignoreCase,s,p1);
2812     if (p1 >= 0) {                                    *
2813       cnt++;                                          *
2814       editRec.deleteInLine(fy, p1, p1 + s.length()); *
2815       editRec.insertInLine(fy, p1, s2);              *
2816       if (!all) {                                     *
2817         return new Point(p1 + s2.length(), fy);      *
2818       }                                               *
2819       p1 = p1 + s2.length();                          *
2820     } else {                                          *
2821       break;                                          *
2822     }                                                 *
2823 }                                                     *
     ...
https://github.com/neoedmund/neoeedit/blob/master/src/neoe/ne/U.java
```

Fig. 3 An example of type-1 code clone pair

2.2 Type-2 Clones

Figure 4 is a case of the type-2 clone pair that exists in two different files. These are complete method definitions overriding a superclass method, and they have the same program structure, but they use different type names such as `Result` and `CharSetParseState`, and different identifiers such as `type` and `mode`. In the case of the overriding methods, similar method definitions may be used, and they frequently form clone pairs as in this example.

Consistent change of all names for the types and identifiers is called *P-match* (parameterized match), which is more formally denoted in such a way that for a

```
       ...
58    public boolean equals(Object other) {
59      if (!(other instanceof Result)) {
60        return false;
61      }
62      Result that = (Result) other;
63      if (this == that) {
64        return true;
65      }
66      return Objects.equals(this.type, that.type) &&
67        Objects.equals(this.codePoint, that.codePoint) &&
68        Objects.equals(this.propertyIntervalSet,
                                  that.propertyIntervalSet) &&
69        Objects.equals(this.parseLength, that.parseLength);
70      }
       ...
     https://github.com/antlr/antlr4/blob/master/tool/src/org/
                  antlr/v4/misc/EscapeSequenceParsing.java


       ...
419  public boolean equals(Object other) {
420    if (!(other instanceof CharSetParseState)) {
421      return false;
422    }
423    CharSetParseState that = (CharSetParseState) other;
424    if (this == that) {
425      return true;
426    }
427    return Objects.equals(this.mode, that.mode) &&
428      Objects.equals(this.inRange, that.inRange) &&
429      Objects.equals(this.prevCodePoint, that.prevCodePoint) &&
430      Objects.equals(this.prevProperty, that.prevProperty);
431  }
       ...
       https://github.com/antlr/antlr4/blob/master/tool/src/
                  org/antlr/v4/automata/LexerATNFactory.java
```

Fig. 4 An example of type-2 code clone pair

type-2 clone pair (X, Y), all occurrences of names a in X are replaced with b in Y. If one occurrence of a in X is replaced with c but others are replaced with b, it is still a type-2 clone pair, but it is not P-match.

For the clones in Fig. 4, all occurrences of class name `Result` are replaced with `CharSetParseState`, and in the same way, variable name `type` to `mode`, `codePoint` to `inRange`, `propertyIntervalSet` to `prevCodePoint`, and `parseLength` to `prevProperty`. Thus, this is the case of P-match.

Analyzing the consistency of the name changes in the clone pairs is an important method of finding bugs created under the copy-and-paste programming. The developer copies a code snippet from the original part and paste it into a different part, and change the variable or type names to fit the new context. In this process, the developer might forget to change a name and create a bug. Such a case could be detected as an inconsistent change of the names.

2.3 Type-3 Clones

Figure 5 contains a type-3 code clone pair of two method definitions (lines 58–63 and lines 66–72) proceeded by the override declarations (lines 57 and 65), respectively. The latter definition has an extra *if* statement at line 67 but other statements constitute type-2 code clone for the former definition. Here, we assume that the similarity

```
        ...
57 @Override
58 public boolean resolvesToToken(String x, ActionAST node) {
59    if ( tokenRefs.get(x)!=null ) return true;
60    LabelElementPair anyLabelDef = getAnyLabelDef(x);
61    if ( anyLabelDef!=null &&
                anyLabelDef.type==LabelType.TOKEN_LABEL ) return true;
62    return false;
63 }
64
65 @Override
66 public boolean resolvesToAttributeDict(String x, ActionAST node) {
67    if ( resolvesToToken(x, node) ) return true;
68    if ( ruleRefs.get(x)!=null) return true;// rule ref in this alt?
69    LabelElementPair anyLabelDef = getAnyLabelDef(x);
70    if ( anyLabelDef!=null &&
                anyLabelDef.type==LabelType.RULE_LABEL ) return true;
71    return false;
72 }
        ...
        https://github.com/antlr/antlr4/blob/master/tool/src/org/
                        antlr/v4/tool/Alternative.java
```

Fig. 5 An example of type-3 code clone pair

threshold θ is, say, two-line difference, so one-line addition to the former definition clears the threshold and they are type-3 code clone pair.

Let's see Fig. 3 again. If we see the overall clauses of while (lines 2788–2801 and 2810–23), these snippets make a type-3 clone pair with the same similarity threshold θ where all the statements are the same except the difference of line 2789 and 2811.

We can take various ways of the similarity threshold. One simple way is to give an absolute value of the different statements, tokens, or characters, e.g., two statement difference shown above. Instead of the absolute value, we would use a relative value for the length of the snippets, like a 10% statement difference. We might employ more sophisticated measure for the similarity, such as the edit distance of two character or token sequences, or the cosine value of two vectors obtained from characteristic values of the code snippets. Recently, machine learning techniques have been used for this purpose [20].

Type-3 clones are created with a small modification after a copy-and-paste operation. Adding, deleting, or changing a few lines in a copied code snippet is very popular after the copy-and-paste. Sometimes we would move statements in the copied fragment. These activities generate type-3 clones.

2.4 Type-4 Clones

It is theoretically infeasible to always determine the functional equivalence of any two code snippets. However, we could identify functionally-equivalent code snippets with specific coding patterns. For example, we sometimes use an array or a linked list for sorting integers, and we can identify that they generate the same result. We can think of various levels of difference, say, different algorithms (e.g., quick sort or bubble sort), data structure (e.g., array or linked list), types (e.g., char or integer), program statements (e.g., "for" or "while"), program structures (e.g., using many copy-and-paste snippets or refactored method), programming languages (e.g., Java or Python), or combination of these.

Figure 6 is an example of a type-4 clone pair that performs the bubble sort algorithm to sort the array element in increasing order. The upper one (Bubble Sort 1) executes the inner loop of if statement for the checking and swapping of the neighbor elements from lower to higher index, while the latter one (Bubble Sort 2) does it from higher to lower. Another distinction is the declaration of the temporary variable *tmp* that is explicitly declared at the beginning of the method in the upper one.

These two code snippets for the method definitions are syntactically different but they compute the same result for the input array. In such a sense, these are a type-4 clone pair.

Compared to other types of code clone detection, type-4 clone detection is more difficult. However, various algorithms for this purpose have been actively studied in recent years. There has been also attempt to relax the condition of type-4 clones to allow the code snippets with similar behavior or semantically similar ones; however,

```
Bubble Sort 1 (ascending inner loop)
1     static void sort(int[] array) {
2         int tmp;
3         for( int i=0; i<array.length-1; i++ ) {
4             for( int j=0; j<array.length-i-1; j++ ) {
5                 if( array[j] > array[j+1] ) {
6                     tmp = array[j];
7                     array[j] = array[j+1];
8                     array[j+1] = tmp;
9                 }
10            }
11        }
12    }

Bubble Sort 2 (descending inner loop)
21    static void sort(int[] array) {
22        for (int i=0; i<array.length-1; i++) {
23            for (int j=array.length-1; j>i; j--) {
24                if (array[j-1] > array[j]) {
25                    int tmp = array[j-1];
26                    array[j-1] = array[j];
27                    array[j] = tmp;
28                }
29            }
30        }
31    }
```

Fig. 6 An example of type-4 code clone pair

formally defining similarity of semantics would not be straightforward and the similarity might be subjective or depend on a specific reference clone corpus that would be used for the evaluation.

3 Factors Affecting Code Clone Detection

Clone detector takes a set of target source code files as its input, and reports code clones, clone pairs, or clone sets as its output. Apart from the formal definition of code clone and clone types, most clone detectors do not report all of the clones in the target files, but they report code clones larger than a minimum report size threshold t. Generally, a smaller t creates many code clones in the output of the clone detector, which are mostly created not by the copy-and-paste operation but by unintentional repeated typing of similar code patterns.

Figure 7a, b show examples of two different threshold t for the same source code in Linux USB device drivers. Figure 7a is the CCFinderX's dot plot of 50 tokens (default) for t, and Fig. 7b is that of 25 tokens, where each dot shows existence of

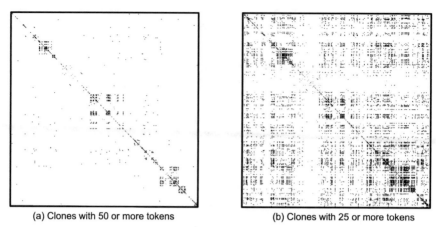

(a) Clones with 50 or more tokens   (b) Clones with 25 or more tokens

linux/drivers/usb/*

Fig. 7 Detected clones with different minimum token lengths

clone pair. The number of the total clone pairs reported in (a) is 1,631, and the one in (b) is 5,907.

Since a smaller threshold t tends to create many code clones, the code clone detector needs to handle all of those and then its performance in the sense of the computation time and usage memory would drop drastically. Also, the huge output might overwhelm further analysis for finding specific code snippets by the human clone analyst. For such reasons, the clone detectors generally have default values such as 50 tokens (CCFinderX) or 10 pretty-printed lines (NiCad) for the threshold t, and the clone pairs smaller than t are discarded and not reported.

As discussed in Sect. 1, the definition of code clones is based on the similarity of the syntactic structure of two code snippets, and it does not rely on the meaning and semantics of those code snippets or the coding action such as copy-and-paste. This might cause to generate many code clones that fit the code clone definition but that are *meaningless* (or uninteresting, useless, boring, ...) for the clone analyst. For example, consecutive assignment statements for table initialization might be repeated in several locations in a system and they would be reported as code clones by clone detector. Machine-generated codes such as the parser generated by the parser generator would contain similar code patterns that can be recognized as code clones. However, these code clones might be meaningless for the clone analyst.

It is not intuitive to determine what are meaningful and meaningless code clones. A code clone analyst would have her/his own subjective criteria for the meaningful clones. Some code clone detectors equip filters to pick up only meaningful ones and reduce the output report, which would help the clone analyst. However, it is important to notice that such filtering would change the statistics of the clone analysis, including the recall and precision values for the evaluation of the clone detectors. Furthermore, some research papers on code clones target the code clones with their subjective filtering of the meaningless clones, which are far away from the formal and syntactic definition of clones. By such deviation of the code clone definition and the actual output we obtain from the clone detector, special care is needed when we compare clone detectors and their empirical evaluation data.

In addition to the discussion of the meaningfulness, it is important to recognize the granularity of the code clone analysis and its effect to the analysis performance and result. Analysis granularity is roughly categorized as follows.

- character
- token
- line or statement
- block
- method or function
- file
- subsystem

For example, a clone detector with the method-level granularity reports only code clones of complete methods in the target language, and it discards similar code snippets that do not form complete methods but parts of those. The fine-grained granularity approach can report the smaller and more precise movement of code in a system, and the coarse-grained one can overview the structure in a single system or duplication among multiple systems.

Figure 8 presents various factors to affect detectable code clones of interest by a clone detector. For all possible pairs of code snippets in the target software system, the analyst determines a clone detection algorithm associated with the similarity threshold θ, the types of detectable clones, analysis granularity, and the minimum size (length) threshold t. Based on these decisions, a code clone detector is executed to get the raw output. For this raw output, the analyst determines what are the meaningful clones in the context of analysis objectives, and she/he would discard the meaningless output by hand or by a filter. The resulting output becomes the detectable

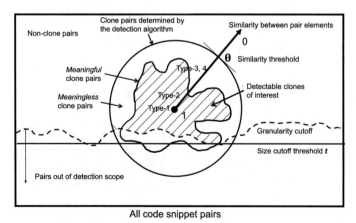

Fig. 8 Detectable code clones of interest

code clones of interest. All of these factors, including this meaningful/meaningless determination, strongly change the resulting code clones. Comparison and evaluation of the empirical data on code clone without clear declaration of those factors might be confusing and could mislead the discussion.

4 Analysis Domain

Figure 9 shows a classification of the target of the clone analysis. As we have been discussing on code clone in this chapter, the target of the code clone analysis is mostly *program text*, or we may say it *software*, or *code* written in some programming language. Programs in popular programming languages such as C/C++ or Java, and scripting languages such as Python or JavaScript are popular examples of the target. Binary code such as X86 machine language and intermediate code such as Java Bytecode are also the target of the code clone analysis [16].

Domain-specific languages (DSL) such as Verilog Hardware Description Language (HDL), SQL, and Model In the Loop Simulation (MILS) are often targeted for the investigation of duplication in those programs [1, 8, 33]. Non-executable software artifacts such as HTML and XML are interesting targets to investigate their redundancy [34]. All of these domains are targets of the code clone analysis here.

Analyzing plane text for finding duplicated strings is an important topic in computer science, especially in the natural language processing area [21]. Also, finding repeated parts in DNA sequence is one of the indispensable techniques in biolog-

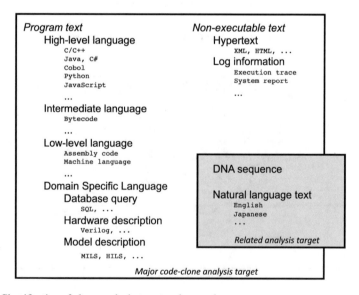

Fig. 9 Classification of clone analysis target and examples

ical science and engineering [30]. These areas are out of the scope in this book, but they have developed various important analysis algorithms and methods that are sometimes very important and useful for our code clone analysis.

5 Overview of Analysis Process

In this section, we overview the process of the code clone detection of a *stand-alone* clone detector that analyzes the whole target source code and reports all of the code clone pairs or clone sets. Recently, a feature for clone detection is popularly provided as a plug-in or an extension of the feature-rich editors and Integrated Development Environments (IDEs) such as Eclipse, Vscode, Visual-Studio, and so on. The process for these is similar but handling the input and output could be simplified from the stand-alone detectors. The discussion here assumes a stand-alone detector that works independently without any editor, IDE, or other development tools.

Figure 10 shows an overview of the process of the code clone detector. It analyzes the overall input target source code and reports all of the code clone pairs or the clone sets in the target. We may sometimes want to know the partial result, such as an incremental difference of the analysis result from a previous one (*incremental clone analysis*), or the matching result for a query snippet (*code clone search*). These require different processes which would be probably lighter than the overall analysis as Fig. 10, and are not discussed here.

5.1 *Front End*

The front end inputs the target source code, and it performs the necessary pre-process and transformation to an internal representation of the code. The features include comment removal, decomposition into atomic chunks (e.g., tokenization, function extraction, …), various transformations (e.g., normalization of identifiers and literals, parsing for tree construction, metrics measurement for chunks, …), and mapping construction between the source and the internal representation.

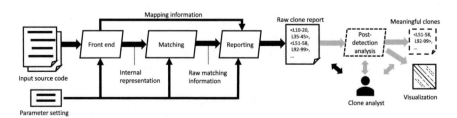

Fig. 10 Overview of code clone analysis processes

For the type-2 clone detection, user-defined names and literals are transformed (normalized) into the special symbols that erase the difference between the names and literals. These features are controlled by the parameters (e.g., similarity threshold θ) given by the clone analyst.

This process requires a language-depend tokenizer (lexical analyzer) or lightweight parser. Sometimes we may want to use an existing fully-featured parser for this purpose, but it would accept only complete and compilable source code and thus the applicability of the clone analysis would be limited.

The output is an internal representation of the original source code, along with the mapping information from the original source code to the internal representation.

5.2 Matching

The matching process is the core of the clone analysis, where the same or similar code snippets in the internal representation of the target source code are identified. There are many approaches to matching, and they are selected based on the analysis granularity, clone types to detect, performance requirement, and so on. We would roughly classify those approaches into the following three categories.

5.2.1 Sequence-Matching Approach

For the fine-grain granularity analysis such as the character level or token-level ones, this approach has been well adopted. The source code is treated internally as a character sequence or token sequence, and for this sequence s, an algorithm to find all *maximal repeats* is applied [10, 30]. A maximal repeat is a subsequence a of s, which has an exactly equal subsequence a' in the different position of s, and the equality cannot be held by extending the subsequences to the left or right of a and a'. Maximal repeats can be found fairly efficiently in $\theta(n + z)$ time by using the *suffix tree* algorithm where n is the size of the sequence and z is the number of the maximal repeats.

A suffix tree is a Patricia trie compactly embedding every suffix of the target sequence on their edges [10]. Figure 11 shows an overview of the construction of the suffix tree, where the sequence is assumed $ABCDABCBC$ and each path from the root to the leaf represents a suffix including the terminate symbol $. An internal node means a share of the preceding subsequence by the suffixes to the leaves, and so a path from the root to an internal node corresponds to a maximal repeat (i.e., clone). The suffix tree algorithm was well used in early code clone detectors [2, 14], but it generally requires large memory space to embed the input sequence and its all suffixes. Thus, these days the suffix array algorithm has become popular, which needs less memory space [3, 10]. Figure 12 shows the suffix array representing the same sequence as Fig. 11, where all the suffixes are sorted and the indices of the sort

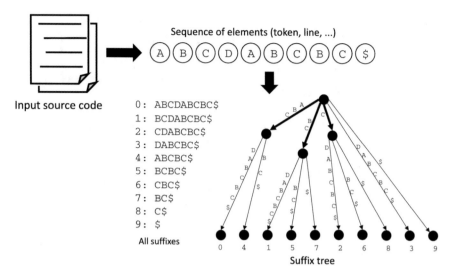

Fig. 11 An example of suffix tree

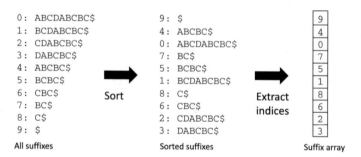

Fig. 12 An example of suffix array

result are kept in the array. Clones can be identified by checking only the header part of the neighboring suffixes.

By using the sequence-matching approach, clone pairs of type-1 and type-2 are exhaustively identified and reported. Type-3 clones can be also identified by connecting the type-1 and type-2 clones, allowing small gaps under the similarity threshold θ. Type-4 clones are not identified by this approach.

This approach generally reports clones clearly defined by the matching algorithm without ambiguity. However, the reported clones could include meaningless sequences for the clone analyst such as the sequences of constant definitions, variable declarations, table initialization, and so on, and the post-detection analysis process for removing the meaningless pairs would be needed.

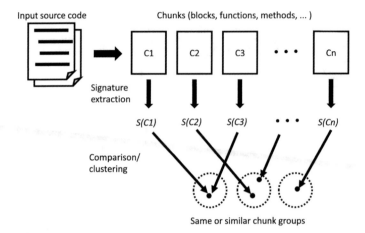

Input source code   Chunks (blocks, functions, methods, ...)

Fig. 13 Overview of chunk comparison approach

5.2.2 Chunk-Comparison Approach

The original source code is decomposed into a sequence of chunks such as blocks of statements, functions (methods), or files based on the analysis granularity. For each chunk, *signatures* (or we may say *features*, *hash*, etc.) to represent the characteristics of the chunk are extracted, and searching for chunks with the same or similar signatures is executed (see Fig. 13).

There are many different implementations of this approach. A simple example would be that we compute a few software metrics values of each function as the signatures, say, Non-comment Lines Of Code (NLOC) and Cyclomatic complexity of functions. Then, we find code clones at the function granularity by searching functions with the same or similar NLOC and Cyclomatic complexity values. A related method is to use techniques for the natural language processing such that we extract keywords from the code and construct word vectors for each function, and find functions with the same or closer vectors, where we can use a simple cosine similarity value or other sophisticated techniques [36]. More sophisticated methods such as Latent Semantic Indexing (LSI) could be employed for the improvement of the matching accuracy for the type-3 and type-4 clones [4]. Various hashing techniques are also used. A simple hash function may only detect type-1 and 2 clones. Locality-Sensitivity-Hashing is one of the methods to allow the type-3 or 4 clones to match [24].

For the chunk of block or function granularity, each chunk may be transformed into a graph (or tree) such as an Abstract Syntax Tree (AST) or (Program Dependence Graph (PDG), and searching for the same or similar graphs can be performed [5, 17]. This method generally requires a longer processing time for parsing the code and constructing AST or PDG, and also for matching graphs. However, it would be easier to identify clone pairs with similar structures on the graph but different representations on the code, and so it fits to detect type-3 and type-4 clones.

Recently, machine learning has been employed for the matching process in research prototype systems. In one of these, the chunk is a single method, and the word (token) frequency of the method is its signature [20]. From the word frequency of two methods, a similarity vector of the method pair is determined. A Deep Neural Net DNN is trained with the collection of the method pair data composed of the similarity vector and a clone/non-clone label. The trained DNN is used to classify a method pair into clone or non-clone. For detecting all clones of the method granularity in the target source code, each method is extracted and all method pairs are enumerated and classified. We can consider various different strategies for the signature extraction, input data for DNN, and hyperparameter of DNN, based on the objectives of the clone detection.

The merits of this approach include flexibility of the algorithm design such that we can choose an appropriate method for the signature extraction and the comparison/clustering of the signatures based on the objectives and requirements of the clone detection. For example, if we would be interested in the semantic similarity in the type-4 function-granularity clone detection, we might extract user-defined names in each function as the signatures and then they would be clustered by the word2vec technique [22], where we can get semantically similar clones in the same cluster. If we would want to have a high-performance clone detector, a light-weight signature extraction, and the comparison algorithms might be chosen, where the accuracy of the reported clones might be lower.

Another merit of this approach is that it is easy to execute the algorithms in parallel. Constructing the chunks and extracting signatures are independent of each other so that we can easily implement them with a multiple process/thread or cluster environment.

To detect all clone pairs from the target, we might need the $O(n^2)$ comparisons for n chunks using the naive approach; however, it would be reduced to the near $O(n)$ comparisons if filtering and optimization techniques are introduced.

It is important to note that a chunk is the finest granularity in the analysis, and finer granularity snippets cannot be detected as clones by this approach. For example, similar statements cannot be detected as clones if we would choose function as a chunk.

5.2.3 Hybrid Approach

Mixing the sequence-matching and the chunk-comparison approaches is applied to fine-grain granularity analyses such as token level, statement-level, or block-level ones. The target source code is transformed into a sequence of the elements in the granularity by the front end, and *n-grams* that is a chunk composed of consecutive *n* elements in the sequence are constructed. Then, the search for the same or similar

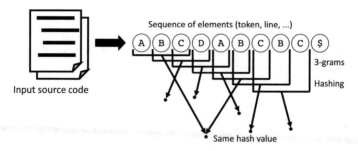

Fig. 14 An example of hybrid approach: 3-gram and hashing method

n-grams is performed using hashing or other fast matching methods. For the found n-grams, expansion to the neighbor elements is tried to find maximal subsequences of the elements.

We can see in Fig. 14 an example of this approach where the 3-gram and hash-based comparison are used. In this case, only ABC with the starting position at 0 and 4 are identified as the same 3-grams, and using those as a core of a clone pair, expansions to the left and right are tried but they will fail. Therefore, only a clone pair ABC at 0 and 4 is reported; however, the smaller but identical pair BC at 1 and 7 is not identified.

This approach is simply implemented and fast for the type-1 and 2 clone analysis [28]. For the type-3 analysis, we may use some techniques to allow gaps in the sequence. Smaller snippets less than n cannot be detected by this approach.

5.3 Reporting

At this process, the matching result is extracted and reported to the clone analyst. The internal representation of the source code at the matching process is generally an abstracted form of the source code, and then a restoration to a human-readable form is needed.

NiCad reports the clone set in an XML or HTML form that is easily browsed by the browsers. On the other hand, CCFinderX reports the found clone pairs in a binary form in the default setting, which is unreadable to the human. This is because the clone detection output tends to become huge and a compact binary form would fit the post-detection analysis.

At this process, the minimum size threshold t is identified, and the smaller snippets than t which match other snippets are cut off and not reported in the output as clones.

5.4 Post-detection Analysis

This process is optional and would be performed with the intention of the clone analyst to extract the clones of interest and to understand the resulting clones properly. Major tasks are as follows.

Measuring Measuring the metric values for the clones is an important basis. The number of the clone pairs and the clone sets are fundamental metrics. Also, the length of the clones is an important metric value to cut off the smaller ones. The code complexity such as the McCabe metrics is a clue to extract meaningful clones. We would want to see the distribution of clone pairs or sets in the same file, different files, different directories, or different systems. To see this, the distance of the clone pairs or the elements in the clone sets is determined and measured. For a single source code file, we might want to know the *clone coverage* of a file, which is the ratio of the components (tokens, lines, statements, …) belonging to any clone in a file to the overall elements in the file. It is an essential metric to observe the characteristics and quality of the source code. For example, a very high clone coverage such as 80–90% would show that the file may not be hand-crafted and would be generated by a source code generator.

Filtering The output from the matching process is generally huge and hard to understand intuitively. To reduce the output and take out only meaningful and interesting clones, various kinds of filters using the metric values can be considered and implemented. For example, we would remove a sequence of continuous assignment statements by using the McCabe complexity value and get only the clones with some control structure as meaningful clones. Note that the resulting clones after the filtering become less than the original ones from the matching process, and taking which set of clones as an evaluation basis heavily affects the results of the evaluation of the code clone detectors.

Visualizing One of the straightforward methods of visualization is to display the source code of the clone information. This is an essential feature to analyze each clone in a detailed statement level. On the other hand, if we would see an overview of the distribution and structure of occurrences of clone pairs in the target software, dot plots such as shown in Fig. 7 are frequently employed [2, 14]. There are many other ways of visualization that will be discussed in another chapter.

6 Application of Code Clone Analysis

Various kinds of applications of the code clone analysis have been proposed and performed as research trials and industrial practices.

6.1 Program Maintenance

Same or Similar Bug Finding
One of the important use cases of the clone analysis is to find the same or similar defects (bugs) in the same or different systems when we identify a bug in a source code file. Since the copy-and-paste practice is very popular, we would guess that the same or similar bugs propagate in the systems and they will eventually cause the same or similar failures in the future. Thus, finding the same or similar code snippets is crucial to prevent the failures again, and clone detection is a very effective method for it. For this purpose, we would use a feature for finding the same or similar code snippets to a query code snippet that contains a bug and could cause a failure to the system. We expect that the query and a found snippet form a clone relation of type-1, 2, or 3, where the code snippets of type-2 and 3 clones cannot be detected by straightforward string matching tools such as *grep* effectively.

Vulnerability Detection
Similar to the bug finding, system-wide code clone search for the code patterns with security risks in the libraries or reused code is a very important issue as a vulnerability analysis method. For this purpose, a scalable clone search approach has to be employed such as the chunk comparison one.

Refactoring
The existence of code clones in a system indicates redundancy of the source code text and the clones are expected to be merged so that the system becomes slim and easy to maintain. Merging the snippets in a clone set into a single method or function is one of the major ways for the refactoring [11]. Type-1 clones are relatively easy to merge, and type-2 and 3 clones need to work with some parameters to erase the gap among the snippets. By the code clone analysis, refactoring opportunities can be effectively sought.

6.2 Program Comprehension

Quality Indicator
There are many reports on the relationship between code clone and program quality such that the existence of clones might be an indicator of program degradation and low quality [23], or that considering clones harmful would be harmful [15]. Although there is no general clue to relate clones to bugs, the existence of many clones in a file or system would indicate the occurrence of the repeated copy-and-paste actions on the file or system, and so the reason for it should be carefully investigated. In such a sense, the clone coverage of each file in a system is computed, and the files with high clone coverage will be specially analyzed. Also, we might have a standard and expected range of the clone coverage of a system, say 10–30%, and if a system that is developed by a subcontractor had the 80% clone coverage, we need to check

the structure of the system and the process of its development. A very low clone coverage such as less than 5% might be also a target of the special care.

Dependence Identification

Knowing the distribution of code clones in a system gives an important clue of the dependence of the system. Sometimes unknown coupling between two subsystems would be identified by finding a clone pair existing between them. We have experienced a case of finding a hidden coupling in a large system where several subsystems had been developed independently by different subcontractors. By the clone analysis, we had found clones between subsystems A and B, but the project managers of A and B did not know why A and B share the code. The further analysis had revealed that A and B use proprietary libraries whose origin was the same but evolution was different.

6.3   Evolution and Provenance Analysis

Evolution Analysis

Clone analysis between two versions X and Y of a system shows the interesting observation of the evolution of the system. The clone coverage of two systems X and Y is the ratio of the sum of the sizes of the clone pairs existing between X and Y over the total size of X and Y. The lower the clone coverage is, the greater the distance between the two versions is. Thus, the clone coverage becomes a similarity measure of two systems, and it can be used to identify the descendants and ancestors of a system. We can construct a *dendrogram (evolution tree)* using it [35]. Figure 15 shows the dendrogram of BSD Unix OS using the clone coverage as the similarity

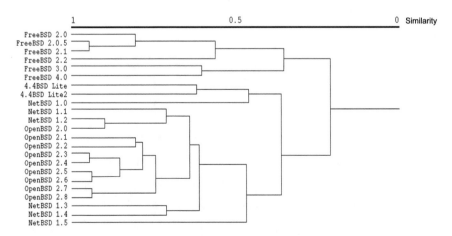

Fig. 15 Dendrogram (evolution tree) of the BSD Unix OS using the clone coverage as similarity measure

measure. As we can see here, closer versions, e.g., FreeBSD 2.0.5 and 2.1, are categorized into nearer clusters, and farther versions, e.g., FreeBSD 2.0 and NetBSD 1.5, are located in farther clusters.

Provenance Analysis

A clone pair of snippets in a system and an old system is a valuable clue of identifying the origin of code [12]. For this purpose, an approach to the code clone search is employed for a corpus of source code which is a collection of Open Source Software (OSS) and/or a proprietary one. For the effective search of the clones, it is important to collect and maintain a sufficiently large and high-quality corpus, but it is not easy for individuals. Companies such as Black Duck provide a service of identifying a code origin in their OSS corpora [32].

6.4 Plagiarism Detection

Investigating clone pairs between two systems is an effective tool for identifying plagiarism of code. The source-code level analysis is fairly easily performed by the clone detectors. Figure 16 shows a case of the clone analysis for the student exercise of a simple compiler construction class. The source code for 5 students was analyzed, and many clones between students S2 and S5 were found. The teacher of the class had asked these students the reason for the many clones.

Considering opportunities for plagiarism detection, the binary-level analysis might be useful more than the source-code level analysis, although the binary-level

Fig. 16 Clones in simple compiler construction exercise of 5 students

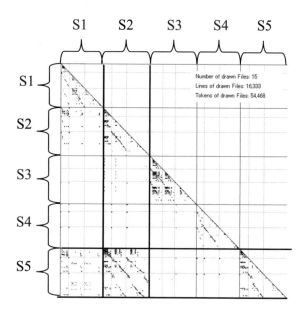

analysis is relatively complex and difficult. A straightforward method for the binary analysis is to decompile or disassemble the binary code into a high-level source code or assembly code, and to perform the clone analysis on the source or assembly code [27]. A threat of this approach is the difference of the binary code for the same source code. Binary code generated by the compilation is heavily affected by the compiler (e.g., gcc or clang), compile options (optimization level, debug, etc.), and execution environment (OS, libraries, etc.). Automatic identification of these distinction has been just explored [25].

7 Conclusion

Nowadays, clone detection is one of the important technologies in software engineering. In this chapter, we have introduced and overviewed the code clone, its analysis, and application. The topics related to the code clone is widely spread now. Thus, we cannot list all of those comprehensively, and so we only sketched some of the important topics here. Comprehensive surveys on code clone researches can be seen in [18, 26, 29, 31].

For the code clone analysis, the basic idea of finding the same or similar code snippets is simple but we can consider many different implementations with new ideas and new applications. We would expect that innovative new approaches might be devised and implemented as new clone detectors in the future.

Acknowledgements We are grateful for the useful comments by Norihiro Yoshida and Eunjong Choi. This work is partially supported by JSPS KAKENHI Grant Number 18H04094.

References

1. F.A. Akbar, S. Rochimah, R.J. Akbar, Investigation of sql clone on mvc-based application. IPTEK J. Proc. Series **2018**(1), 72–77 (2018)
2. B. Baker, A program for identifying duplicated code, in *Proceedings of Computing Science and Statistics: 24th Symposium on the Interface*, vol. 24, pp. 49–57 (1992)
3. H.A. Basit, D.C. Rajapakse, S. Jarzabek, Beyond templates: a study of clones in the STL and some general implications, in *27th International Conference on Software Engineering (ICSE 2005)* (St. Louis, Missouri, USA, 2005), pp. 451–459
4. V. Bauer, T. Völke, S. Eder, Combining clone detection and latent semantic indexing to detect re-implementations, in *2016 IEEE 23rd International Conference on Software Analysis, Evolution, and Reengineering (SANER)*, vol. 3 (IEEE, 2016), pp. 23–29
5. I.D. Baxter, A. Yahin, L. Moura, M. Sant'Anna, L. Bier, Clone detection using abstract syntax trees, in *Proceedings of International Conference on Software Maintenance* (IEEE, 1998), pp. 368–377
6. S. Carter, R. Frank, D. Tansley, Clone detection in telecommunications software systems: a neural net approach, in *Proceedings of International Workshop on Application of Neural Networks to Telecommunications* (1993), pp. 273–287

7. N. Davey, P. Barson, S. Field, R. Frank, D. Tansley, The development of a software clone detector. Int. J. Appl. Soft. Technol. (1995)
8. F. Deissenboeck, B. Hummel, E. Jürgens, B. Schätz, S. Wagner, J.F. Girard, S. Teuchert, Clone detection in automotive model-based development, in *2008 ACM/IEEE 30th International Conference on Software Engineering (ICSE2008)* (IEEE, 2008), pp. 603–612
9. S. Ducasse, M. Rieger, S. Demeyer, A language independent approach for detecting duplicated code, in *Proceedings IEEE International Conference on Software Maintenance (ICSM'99)* (IEEE, 1999), pp. 109–118
10. D. Gusfield, *Algorithms on Strings, Trees and Sequences* (Cambridge University Press, New York, NY, 1997)
11. Y. Higo, Y. Ueda, T. Kamiya, S. Kusumoto, K. Inoue, On software maintenance process improvement based on code clone analysis, in *International Conference on Product Focused Software Process Improvement* (Springer, 2002), pp. 185–197
12. K. Inoue, Y. Sasaki, P. Xia, Y. Manabe, Where does this code come from and where does it go?—integrated code history tracker for open source systems, in *2012 34th International Conference on Software Engineering (ICSE12)* (2012), pp. 331–341
13. L. Jiang, G. Misherghi, Z. Su, S. Glondu, Deckard: scalable and accurate tree-based detection of code clones, in *29th International Conference on Software Engineering (ICSE '07)* (IEEE, 2007), pp. 96–105
14. T. Kamiya, S. Kusumoto, K. Inoue, Ccfinder: a multilinguistic token-based code clone detection system for large scale source code. IEEE Trans. Software Eng. **28**, 654–670 (2002)
15. C.J. Kapser, M.W. Godfrey, "Cloning considered harmful" considered harmful: patterns of cloning in software. Emp. Soft. Eng. **13**(6), 645 (2008)
16. I. Keivanloo, C.K. Roy, J. Rilling, Java bytecode clone detection via relaxation on code fingerprint and semantic web reasoning, in *2012 6th International Workshop on Software Clones (IWSC)* (IEEE, 2012), pp. 36–42
17. R. Komondoor, S. Horwitz, Semantics-preserving procedure extraction, in *Proceedings of the 27th ACM SIGPLAN-SIGACT Symposium on Principles of Programming Languages* (2000), pp. 155–169
18. R. Koschke, Survey of research on software clones, in *Dagstuhl Seminar Proceedings*. Schloss Dagstuhl-Leibniz-Zentrum für Informatik (2007)
19. B. Lague, D. Proulx, J. Mayrand, E.M. Merlo, J. Hudepohl, Assessing the benefits of incorporating function clone detection in a development process, in *1997 Proceedings International Conference on Software Maintenance* (IEEE, 1997), pp. 314–321
20. L. Li, H. Feng, W. Zhuang, N. Meng, B. Ryder, Cclearner: a deep learning-based clone detection approach, in *2017 IEEE International Conference on Software Maintenance and Evolution (ICSME)* (IEEE, 2017), pp. 249–260
21. C. Manning, H. Schutze, *Foundations of Statistical Natural Language Processing* (MIT Press, 1999)
22. T. Mikolov, K. Chen, G. Corrado, J. Dean, Efficient estimation of word representations in vector space. arXiv:1301.3781 (2013)
23. A. Monden, D. Nakae, T. Kamiya, S. Sato, K. Matsumoto, Software quality analysis by code clones in industrial legacy software, in *Proceedings Eighth IEEE Symposium on Software Metrics* (IEEE, 2002), pp. 87–94
24. T.T. Nguyen, H.A. Nguyen, J.M. Al-Kofahi, N.H. Pham, T.N. Nguyen, Scalable and incremental clone detection for evolving software, in *2009 IEEE International Conference on Software Maintenance* (IEEE, 2009), pp. 491–494
25. D. Pizzolotto, K. Inoue, Identifying compiler and optimization options from binary code using deep learning approaches, in *2020 IEEE International Conference on Software Maintenance and Evolution (ICSME)* (2020), pp. 232–242
26. C.K. Roy, J.R. Cordy, R. Koschke, Comparison and evaluation of code clone detection techniques and tools: a qualitative approach. Sci. Comput. Program. **74**(7), 470–495 (2009)
27. A. Sæbjørnsen, J. Willcock, T. Panas, D. Quinlan, Z. Su, Detecting code clones in binary executables, in *Proceedings of the Eighteenth International Symposium on Software Testing and Analysis, ISSTA '09* (ACM, 2009), pp. 117–128

28. Y. Semura, N. Yoshida, E. Choi, K. Inoue, Ccfindersw: clone detection tool with flexible multilingual tokenization, in *2017 24th Asia-Pacific Software Engineering Conference (APSEC)* (2017), pp. 654–659
29. A. Sheneamer, J. Kalita, A survey of software clone detection techniques. Int. J. Comput. Appl. **137**(10), 1–21 (2016)
30. W. Smyth, *Computing Patterns in Strings* (Addison-Wesley, New York, 2003)
31. J. Svajlenko, C.K. Roy, A survey on the evaluation of clone detection performance and benchmarking (2020)
32. Synopsys: Black duck open source security and license compliance (2020). https://www.blackducksoftware.com/
33. K. Uemura, A. Mori, K. Fujiwara, E. Choi, H. Iida, Detecting and analyzing code clones in hdl, in *2017 IEEE 11th International Workshop on Software Clones (IWSC)* (IEEE, 2017), pp. 1–7
34. M. Weis, F. Naumann, F. Brosy, A duplicate detection benchmark for xml (and relational) data, in *Proceedings of Workshop on Information Quality for Information Systems (IQIS)* (2006)
35. T. Yamamoto, M. Matsushita, T. Kamiya, K. Inoue, Measuring similarity of large software systems based on source code correspondence, in *6th International PROFES (Product Focused Software Process Improvement), LNCS3547* (2005), pp. 530–544
36. K. Yokoi, E. Choi, N. Yoshida, K. Inoue, Investigating vector-based detection of code clones using bigclonebench, in *2018 25th Asia-Pacific Software Engineering Conference (APSEC)* (IEEE, 2018), pp. 699–700

Code Clone Analysis Tools

CCFinderX: An Interactive Code Clone Analysis Environment

Toshihiro Kamiya

Abstract CCFinderX is a successor tool that advances the concepts of CCFinder (2002) and Gemini (2002), and is a standalone environment for code clone detection and analysis. CCFinderX is designed as an interactive analysis environment that allows users to switch between views of scatter plot, file, metrics, and source text, for applying to large code bodies. This chapter describes the features of these views, such as the display content, operations for coordination between views, metrics for files and clone classes, and the revamped code clone detection algorithm.

1 Introduction

CCFinderX is an environment for interactive code clone detection and analysis, with functions such as code clone detection, code clone metrics measurement, and code clone visualization. It was developed to detect code clones from given source files of up to several million lines and analyze the detected code clones, through a closed environment without using other tools.

At the time CCFinderX was released, to the best of the author's knowledge, there were few tools available to interactively analyze code clones for application to large code bodies with various visualization methods. Analyzing the code clones detected by the code clone detection tool was a time-consuming task to do. In particular, when code clones were detected for millions of lines of source code, thousands or tens of thousands (or more) of code clones could be detected, and deciding which code clones to analyze was important but difficult to do manually. For example, suppose only a code clone detection tool and a tool to display a scatter plot of the code clones are available. In that case, this task can be accomplished by creating and displaying a scatter plot (image) of the entire product, picking up interesting directories and detecting the code clones again using some of the directories as input, and then again rebuilding and displaying the scatter plot. To examine the actual source code of the

T. Kamiya (✉)
Shimane University, Matsue, Japan
e-mail: kamiya@cis.shimane-u.ac.jp

© The Author(s), under exclusive license to Springer Nature Singapore Pte Ltd. 2021
K. Inoue and C. K. Roy (eds.), *Code Clone Analysis*,
https://doi.org/10.1007/978-981-16-1927-4_2

code clones shown in the scatter plot, we had to repeatedly find the file names and open the files with a text editor or diff tool.

In this chapter, we will explain the purpose, features, design, and algorithms of CCFinderX. The CCFinderX implementation referred to in this chapter is the last version released in April 2010. All execution results and screenshots in this chapter are based on this implementation.

2   Code Clone Detection and Analysis Tools

There several methods for detecting similar code in source code were proposed; text-based methods such as [6], token-based methods such as [1, 7], AST-based methods such as [2], metric-based methods such as [9] (similarity of metric values of procedures), and dependency-graph-based methods such as [8, 10]. With the emergence of many code clone detection tools, the benchmarking [3] of code clone detection tools was about to start, which used the source code of actual products as the input of the tools.

A view that visualizes similarities in a multi-million line text file utilizing a scatter plot and interactively references the text was proposed by [4]. It is also used as a visualization technique in [1].

CCFinder[7] was first introduced as a token-based code clone detection tool for multiple programming languages. Then, Gemini [5, 13] was developed as a GUI code clone analysis environment for CCFinder with interactive views such as a scatter plot [4] and metrics tables. CCFinderX has been redesigned to revamp the detection algorithm of its predecessor, CCFinder, and to enhance its integration with Gemini, a GUI analysis tool, making it available as an integrated environment for code clone detection and analysis.

3   Interactive Code Clone Analysis

A possible usage scenario of CCFinderX is to analyze code clones given a source file of a target product (or products of a product line developed from one product). The analyst has to decide in what order to analyze or proceed to deal with the many code clones detected in the product. In this situation, not only the internal characteristics of the cloned code fragment (whether it is complex code, long code, etc.), but also the location where the code fragment appears (whether it is a code fragment that appears only in a specific file, a similar code between files in different directories of a product, or a code fragment that appears commonly among multiple products in a product line) is an important clue.

CCFinderX has four views for interactive analysis, alternately examining the contents of the cloned code fragments and the locations where the code clones appear.

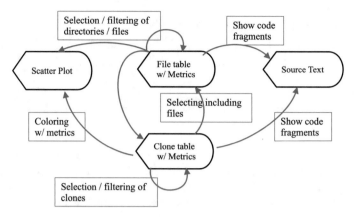

Fig. 1 Views and collaborations between the views

- Scatter Plot
- Clone Table with Clone Metrics
- File Table with File Metrics
- Source Text

Figure 1 shows the views of CCFinderX and the operations of the views to collaborate (influence) each other. By manipulating and switching between these views, the user can narrow down the code fragments to be focused on from the entire source code. For example, the user can find a directory of interest in the scatter plot and then proceed with the analysis by looking at the source files in that directory one by one.

3.1 Scatter Plot View

CCFinderX provides a scatter plot [4] as an overview to understand the distribution of code clones within or between products.

The scatter plot's vertical and horizontal axes consist of the indices of each token in the token sequence extracted from the source files (Intuitively, imagine that all the lines of all the source files are lined up on the vertical and horizontal axes). Each square on the main diagonal in the scatter plot represents a directory. The nesting of the squares directly indicates the tree structure of the directory. The descending right line segments in the scatter plot indicate code fragments that are code clones. In other words, the token sequence in the vertical axis range corresponding to the line segment and the token sequence in the horizontal axis range is code clones (Table 1).

Table 1 Size statistics for source code of the three OSs

Product	Files	LOC	Tokens
FreeBSD	42,396	22,290,241	68,768,315
Linux	50,497	26,336,521	71,956,559
NetBSD	71,698	28,328,173	84,493,290

Note The source files using C++ macros and could not be parsed properly had been removed

Figure 2 shows a scatter plot of inner-product and inter-product clones detected from three software products, FreeBSD OS,[1] Linux OS,[2] and NetBSD OS,[3] displayed by CCFinderX. The size of each product is more than 22 MLoc of the source file.[4] The code clones were detected from the source code tarball with the condition that the length of the token sequence was 200 or more.

The three largest squares (not included by other squares) on the diagonal are "free_bsd", "linux", and "net_bsd" in order from the top left to the bottom right. These three squares are the root directories where the source files for of three OSs are placed. From this scatter plot, we can see that there are many code clones between the two products, FreeBSD and NetBSD, and in comparison, there are not so many code clones between Linux and FreeBSD or Linux and NetBSD. It can be inferred that there would be many similar or the same source files between FreeBSD's "contrib" directory and NetBSD's "external" directory, but these files are arranged in a different order on the scatter plot axis due to the difference in directory structure.

As a reference for execution performance, Table 2 shows the settings and the time required for execution of detecting code clones from the source code of the three operating systems.

3.2 Clone Table View

The clone table view displays the following metrics, called clone metrics, for each of the detected clone classes. The clone table has the ability to filter these metrics by specifying a range of values, which can be used to narrow down the code clones in a code clone analysis.

- LEN: Length of code fragment.
- POP: The number of code fragments that the clone class contains.

---

[1] Index of /pub/FreeBSD/development/tarballs/, http://ftp.freebsd.org/pub/FreeBSD/development/tarballs/.

[2] The Linux Kernel Archives, https://www.kernel.org/.

[3] NetBSD Mercurial, https://anonhg.netbsd.org/.

[4] A CCFinder paper from 2002 [7] also shows a scatter plot of the results of similar code clone detection at that time. At that time, the size of each product was about 2M to 2.5M LOC of source files, so we can see that the size has increased about 10 times in 20 years.

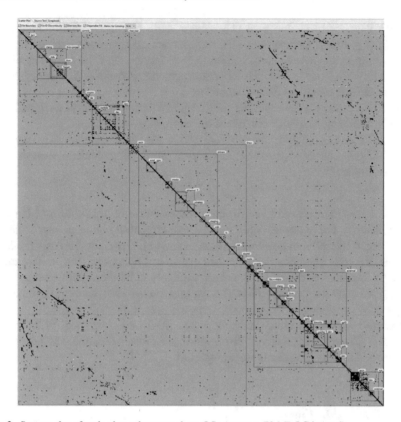

Fig. 2 Scatter plot of code clones between three OSs (apporx. 73 MLOC in total)

Table 2 Setting up ccfx execution and resources required for execution

CPU	6 Core i7-6800K 3.4 GHz (6 cores*)
Memory	128 GiB (32 GiB*)
OS	Windows 10 in a virtual environment on Ubuntu host
Dependencies	Python 2.6.6 32 bit, Java 1.8.0 32 bit
CCFinderX	10.2.7.2 for Windows XP/Vista 32 bit
Step (1)	91 minutes with peak memory usage less than 100 MiB
	for running `ccfx.exe d cpp -d . -p -threads=4`
Step (2) to (4)	58 minutes with peak memory 1,470 MiB
	for running `ccfx.exe d cpp -b 200 -d . -v -j-`

Note The value marked with an asterisk represents the value of the resource allocated to the guest OS in the virtual environment. See Sect. 4.1 for steps (1) through (4). Peak memory usage is measured as the maximum value of the log that records the memory used by the process every second, so it may be smaller than the actual value. However, since the executable binary was 32-bit one, the memory usage never exceeded 4 GiB.

- NIF: Number of source files that contain code fragments of the clone class. $NIF(c) \le POP(c)$, because one file may contain multiple code fragments.
- RAD: Spread of source files containing code fragments of the clone class in the directory. $RAD(C) \ge 0$. When all code fragments of a clone class are contained in a single source file, RAD is defined as 0.
- RNR: Percentage of tokens in the code fragment that are not part of the repetitions.
- TKS: Number of kinds of the tokens the code fragment contains.
- LOOP: Number of appearances of reserved words for loops in the code fragment.
- COND: Number of appearances of reserved words for conditional branch in the code fragment.
- McCabe: $McCabe(c) = LOOP(c) + COND(c)$.

These metrics are used to select the code clones to be focused on in the code clone analysis. For example, code clones with a large RAD value are more likely to be managed by different developers (or maintainers), especially for large products, because the code fragments are contained in distant directories of the product source files. Code clones with low RNR values are likely to be those with a sequence of boilerplate code such as repetition of assignment statements, and such code clones may not be considered as targets to be removed even if they are detected.

Figure 3 shows the clone table view and the source text view (described in Sect. 3.4). From the code clones displayed in the clone table, one was selected by metrics and its code fragments were displayed.

3.3 File Table View

In the File Table view, for each of the input source files, in addition to the source file path, the following metrics, called file metrics, are displayed. The file table has the ability to specify and filter the values of these metrics, which can be used to narrow down the source files in code clone analysis.

- CLN: The number of clone classes that contain at least one code fragment of the source file.
- NBR: Number of other source files that have any code fragment of a clone pair with a code fragment in the source file.
- RSA: Percentage of the tokens in the source file that are covered by a code fragment of a clone pair with a code fragment of one of the other source files.
- RSI: Percentage of the tokens in the source file that are covered by a code fragment of a clone pair with another code fragment of the same source file.
- CVR: Percentage of the tokens in the source file that are covered by a code fragment of a code clone. By definition, $max(RSA(F), RSI(F)) \le CVR(F) \le RSA(F) + RSI(F)$.

These metrics are used to narrow down the files that should be focused on in the code clone analysis. For example, a source file with an NBR of 0 has no code

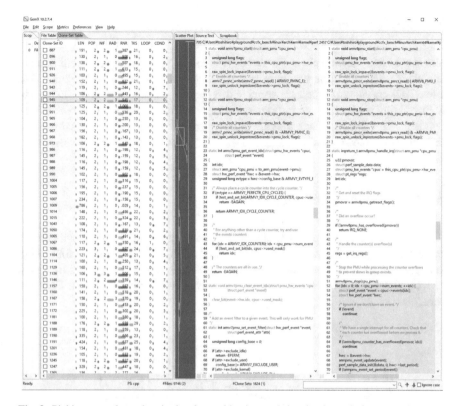

Fig. 3 Picking up a clone class in the clone table view and showing its code fragments in source text view

clones between it and other source files, so even when a code fragment of the code clone needs to be modified, such modification is limited to within that source file and therefore is considered to be easier to modify and maintain than a code clone spread over many directories of source files. While the metric CVR is useful for identifying source files where a large percentage of the code is code clones, the metrics RSA and RSI provide clues to identify more detailed situations. For example, when you copy an entire source file to create another source file in a project, the RSA value of these two source files will be close to 1. A source file with a sequence of boilerplate code such as assignment statements and constructor calls will have an RSI value close to 1.

The file table also has the ability to specify a directory at a relative depth from a specified file, and select or filter only the files in that directory. Since directories are often used as the unit of modules and packages in the software development process, specifying a directory allows you to perform analysis on a specific module or between specific modules.

3.4 Source Text View

The source text view displays the text of two source files (or two different parts of one source file) with line numbers, and shows the parts that are code clones with a text background color and (in some text editors) a so-called minimap-like view. In the minimap-like view, code fragments that are code clones are displayed as line segments, and line segments that are code fragments belonging to the same clone class are connected by a curve. Figure 3 includes an example of the source view.

4 Structure of CCFinderX

Figure 4 shows the structure of CCFinderX. The functions of detecting code clones and calculating metrics values are implemented as a CLI tool ccfx. The four views to analyze code clones introduced in Fig. 1 in Sect. 3 and the operations to switch between these views for interactive analysis have been implemented in a GUI tool gemx.

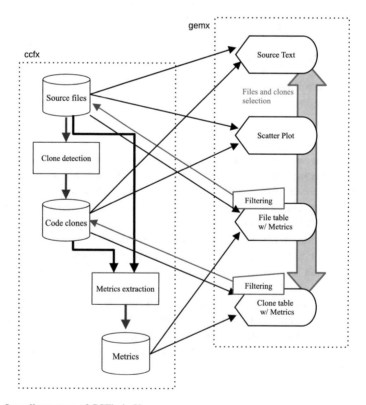

Fig. 4 Overall structure of CCFinderX

The cooperation between gemx and ccfx is done by passing data as files and by launching processes; gemx accesses source files and data files generated by ccfx, i.e., code clones and metrics, and visualizes these data in a scatter plot, etc. On the other hand, when the user selects a source file or a clone class directly on the GUI and requests recalculation, or when the user requests filtering by the value of metrics in the source file or clone class, gemx invokes a ccfx process to update the data files.

4.1 Code-Clone Detection

The code clone detection engine of CCFinderX is designed to detect Type I and II code clones. Figure 5 shows the structure of the code clone detection engine. Note, however, that the code fragments of the detected clone classes may not match as a

Fig. 5 Structure of code-clone detection engine of CCFinderX

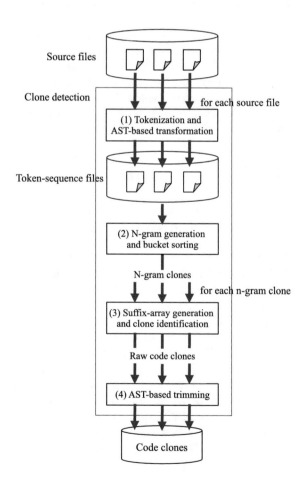

sequence of tokens because the token sequence is pre-processed before the detection algorithm (as marked "AST-based transformation" in the figure).

Each step of the code clone detection function is described below. Of these, step (3) in particular is a new algorithm from CCFinder[7] that uses a more concise data structure to improve the scalability to the input data.

(1) Tokenization and AST-based Transformation

From the input source file, it extracts the tokens and constructs the AST according to the grammar of the programming language, and then transforms the AST according to the transformation rules. For this parsing and AST transformation, we have implemented our own routines for the programming languages: Java, C/C++, COBOL, VB, and C#. The purpose of transforming the AST is to prevent trivial syntactic differences making a difference in code clone detection by supplementing such as missing "{" or "}" of code blocks, and to suppress detection code clones having code fragments that would be of little interest to the analyst by removing token sequences such as import statements or array initialization tables.

This step is done in parallel for each source file, and the output token sequence is saved as a separate file ("*.ccfxprep") for each source file. The output files act as a kind of cache, allowing you to skip the tokenization and transformation process the next time you detect a code clone for a set of input files including the same source files.

(2) N-Gram Generation and Bucket Sorting

Extract n-grams from the token sequence generated from the source file with the length of the minimum code fragment length specified in the code clone detection parameters (as explained later, each n-gram is extended in later steps, so that this n-gram is the shortest code fragment of the code clones to be detected). Bucket sort the n-grams to find clone class; generate a hash map of key-value pairs, which has a hash value of n-gram as a key and a list of positions where the n-gram appears as the value, for each of n-gram occurrences in the input token sequences. When the generation of the hash map is completed, each of the lists of n-gram positions (as values of the hash map) is identified as a candidate of a clone class. That is, each n-gram at the position represented by each element in the list represents a code fragment that matches each other with at least the minimum specified length. When a list of n-grams has two or more elements, make it be an *n-gram clone*.

Figure 6 shows an illustration of this step. Assume that the input is a token sequence "^abababcabdabc$" extracted from some source file F. Here, "^" is a special token that represents the beginning of the file, and "$" is a special token that represents the end of the file. The hash map generated has a value of a list of positions of n-grams of length 2.

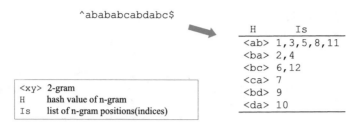

Fig. 6 Illustration of n-gram generation and bucket sorting

The resulting n-gram clones are follows:

- 2-gram <ab>s at positions 1, 3, 5, 8, and 11
- 2-gram <ba>s at positions 2 and 4
- 2-gram <bc>s at positions 6 and 12

Note that "^" and "$" are treated as different tokens from each other or from any other token, and are never included in an n-gram. In a more general case, when there are multiple files as input, "^" and "$" are prepared for each input file. That is, for each input file F_j, we prepare special tokens ^_j and $\$_j$, all of which are different from each other or from any other token.

(3) Suffix-Array Generation and Clone Identification

For each n-gram clone (l), a suffix array is generated to identify clone classes. The algorithm identifies clone classes having either maximal POP or maximal LEN.

Let $f_1, f_2, \ldots, f_n$ be the code fragments in l. The attributes of each f_i are its position on the source file (i.e., file name and index in a token sequence from the file), and length.

(3-1) If the size of l (the number of code fragments) ≤ 1, exit the algorithm (Because the clone class needs to have two or more code fragment). Otherwise, for each of f_i, let b_i be the token immediately preceding it. If $b_1, b_2, \ldots, b_n$ are tokens of the same kind, exit the algorithm (By extending the preceding token to each of the code fragments, we can create a clone class having longer code fragments from l', and the hash map includes such l' as one of the other values).

(3-2) For each of f_i, let a_i be the token immediately following it. Extend the length of all f_i's while all a_i are all tokens of the same type. If a f_i has reached the end of the file and cannot be extended, remove such f_i from l. By removing it, if the number of elements in l decreases to ≤ 1, exit the algorithm.

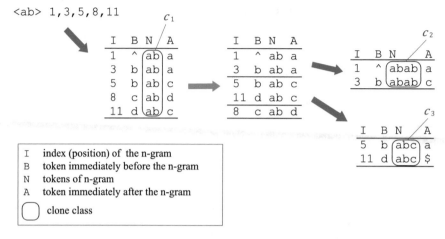

Fig. 7 Illustration of generating a suffix array and identifying clone classes

(3-3) Identify l, that is, code fragments $f_1, f_2, \ldots, f_n$, as a clone class.

(3–4) Divide l into sub-lists according to the kind of tokens of a_i, and apply the algorithm in (3) recursively to each of the sub-lists.

Figure 7 shows an illustration of generating suffix arrays. The input is an n-gram clone of the 2-gram <ab>, which is the first row of the table to the right of Fig. 6. As a result, three clone classes are identified: a clone class (c_1 in the figure) consisting of code fragments starting at positions 1, 3, 5, 8, and 11 with length 2, a clone class (c_2) consisting of code fragments starting at positions 1 and 3 with length 4, and a clone class (c_3) consisting of code fragments starting at positions 5 and 11 with length 3.

Note that code fragments overlapping each other starting at position 1 are included in the clone classes c_1 and c_2, but each of the clone classes contains the largest number of code fragments (POP) for the length of code fragments (LEN), so that one clone class is never completely "covered" by the other. For example, c_1 and c_3 have POP and LEN values of (4, 2) and (2, 3), respectively, and neither clone class is larger than the other in both metrics.

From Fig. 5, it might seem that step (3) can be executed in a parallel way, but since the amount of memory required depends on the number of elements in the n-gram clones, and the number could be large, the implementation uses a loop to process each n-gram clone sequentially instead of executing in parallel.

(4) AST-Based Trimming

Trim the detected code fragments of the clone class by comparing them with the nested structure of the blocks of source code, i.e., remove code fragments that start near the end of a code block and end just after the beginning of another code block. This feature prevents the detection of many code clones, especially those that are coincidental matches for short code fragments.

5 Summary and Last Words

In this chapter, we have introduced the code cloning analysis environment CCFinderX, including the situation at the time of its release, the targeted analysis workflow, the functions and design to realize that workflow, and the detection algorithm that has been renewed from CCFinder.

CCFinderX was a code cloning analysis environment that was intended to be used in a development environment beyond the framework of a research tool. Due to its ease of use and good (for the time) performance, it was used by many companies after its release, and we received verbal and e-mail comments/feedbacks. More than 5,000 user licenses were issued, and it was then transitioned to open source with no license issuance process. Its successor tool, [11, 12], bearing the CCFinder name has also been published and announced.

I would like to conclude this chapter by expressing my gratitude to everyone who has been involved in CCFinderX collaborations and to everyone who has used CCFinderX, whether in industry or academia.

References

1. B. Baker, On finding duplication and near-duplication in large software systems, in *Proceedings of the 2nd Working Conference on Reverse Engineering (WCRE 1995)* (1995), pp. 86–95
2. Baxter, I., Yahin, A., Moura, L., Anna, M., Clone detection using abstract syntax trees, in *Proceedings of the 14th International Conference on Software Maintenance (ICSM 1998)* (1998), pp. 368–377
3. S. Bellon, R. Koschke, G. Antoniol, J. Krinke, E. Merlo, Comparison and evaluation of clone detection tools. IEEE Trans. Softw. Eng. **33**(9), 577–591 (2007)
4. K. Church, J. Helfman, Dotplot: a program for exploring self-similarity in millions of lines for text and code. J. Am. Stat. Assoc. **2**(2), 153–174 (1993)
5. Higo, Y., Ueda, Y., Kamiya, T., Kusumoto, S., Inoue, K., On software maintenance process improvement based on code clone analysis, in *Proceedings of the 4th International Conference on Product Focused Software Process Improvement, (PROFES 2002)* (2002), pp. 185–197
6. Johnson, J., Substring matching for clone detection and change tracking, in *Proceedings of the 10th International Conference on Software Maintenance, ICSM 1994* (1994), pp. 120–126
7. T. Kamiya, S. Kusumoto, K. Inoue, CCFinder: a multilinguistic token-based code clone detection system for large scale source code. IEEE Trans. Softw. Eng. **28**(7), 654–670 (2002)
8. Komondoor, R., Horwitz, S., Using slicing to identify duplication in source code, in *Proceedings of the 8th International Symposium on Static Analysis, SAS 2001* (2001), pp. 40–56
9. K. Kontogiannis, R. DeMori, E. Merlo, M. Galler, M. Bernstein, Pattern matching for clone and concept detection. J. Autom. Softw. Eng. **3**(1–2), 77–108 (1996)
10. Krinke, J., Identifying similar code with program dependence graphs, in *Proceedings of the 8th Working Conference on Reverse Engineering (WCRE 2001)* (2001), pp. 301–309

11. Livieri, S., Higo, Y., Matsushita, M., Inoue, K., Very-large scale code clone analysis and visualization of open source programs using distributed CCFinder, in *Proceedings of the 29th International Conference on Software Engineering (ICSE 2007)* (2007), pp. 106–115
12. Y. Semura, N. Yoshida, E. Choi, K. Inoue, CCFinderSW: clone detection tool with flexible multilingual tokenization, in *Proceedings of the 24th Asia-Pacific Software Engineering Conference (APSEC 2017)* (2017), pp. 654–659
13. Y. Ueda, Y. Higo, T. Kamiya, S. Kusumoto, K. Inoue, Gemini: code clone analysis tool, in *Proceedings of the 2002 International Symposium on Empirical Software Engineering (ISESE2002), vol. 2* (2002), pp. 31–32

NiCad: A Modern Clone Detector

Manishankar Mondal, Chanchal K. Roy, and James R. Cordy

Abstract Code clones are exactly or nearly similar code fragments in the code-base of a software system. Studies have revealed that such code fragments can have mixed impact (both positive and negative) on software evolution and maintenance. In order to reduce the negative impact of code clones and benifit from their advantages, researchers have suggested a number of different clone management techniques. Clone management begins with clone detection. Clone detection has thus been a hot research topic, resulting in many different clone detectors [26, 32] that have been used in a range of applications, including clone analysis, refactoring, and tracking. One of those that has been widely used and investigated is NiCad [3, 27]. What follows is a brief overview of the NiCad detection mechanism and its application in various studies of code clones.

1 A Brief Overview of NiCad

NiCad (Accurate Detection of Near-miss Intentional Clones) is a popular and widely used modern clone detector. NiCad was originally developed by Chanchal K. Roy as part of his PhD thesis work under the supervision of James R. Cordy at Queen's University in Canada. NiCad is a hybrid tool that uses a combination of parsing and approximate text comparison to detect near-miss clones [3]. Svajlenko and Roy [33]

The original version of this chapter was revised. The affiliation of author "J. R. Cordy" has been changed as "Queen's University, Kingston, Canada". An erratum to this chapter can be found at https://doi.org/10.1007/978-981-16-1927-4_17

M. Mondal (✉)
Khulna University, Khulna, Bangladesh
e-mail: mshankar@cseku.ac.bd

C. K. Roy
University of Saskatchewan, Saskatoon, Canada
e-mail: chanchal.roy@usask.ca

J. R. Cordy
Queen's University, Kingston, Canada
e-mail: cordy@cs.queensu.ca

45

K. Inoue and C. K. Roy (eds.), *Code Clone Analysis*,
https://doi.org/10.1007/978-981-16-1927-4_3

showed that it can be a promising choice among the modern clone detection tools on the basis of its measured accuracy in detecting each of the three major clone types (Types 1, 2, and 3). Because of its high precision and recall, it has been used as the clone detection engine in many studies of clones in both open source and industrial software systems. NiCad's high impact on the research community has been recognized with a ten-year Most Influential Paper (MIP) award at ICPC 2018 [28], and its evaluation framework received the MIP award at SANER 2018 [29]. In addition, the SimCad [35, 36] extension to NiCad received the MIP award at SANER 2021 [37].

1.1 The NiCad Method

NiCad works in four steps: parsing, normalization, comparison, and clustering. In brief, each of these steps can be described as follows.

- **Parsing**: In this step, NiCad uses the TXL source transformation system [2] to parse and extract all code fragments of a particular source granularity from the entire source code base. Extracted fragments are converted to a standardized form by removing noise such as spacing, formatting and comments, and reformatting using pretty-printing. NiCad currently supports extraction of code fragments in three granularities: functions, blocks, and whole source files. NiCad automatically adapts to any programming language for which there exists a TXL grammar, and currently comes pre-loaded with grammars and extractors for ATL, C, C#, Java, PHP, Python, Ruby, Rust, Solidity, Swift, and WSDL.
- **Normalization**: In this second step, the extracted code fragments from the first step can be further normalized, filtered, or abstracted using blind or consistent renaming (to expose Type 2 similarity), filtering or abstraction of irrelevant features such as declarations, and normalization of alternatives to remove irrelevant differences.
- **Comparison**: In the third step, the extracted and normalized code fragments are compared using an optimized longest-common-subsequence (LCS) text comparison algorithm to discover if they form clone pairs. The comparison uses a user-specified difference threshold (0.0, 0.1, 0.2, ...) to allow for detection of near-miss (Type 3) clones. Identical (Type 1) code clones are detected using a difference threshold of 0.0, and a difference threshold of 0.1 allows for clones with up to 10% dissimilarity (i.e., at least 90% similarity).
- **Clustering**: NiCad can report clone detection results either as clone pairs, or as clone classes. Following comparison, clone pairs are clustered using a threshold-sensitive transitive closure to expose clone classes.

NiCad works on a directory containing the source code of a software system and outputs the code clones in the system as either clone pairs or classes, reported either as an XML database or as an interactive HTML webpage that allows for side-by-side viewing of original source fragments. While the XML form provides as easy form for further analysis, the HTML webpages allow for convenient browsing and hand-analysis of results.

1.2 Cross-Clones and Extensibility

NiCad supports cross-clone detection, the detection of code clones between versions of a single software system, or across different software systems, by reporting only those clones that cross between the two versions or systems. For example, it can be used to detect subtle differences between releases of a system in code evolution analysis, to detect licensing violations and code borrowing between systems or code bases, and to detect plagiarism in programming assignments. NiCad was designed to be extensible, using a plugin architecture that allows for easy addition of other programming languages and granularities. A detailed explanation of the NiCad plugin architecture can be found in earlier work [27].

2 Clone Analysis and Management Using NiCad

Many studies [4, 5, 9–18, 20, 23–25] have used NiCad for detecting, analyzing, and managing code clones. For example, Mondal et al. [9–15, 24, 25] used NiCad to analyze the comparative stability of cloned and non-cloned code [14], for detecting and analyzing clone-related bugs [5, 21], to investigate the impact of late propagation in code clones [19], to identify clones that are important for refactoring and tracking [16, 17, 20, 23], visualizing clone evolution [8], and for change impact analysis by suggesting co-change candidates [12]. NiCad can easily detect all the three major types of code clones (Types 1, 2, and 3) separately, making clone-type centric analysis more convenient.

Tsantalis et al. [34] automatically assessed the refactorability of three types of code clones detected by NiCad and found that Type 1 clones are more refactorable compared to other clone-types. Fontana et al. [4] devised a clone refactoring advisor by analyzing code clones detected by NiCad. Saha et al. [30] implemented a clone evolution tracker, called gCad, which is capable of extracting genealogies of near-miss code clones using NiCad.

NiCad has also been used for investigating micro-clones (code clones of at most 4 LOC) in software systems [25], and Mondal et al. [13] have detected and analyzed near-miss micro-clones using it. Islam et al. [6] have compared the bug-proneness of regular and micro-clones and have investigated bug-replication in micro-clones [7] using NiCad.

Asaduzzaman et al. [1] developed a tool called visCad for flexible analysis of code clones detected by NiCad. Mondal et al. [31] used NiCad for investigating inconsistent changes in code clones. As NiCad helps us detect three types of code clones separately, they performed their investigations on three clone-types separately.

Mondal et al. [18] also investigated evolutionary couplings in three different types of code clones using the NiCad clone detector.

NiCad has also been used for investigating change recommendation [22] by analyzing code clones. The latest version of NiCad, NiCad6, is scalable to very large software systems consisting of tens of millions of lines of code. It can be installed as a command line tool on Linux, Mac OS, Cygwin, and MinGW, and can be easily integrated with IDEs and other environments.

3 Future Research Directions

Wang et al. [38] performed a rigorous study on different clone detectors in order to find the best thresholds for detecting code clones using those detectors. According to their study, the best minimum line threshold for detecting code clones using NiCad from C and Java systems is 5 LOC. Most recent studies, however, analyze code clones at a higher minimum-line threshold, such as NiCad's default 10 LOC. Microclones (code clones of at most 4 LOC) have become a recent concern in the clone research community, and it is important to investigate whether NiCad is suitable for detecting micro-clones as well. Although a number of studies [13, 25] have already used NiCad for detecting and analyzing micro-clones, a comprehensive evaluation of NiCad in detecting such small clones would be interesting, and future research on tuning NiCad for better detection of micro-clones would add value for clone detection research.

Currently, if we apply NiCad on the entire source code of a software system, we get all the clone classes from the system. However, in a real-time coding environment programmers often need to make a focused search of the code clones of a particular target/seed fragment. NiCad does not directly provide such a targeted clone detection mode, and rather uses its cross-clone detection capability to allow for fragment search by synthesizing a system containing only the fragment. Future research on customizing NiCad to more efficiently support targeted clone search would be beneficial to the programmers, and research in this direction might also play a significant role in the wider industrialization of NiCad.

References

1. M. Asaduzzaman, C.K. Roy, K.A. Schneider, Viscad: flexible code clone analysis support for nicad, in *IWSC*, pp. 77–78 (2011)
2. J.R. Cordy, The TXL source transformation language. Sci. Comput. Program. **61**(3), 190–210 (2006)
3. J.R. Cordy, C.K. Roy, The NiCad clone detector, in *Proceedings of the 2011 IEEE 19th International Conference on Program Comprehension (ICPC' 11)*, pp. 219–220 (2011)
4. F.A. Fontana, M. Zanoni, F. Zanoni, A duplicated code refactoring advisor, in *Agile Processes, in Software Engineering, and Extreme Programming*, LNBIP(212), pp. 3–14 (2015)

5. J.F. Islam, M. Mondal, C.K. Roy, Bug replication in code clones: an empirical study, in *Proceedings of the 23rd IEEE International Conference on Software Analysis, Evolution, and Reengineering (SANER'16)*, pp. 68–78 (2016)
6. J.F. Islam, M. Mondal, C.K. Roy, A comparative study of software bugs in micro-clones and regular code clones, in *SANER*, pp. 1–11 (2019)
7. J.F. Islam, M. Mondal, C.K. Roy, K.A. Schneider, Comparing bug replication in regular and micro code clones, in *ICPC*, pp. 1–11 (2019)
8. D. Mondal, M. Mondal, C.K. Roy, K.A. Schneider, Y. Li, S. Wang, Clone-world: a visual analytic system for large scale software clones. Vis. Inform. **3**(1), 18–26 (2019)
9. M. Mondal, M.S. Rahman, C.K. Roy, K.A. Schneider, Is cloned code really stable? Empir. Softw. Eng. **23**(2), 693–770 (2018)
10. M. Mondal, B. Roy, C.K. Roy, K.A. Schneider, An empirical study on bug propagation through code cloning. J. Syst. Softw. (2019)
11. M. Mondal, B. Roy, C.K. Roy, K.A. Schneider, Investigating context adaptation bugs in code clones, in *ICSME*, pp. 157–168 (2019)
12. M. Mondal, B. Roy, C.K. Roy, K.A. Schneider, Associating code clones with association rules for change impact analysis, in *SANER*, pp. 93–103 (2020)
13. M. Mondal, B. Roy, C.K. Roy, K.A. Schneider, Investigating near-miss micro-clones in evolving software, in *ICPC*, p. 11 (2020)
14. M. Mondal, C.K. Roy, M.S. Rahman, R.K. Saha, J. Krinke, K.A. Schneider, Comparative stability of cloned and non-cloned code: an empirical study, in *Proceedings of the 27th Annual ACM Symposium on Applied Computing (SAC'12)*, pp. 1227–1234 (2012)
15. M. Mondal, C.K. Roy, K.A. Schneider, An insight into the dispersion of changes in cloned and non-cloned code: a genealogy based empirical study. Sci. Comput. Program. J. **95**(4), 445–468 (2013)
16. M. Mondal, C.K. Roy, K.A. Schneider, Automatic identification of important clones for refactoring and tracking, in *Proceedings of the IEEE 14th International Working Conference on Source Code Analysis and Manipulation (SCAM'14)*, pp. 11–20 (2014)
17. M. Mondal, C.K. Roy, K.A. Schneider, Automatic ranking of clones for refactoring through mining association rules, in *Proceedings of the IEEE Conference on Software Maintenance, Reengineering and Reverse Engineering (CSMR-WCRE'14), Software Evolution Week*, pp. 114–123 (2014)
18. M. Mondal, C.K. Roy, K.A. Schneider, A fine-grained analysis on the evolutionary coupling of cloned code, in *Proceedings of the 30th IEEE International Conference on Software Maintenance and Evolution (ICSME'14)*, pp. 51–60 (2014)
19. M. Mondal, C.K. Roy, K.A. Schneider, Late propagation in near-miss clones: an empirical study, in *Proceedings of the 8th International Workshop on Software Clones (IWSC'14)*, pp. 1–15 (2014)
20. M. Mondal, C.K. Roy, K.A. Schneider, Prediction and ranking of co-change candidates for clones, in *Proceedings of the 11th Working Conference on Mining Software (MSR'14)*, pp. 32–41 (2014)
21. M. Mondal, C.K. Roy, K.A. Schneider, A comparative study on the bug-proneness of different types of code clones, in *Proceedings of the 31st IEEE International Conference on Software Maintenance and Evolution (ICSME'15)*, pp. 91–100 (2015)
22. M. Mondal, C.K. Roy, K.A. Schneider, An empirical study on change recommendation, in *Proceedings of the 25th Annual International Conference on Computer Science and Software Engineering (CASCON'15)*, pp. 141–150 (2015)
23. M. Mondal, C.K. Roy, K.A. Schneider, SPCP-Miner: a tool for mining code clones that are important for refactoring or tracking, in *Proceedings of the 22nd IEEE International Conference on Software Analysis, Evolution, and Reengineering (SANER'15)*, pp. 482–486 (2015)
24. M. Mondal, C.K. Roy, K.A. Schneider, A comparative study on the intensity and harmfulness of late propagation in near-miss code clones. Softw. Qual. J. **24**(4), 883–915 (2016)
25. M. Mondal, C.K. Roy, K.A. Schneider, Micro-clones in evolving software, in *SANER*, pp. 50–60 (2018)

26. C.K. Roy, J.R. Cordy, A survey on software clone detection research, in *Tech Report TR 2007-541, School of Computing, Queens University, Canada*, pp. 1–115 (2007)
27. C.K. Roy, J.R. Cordy, NICAD: accurate detection of near-miss intentional clones using flexible pretty-printing and code normalization, in *Proceedings of the 16th IEEE International Conference on Program Comprehension (ICPC'08)*, pp. 172–181 (2008)
28. C.K. Roy, J.R. Cordy, Adventuures in NICAD: a ten-year retrospective. In *ICPC*, p. 19 (2018) (MIP Abstract)
29. C.K. Roy, J.R. Cordy, Benchmarks for software clone detection: a ten-year retrospective. In *SANER*, pp. 26–37 (2018)
30. R.K. Saha, C.K. Roy, K.A. Schneider, An automatic framework for extracting and classifying near-miss clone genealogies, in *Proceedings of the 27th IEEE International Conference on Software Maintenance (ICSM'11)*, pp. 293–302 (2011)
31. K.A. Schneider, M. Mondal, C.K. Roy, A fine-grained analysis on the inconsistent changes in code clones, in *ICSME*, pp. 220–231 (2020)
32. A. Sheneamer, J. Kalita, Article: a survey of software clone detection techniques. Int. J. Comput. Appl. **137**(10), 1–21 (2016)
33. J. Svajlenko, C.K. Roy, Evaluating modern clone detection tools, in *Proceedings of the 2014 IEEE International Conference on Software Maintenance and Evolution (ICSME'14)*, pp. 321–330 (2014)
34. N. Tsantalis, D. Mazinanian, G.P. Krishnan, Assessing the refactorability of software clones. IEEE Trans. Softw. Eng. **41**(11), 1055–1090 (2015)
35. S. Uddin, C.K. Roy, K.A. Schneider, SimCad: an extensible and faster clone detection tool for large scale software systems, in *Proceedings of the IEEE 21st International Conference on Program Comprehension (ICPC'13)*, pp. 236–238 (2013)
36. S. Uddin, C.K. Roy, K.A. Schneider, A. Hindle, On the effectiveness of simhash for detecting near-miss clones in large scale software systems, in *WCRE*, pp. 13–22 (2011)
37. S. Uddin, C.K. Roy, K.A. Schneider, A. Hindle, Simcad: a ten-year retrospective, in *SANER* (2021) (oral presentation)
38. T. Wang, M. Harman, Y. Jia, J. Krinke, Searching for better configurations: a rigorous approach to clone evaluation, in *Proceedings of the 9th Joint Meeting on Foundations of Software Engineering (ESEC/FSE'13)*, pp. 455–465 (2013)

SourcererCC: Scalable and Accurate Clone Detection

Hitesh Sajnani, Vaibhav Saini, Chanchal K. Roy, and Cristina Lopes

Abstract Clone detection is an active area of research. However, there is a marked lack in clone detectors that scale to very large repositories of source code, in particular for detecting near-miss clones where significant editing activities may take place in the cloned code. SourcererCC was developed as an attempt to fill this gap. It is a widely used token-based clone detector that targets three clone types, and exploits an index to achieve scalability to large inter-project repositories using a standard workstation. SourcererCC uses an optimized inverted-index to quickly query the potential clones of a given code block. Filtering heuristics based on token ordering are used to significantly reduce the size of the index, the number of code-block comparisons needed to detect the clones, as well as the number of required token-comparisons needed to judge a potential clone. In the evaluation experiments, SourcererCC demonstrated both high recall and precision, and the ability to scale to a large inter-project repository (250MLOC) even using a standard workstation. This chapter reflects on some of the principle design decisions behind the success of SourcererCC and also presents an architecture to scale it horizontally.

1 Introduction

With the amount of source code increasing steadily, large-scale clone detection has become a necessity. Large code bases and repositories of projects have led to several new use cases of clone detection including mining library candidates [11], detecting similar mobile applications [3], license violation detection [14], reverse engineering product lines [8], finding the provenance of a component [5], and code search [12].

H. Sajnani (✉) · V. Saini
Microsoft, Redmond, USA
e-mail: hsajnani@uci.edu

C. K. Roy
University of Saskatchewan, Saskatoon, Canada

C. Lopes
University of California, Irvine, USA

While presenting new opportunities for the application of clone detection, these modern use cases also pose scalability challenges.

1.1 Motivation

To further illustrate the problem and its scale in practice, consider a real-life scenario where a retail banking software system is maintained by Tata Consultancy Services (TCS). A team at TCS deployed the banking system for many different banks (clients) and maintained a separate code base for each of these banks. After following this practice for a while, they decided to form a common code base for all these banks to minimize expenses occurring due to (i) duplicated efforts to deliver the common features and (ii) separately maintaining existing common parts of different code bases.

As part of this bigger goal, the team decided to first identify common code blocks across all the code bases. In order to assess the feasibility of using clone detection tools for this task, the team[1] ran CloneDR, an AST-based commercial clone detection tool on ML0000, a single COBOL program consisting of 88K LOC. The clone detection process took around 8 h on an IBM T43 Thinkpad default specification[2] machine. Each bank's code base (8 of them) ran into multi-million lines of code spanning across thousands of such COBOL programs in different dialects, posing a major scalability challenge.

This situation at TCS is not unique and in fact represents the state of many companies in the service industry that are now moving away from the greenfield development model and adopting the packaging model to build and deliver software. In fact, as Cordy points out, it is a common practice in industry to clone a module and maintain it in parallel [4]. Similarly in open source development, developers often clone modules or fork projects to meet the needs of different clients, and may need large-scale clone detectors to merge these cloned systems toward a product-line style of development.

While the above use cases are more pertinent to industry, researchers are also interested in studying cloning in large software ecosystems (e.g., Debian), or in open-source development communities (e.g., GitHub) to assess its impact on software development and its properties. However, very few tools can scale to the demands of clone detection in very large code bases [20]. For example, Kim and Notkin [13] reflected how they wanted to use clone detection tools for doing origin analysis of software files but were constrained by its speed due to n-to-n file comparison. In his work on using clone detection to identify license violations, Koschke [14] reflects the following: "Detecting license violations of source code requires to compare a suspected system against a very large corpus of source code, for instance, the Debian source distribution. Thus, code clone detection techniques must scale in

---

[1] The author was part of the team that carried out the analysis.

[2] i5 processor, 8 GB RAM, and 500 GB disk storage.

terms of resources needed". In 2014, Debian had 43,000[3] software packages and approximately 323 million lines of code. In one of their studies to investigate cloning in FreeBSD, Livieri et al. [16] motivate the need for scalable code clone detection tools as follows: "Current clone detection tools are incapable of dealing with a corpus of this size, and might either take literally months to complete a detection run, or might simply crash due to lack of resources".

1.2 Challenges

While a few novel algorithms [10, 16] in the last decade demonstrated scalability, they do not support Type-3 near-miss clones, where minor to significant editing activities might have taken place in the copy/pasted fragments. These tools therefore miss a large portion of the clones, since there are more number of Type-3 clones in the repositories than the other types. Furthermore, the ability to detect Type-3 clones is most needed in large-scale clone detection applications [18].

Many techniques have also been proposed to achieve a few specific applications of large-scale clone detection [3, 14], however, they make assumptions regarding the requirements of their target domain to achieve scalability, for example, detecting only file-level clones to identify copyright infringement, or detecting clones only for a given block (clone search) in a large corpus. These domain-specific techniques are not described as general large-scale clone detectors, and face significant scalability challenges for general clone detection.

The scalability of clone detection tools is also constrained by the computational nature of the problem itself. A fundamental way of identifying if two code blocks are clones is to measure the degree of similarity between them, where similarity is measured using a similarity function. A higher similarity value indicates that code blocks are more similar. Thus we can consider pairs of code blocks with high similarity value as clones. In other words, to detect all the clones in a system, each code block has to be compared against every other code block (also known as candidate code blocks), bearing a prohibitively $O(n^2)$ time complexity. Hence, it is an algorithmic challenge to perform this comparison in an efficient and scalable way. This challenge, along with modern use cases and today's large systems, makes large-scale code clone detection a difficult problem.

The above challenges can be characterized in the form of the following research questions.

Research Question 1. [Design]—How can we be more robust to modifications in cloned code to detect Type-3 clones?

Research Question 2. [Computational Complexity]—How can we reduce the $O(n^2)$ candidate comparisons to $O(c.n)$, where $c << n$?

Research Question 3. [Engineering]—How can we make faster candidate comparisons without requiring much memory?

---

[3] https://en.wikipedia.org/wiki/Debian.

Research Question 1 has a direct implication on the accuracy of the clone detection technique, and Research Questions 2 and 3 focus on improving the scalability and efficiency of the clone detection technique.

SourererCC [19] addresses the above challenges leading to an accurate and fast approach to clone detection that is both scalable to very large software repositories and robust against code modifications.

2 SourcererCC

The core idea of SourcererCC is to build an optimized index of code blocks and compare them using a simple and fast bag-of-tokens[4] strategy which is resilient to Type-3 changes (Research Question 1). Several filtering heuristics are used to reduce the size of the index, which significantly reduces the number of code block comparisons to detect the clones. SourcererCC also exploits the ordering of tokens in a code block to measure a live upper-bound on the similarity of code blocks in order to reject or accept a clone candidate with minimal token comparisons (Research Question 2 and 3).

2.1   Bag-of-Tokens Model

SourcererCC represents a code block using a bag-of-tokens model where tokens are assumed to appear independently of one another and their order is irrelevant. The idea is to transform code blocks in a form that enables SourcererCC to detect clones that have different syntax but similar meaning. Moreover, this representation also filters out code blocks with specified structure patterns. Since SourcererCC matches tokens and not sequences or structures, it has a high tolerance to minor modifications, making it effective in detecting Type-3 clones, including clones where statements are swapped, added, and/or deleted.

The overlap similarity measure simply computes the intersection between the code fragments by counting the number of tokens shared between them. The intuition here is simple. *If two code fragments have many tokens in common, then they are likely to be similar to some degree.*

It is interesting to note that such a simple strategy could prove to be so effective in a complex software engineering task of identifying code clones. The primary reason for the effectiveness of bag-of-tokens and overlap similarity measure is rooted in the program vocabulary used by the developers while writing code. While programming languages in theory are complex and powerful, the programs that real people write are mostly simple and rather repetitive and similar [9]. This similarity is manifested in the source code in the form of tokens, and particularly in identifiers. In source code,

---

[4] Similar to the popular bag-of-words model [22] in Information Retrieval.

identifiers (e.g., names of variables, methods, classes, parameters, and attributes) account for approximately more than 70% of the linguistic information [6]. Many researchers have concluded that identifiers reflect the semantics and the role of the named entities they are intended to label [1, 7, 15]. Therefore, code fragments having similar semantics are likely to have similarities in their identifiers. Furthermore, oftentimes, during copy-paste-modify practice, developers preserve identifier names as they reflect the underlying functionality of the code that is copied. They seem to be aware of the fact that different names used for the same concept or even identical names used for different concepts reflect misunderstandings and foster further misconceptions [6]. As a result, while copied fragments are edited to adapt to the context in which they are copied, they often have enough syntactical similarity associated with the original fragment. This similarity is effectively captured by the bag-of-tokens model in conjunction with the overlap similarity measure.

Of course, there are scenarios when programmers may deliberately obfuscate code to conceal its purpose (security through obscurity) or its logic, in order to prevent tampering, deter reverse engineering, hide plagiarism, or as a puzzle or recreational challenge for someone reading the source code. The simple bag-of-tokens model of SourcererCC may not be effective in detecting clones in such cases. Other tools like Deckard that rely on AST, or NiCad that uses heavy normalization, may be effective under such scenarios.

2.2 Filtering Heuristics to Reduce Candidate Comparisons

In order to detect all clone pairs in a project or a repository, the above approach of computing the similarity between two code blocks can simply be extended to iterate over all the code blocks and compute pairwise similarity for each code block pair. For a given code block, all the other code blocks compared are called candidate code blocks or candidates in short. While the approach is very simple and intuitive, it is also subject to a fundamental problem that prohibits scalability—$O(n^2)$ time complexity. Figure 1 describes this by plotting the number of total code blocks (X-axis) versus the number of candidate comparisons (Y-axis) in 35 Apache Java projects. Note that the granularity of a code block is taken as a method. Points denoted by o show how the number of candidates compared increases quadratically[5] with the increase in the number of methods. SourcererCC uses advanced index structures and filtering heuristics—*sub-block overlap filtering and token position filtering*—to significantly reduce the number of candidate comparisons during clone detection. These heuristics are inspired by the work of Chaudhuri et al. [2] and Xiao et al. [21] on efficient set similarity joins in databases. Sub-block overlap filtering follows an intuition that when two sets have a large overlap, even their smaller subsets should overlap. Since

---

[5] The curve can also be represented using $y = x(x-1)/2$ quadratic function where x is the number of methods in a project and y is the number of candidate comparisons carried out to detect all clone pairs.

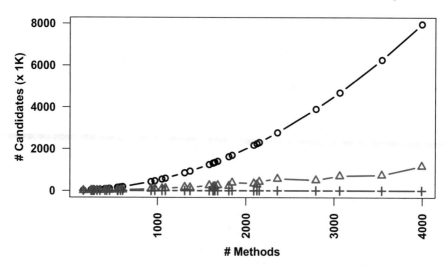

Fig. 1 Growth in the number of candidate comparisons with the increase in the number of code blocks. ○ show quadratic increase in candidate comparisons; △ denote the number of candidate comparisons after applying the sub-block overlap filtering; + denote the number of candidate comparisons after applying the token position filtering

we represent code blocks as bag-of-tokens (i.e., a multiset), we can extend this idea to code blocks, i.e., when two code blocks have a large overlap, even their smaller sub-blocks should overlap. This constraint allows one to reduce the number of candidate comparisons by eliminating candidates that do not share a similarity in their sub-blocks. Revisiting Fig. 1, the points denoted by △ show the number of candidate comparisons after applying the sub-block overlap filtering. The large difference from the earlier curve (○) shows the impact of filtering in eliminating candidate comparisons. It turns out that if the tokens in the code block are further arranged to follow a pre-defined order (e.g., order of popularity of tokens in the corpus), we can further reduce the number of token and candidate comparisons by computing a safe upper-bound (without violating the correctness). This filtering is termed token position filtering. The points denoted by + in Fig. 1 show the number of candidate comparisons after applying the token position filtering. The reduction is so significant that empirically on this dataset, the function seems to be *near-linear*. This is a massive reduction in the number of comparisons when compared to the quadratic number of comparisons shown earlier without any filtering.

3 Distributed SourcererCC: Scaling SourcererCC Horizontally

SourcererCC advances the state of the art in code clone detection tools that can scale vertically using high-power CPUs and memory added to a single machine. While this approach works well in most of the cases, in certain scenarios using vertical scalable approaches may not be feasible as they are bounded by the amount of data that can fit into the memory of a single machine. In such scenarios, timely computing clones in ultra-large datasets are beyond the capacity of a single machine.

Under such scenarios, efficient parallelization of the computation process is the only feasible option. Previously, research in this direction was limited due to the lack of the availability of resources and the cost of setting up the infrastructure. But the recent developments in the field of cloud computing and the availability of low-cost infrastructure services like Amazon Web Services (AWS), Azure, and Google Cloud have enabled the research in this area.

However, it is important to note that simply dividing the input space and parallelizing the clone detection operation do not solve the problem, because running tools on projects individually, and then combining the results in the later step, would lead to a collection of common clones, but would not identify clones across division boundaries [16]. Thus, efficient parallelization of the computation process is necessary.

SourcererCC's extensible architecture can be easily adapted to horizontally scale to multiple processors and efficiently detect the first three types of clones on large datasets preserving the same detection quality (recall and precision). We call this extension of SourcererCC Distributed SoucererCC or SourcererCC-D.

SourcererCC-D operates on a cluster of nodes by constructing the index of the entire corpus that is shared across all the nodes, and then parallelizes the clone searching process by distributing the tasks across all the nodes in the cluster. In order to achieve this, SourcererCC-D follows a standard *Shared disk* (see Fig. 2) or a *Shared memory* (see Fig. 3) architecture style.

A shared disk architecture (SD) is a distributed computing paradigm in which all disks are accessible from all the cluster nodes. While the nodes may or may not have their own private memory, it is imperative that they at least share the disk space. A

Fig. 2 Shared disk architecture style

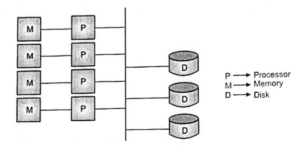

Fig. 3 Shared memory
architecture style

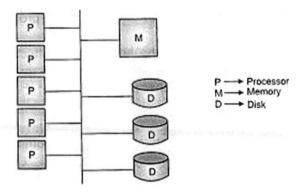

shared memory architecture (SM) is a distributed computing paradigm in which the cluster nodes not only share the disks but also have access to global shared memory.

Figure 4 describes SourcererCC-D's clone detection process. Let us assume a cluster of $N + 1$ nodes.[6] Initially, a master node (any one of the cluster nodes) runs the parser on the entire corpus and produces a parsed input file containing code blocks according to the granularity set by the user. Next, the master node runs SourcererCC's Indexer on the parsed input file to build an index. The constructed index, also known as a global index, resides on the shared disk and hence is accessible by all the nodes in the cluster. After the global index is constructed, the master node splits the parsed input file into N different files namely Q_1, Q_2, Q_3,...Q_N and distributes them to each node in the cluster. Each node is now responsible to locally compute clones of code blocks in its respective query file using SourcererCC's Searcher. Note that since each node has access to the global index, it can find all the clones in the entire corpus for its given input, i.e., clones present across other nodes. It is for this reason, nodes must have a shared disk space to store the global index. When all the nodes finish executing the Searcher, all the clones in the corpus are found.

Note that in the above design, while the search phase is distributed and happens in parallel, the index construction phase is not parallelized (only the master node constructs the index). However, this hardly impacts the overall clone detection performance because we found that index construction takes less than 4% of the total time to detect clones.

SourcererCC-D can be deployed on in-house clusters, cloud services like AWS, Azure, or even in-house multi-processor machines. The ability to scale to multiple machines enables SourererCC to be effectively used for ultra-large datasets (e.g., entire corpus of GitHub) as demonstrated in [17].

---

[6] In case of a single high-performance multi-processor machine, $N + 1$ is the number of processors available on that machine.

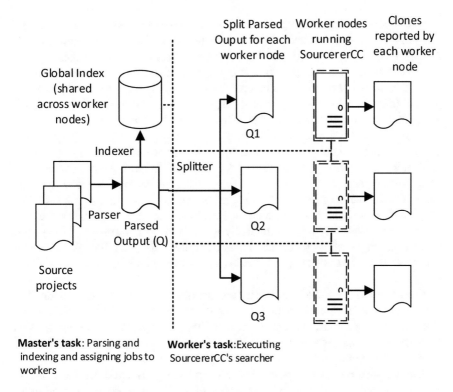

Master's task: Parsing and indexing and assigning jobs to workers

Worker's task:Executing SourcererCC's searcher

Fig. 4 SourcererCC-D's clone detection process

4   Lessons Learned During Implementation

There were many lessons learned during the design, development, and testing of SourcererCC. While these lessons are not new, this section reflects upon them, as they played an important role in the successful development and adoption of the SourcererCC tool in the academic community. We believe tool designers could benefit from our experience and reflection.

Everything breaks at scale. One of the key lessons during SourcererCC's development can be aptly described in a phrase—"Everything breaks at scale, so expect the unexpected". We realized that at scale, we cannot test for every error. As a result, we used assertions and exception handlers for things that can't happen. We added diagnostic code, logging, and tracing to help explain what is going on at run-time, especially when we ran into problems during development. The philosophy—if this failed, look for what else can fail—played a very important role during SourcererCC's development.

Fault Tolerance. During the initial stages of the development, SourcererCC crashed at times while running on large datasets after several hours of execution due to unexpected reasons. Since SourcererCC did not have the mechanism to preserve its execution state during that time, such failures resulted in a loss of several hours of computation time and effort, not to mention the frustration that comes along. Based on these experiences, we realized that SourcererCC's exception handler must preserve its state of the execution (i.e., keeping track of how much data is already processed), so when interrupted, SourcererCC's execution can resume correctly from the point of failure at a later time. The necessity of logging how much data is processed by the tool is an important lesson that we learned the hard way.

Memory Leaks. SourcererCC is written in Java programming language which has its own garbage collection mechanism. However, we encountered bugs related to memory leaks while testing SourcererCC on large datasets. What I learned from debugging memory leak issues is that while there are simple solutions to detect and deal with memory leaks (e.g., logging the size of your data structures when you modify them, and then searching the logs for data structures that grow beyond a reasonable size), a tool is undoubtedly a big help. In the absence of the right tools, debugging such issues could take unreasonable time and effort. We were able to resolve these issues much faster using open-source tools like VisualVM[7] and Profiler4J.[8]

The problem could be in the data too. Oftentimes when we noticed anomalies in the execution of SourcererCC, we thought that the issue would be in the code. However, it was not unusual to find issues with either the input data or our assumptions about the input data. As a result, we realized that it is always useful to check for data consistency and integrity even before any experimentation.

Tuning parameters to optimize SourcererCC's performance. SourcererCC has a few parameters (e.g., similarity threshold, tokenization strategies, and minimum size threshold of a code block) that had to be tuned to optimize for accuracy, scalability, and efficiency. This resulted in countless experiments, and keeping track of these experiments and their settings posed a severe challenge.

To do this exercise systematically, we adopted the following process that indeed turned out to be very effective.

We created a smaller dataset for parameter tuning experiments. Apart from the smaller size, this dataset had characteristics very similar to the large datasets on which SourcererCC is intended to be used. Executing SourcererCC on a smaller dataset took less time, thus giving us more freedom to experiment.

In order to better keep track of SourcererCC's performance on different parameter configurations, we created a SourcererCC revision (using Git) for each configuration of parameters. This not only enabled us to run several experiments in parallel but also helped to easily switch back-and-forth across various parameter configurations.

To summarize, creating SourcererCC's revisions for various parameter configurations and running them in parallel on a smaller dataset greatly reduced the turnaround time for performing experiments to tune SourcererCC.

SourcererCC is publicly available and actively maintained. It can be downloaded from https://github.com/Mondego/SourcererCC.

---

[7] https://visualvm.java.net/.

[8] http://profiler4j.sourceforge.net/.

5 Going Forward

Code Clone detection research has come a long way in the last couple of decades. We conclude by identifying some of the relevant areas that might shape the future research in this field. There are many tools available for clone detection. In contrast, there are relatively few tools that help in removing or effectively managing clones. Identifying various means of eliminating harmful clones through automated tool support is an interesting venue to explore in the future. Large-scale clone detection is often faced with the challenge of how to make sense of the large data produced by the clone detection tools. Visual and interactive representations of the output to reinforce human cognition and produce actionable insight is another useful direction for the future. The utility of clone detection is not just limited to source code. Clone detection in other software artifacts, including models, bug-reports, requirement documents, and binaries, is turning out to be a necessity for several use cases. For example, the ability to detect clones in software binaries is necessary for effectively detecting Malwares and License Infringement. Therefore, extending code clone detection research to other software artifacts is a promising area for the future. Clone research should also focus on clone management by (i) identifying and prioritizing the clones that are of interest to the developers for a given task, (ii) helping developers pro actively assess the negative consequence of cloning, and (iii) categorizing clones as harmful and harmless after detection. With the several new use cases of clone detection emerging, a reorientation of research focus toward application-oriented clone detection might be useful. In many cases, state-of-the-art clone detection tools do not behave well for these specific use cases. These observations point to the new research opportunities to enhance clone detection technologies. Moreover, use case-specific benchmarking to evaluate various tools and techniques might be another area to focus on in the future.

References

1. C. Caprile, P. Tonella, Nomen est omen: analyzing the language of function identifiers, in *Reverse Engineering. Proceedings. Sixth Working Conference on* (1999), pp 112–122. https://doi.org/10.1109/WCRE.1999.806952
2. S. Chaudhuri, V. Ganti, R. Kaushik, A primitive operator for similarity joins in data cleaning, in *Proceedings of the 22nd International Conference on Data Engineering, IEEE Computer Society, Washington, DC, USA, ICDE '06* (2006), pp 5. https://doi.org/10.1109/ICDE.2006.9
3. K. Chen, P. Liu, Y. Zhang, Achieving accuracy and scalability simultaneously in detecting application clones on android markets, in *Proceedings of the 36th International Conference on Software Engineering, ACM, New York, NY, USA,* (ICSE 2014), pp 175–186
4. J.R. Cordy, Comprehending reality-practical barriers to industrial adoption of software maintenance automation, in *Program Comprehension, 2003. 11th IEEE International Workshop on* (IEEE, 2003), pp 196–205
5. J. Davies, D. German, M. Godfrey, A. Hindle, Software Bertillonage: finding the provenance of an entity, in *Proceedings of MSR* (2011)

6. F. Deissenboeck, M. Pizka, Concise and consistent naming. Softw. Qual. J. **14**(3), 261–282. https://doi.org/10.1007/s11219-006-9219-1
7. L. Guerrouj, Normalizing source code vocabulary to support program comprehension and software quality, in *Software Engineering (ICSE), 2013 35th International Conference on*(2013), pp 1385–1388. https://doi.org/10.1109/ICSE.2013.6606723
8. A. Hemel, R. Koschke, Reverse engineering variability in source code using clone detection: a case study for linux variants of consumer electronic devices, in *Proceedings of Working Conference on Reverse Engineering* (2012), pp 357–366
9. A. Hindle, E. T. Barr, Z. Su, M. Gabel, P. Devanbu, On the naturalness of software, in *Proceedings of the 34th International Conference on Software Engineering* (IEEE Press, Piscataway, NJ, USA, ICSE '12, 2012), pp 837–847. http://dl.acm.org/citation.cfm?id=2337223.2337322
10. B. Hummel, E. Juergens, L. Heinemann, M. Conradt, Index-based code clone detection:incremental, distributed, scalable, in *Proceedings of ICSM* (2010)
11. T. Ishihara, K. Hotta, Y. Higo, H. Igaki, S. Kusumoto, Inter-project functional clone detection toward building libraries: an empirical study on 13,000 projects, in *Reverse Engineering (WCRE), 2012 19th Working Conference on* (2012), pp 387–391. https://doi.org/10.1109/WCRE.2012.48
12. I. Keivanloo, J. Rilling, P. Charland, Internet-scale real-time code clone search via multi-level indexing, in *Proceedings of WCRE* (2011)
13. M. Kim, D. Notkin, Program element matching for multi-version program analyses, in *Proceedings of the 2006 International Workshop on Mining Software Repositories* (ACM, New York, NY, USA, MSR '06, 2006), pp 58–64. https://doi.org/10.1145/1137983.1137999
14. R. Koschke, Large-scale inter-system clone detection using suffix trees, in *Proceedings of CSMR* (2012), pp. 309–318
15. D. Lawrie, C. Morrell, H. Feild, D. Binkley, What's in a name? a study of identifiers, in *14th IEEE International Conference on Program Comprehension (ICPC'06)* (2006), pp. 3–12. https://doi.org/10.1109/ICPC.2006.51
16. S. Livieri, Y. Higo, M. Matsushita, K. Inoue, Very-large scale code clone analysis and visualization of open source programs using distributed ccfinder: D-ccfinder, in *Proceedings of ICSE* (2007)
17. C. V. Lopes, P. Maj, P. Martins, V. Saini, D. Yang, J. Zitny, H. Sajnani, J. Vitek, Déjàvu: a map of code duplicates on github, in *Proceedings of the ACM Program Lang 1(OOPSLA)* (2017). https://doi.org/10.1145/3133908
18. C. Roy, M. Zibran, R. Koschke, The vision of software clone management: past, present, and future (keynote paper), in *Software Maintenance, Reengineering and Reverse Engineering (CSMR-WCRE), 2014 Software Evolution Week–IEEE Conference on* (2014), pp. 18–33
19. H. Sajnani, V. Saini, J. Svajlenko, C.K. Roy, C.V. Lopes, Sourcerercc: scaling code clone detection to big-code, in *Proceedings of the 38th International Conference on Software Engineering, Association for Computing Machinery* (New York, NY, USA, ICSE '16, 2016), pp. 1157–1168. https://doi.org/10.1145/2884781.2884877
20. J. Svajlenko, I. Keivanloo, C. Roy, Scaling classical clone detection tools for ultra-large datasets: an exploratory study, in *Software Clones (IWSC), 2013 7th International Workshop on* (2013), pp. 16–22
21. C. Xiao, W. Wang, X. Lin, J. X. Yu, Efficient similarity joins for near duplicate detection, in *Proceedings of the 17th International Conference on World Wide Web* (ACM, New York, NY, USA, WWW '08, 2008), pp. 131–140. https://doi.org/10.1145/1367497.1367516
22. Y. Zhang, R. Jin, Z.H. Zhou, Understanding bag-of-words model: a statistical framework. Int. J. Mach. Learn. Cybern. **1**(1-4), 43–52 (2010). https://doi.org/10.1007/s13042-010-0001-0

Oreo: Scaling Clone Detection Beyond Near-Miss Clones

Vaibhav Saini, Farima Farmahinifarahani, Hitesh Sajnani, and Cristina Lopes

Abstract With recent advancements in the field of code clone detection, researchers have made it possible to scale large datasets. The scope of scalable and accurate clone detection, however, was limited to Type-1, Type-2, and near-miss Type-3 clones. Most clone detectors fail to detect clones beyond the near-miss Type-3 category as it becomes hard to detect such clones in a scalable manner. There are two main challenges in identifying clones beyond the Type-3 category: (1) Syntactical similarity is low between such complex clones and (2) comparing code snippets leads to prohibitive quadratic comparisons, which causes candidate explosion and leads to scalability issues. Oreo introduces a novel semantic filter named *Action filter* which filters out a large number of code pairs that do not share semantic similarities, thereby addressing the candidate explosion issue. Moreover, the candidates that pass this filter have high semantic similarity which leads to the detection of complex and semantically similar clones. As many semantically similar candidates may not be clones, Oreo uses a deep learning model to validate the structural similarity between the semantically similar candidates, which leads to greater accuracy in clone detection. Oreo demonstrated broader range of clone detection, high recall, precision, speed, and ability to scale to a large inter-project repository (250MLOC) using a standard workstation. This chapter aims to describe the design decisions and concepts which enabled Oreo to take scalable and accurate clone detection beyond the near-miss clones.

V. Saini (✉) · H. Sajnani
Microsoft, Redmond, USA
e-mail: hsajnani@uci.edu

F. Farmahinifarahani · C. Lopes
University of California Irvine, Irvine, USA
e-mail: lopes@uci.edu

© The Author(s), under exclusive license to Springer Nature Singapore Pte Ltd. 2021
K. Inoue and C. K. Roy (eds.), *Code Clone Analysis*,
https://doi.org/10.1007/978-981-16-1927-4_5

1 Introduction

Most clone detectors in the literature tend to aim for detecting specific types of clones, usually up to Type-3. Very few of them attempt at detecting pure Type-4 clones, since it requires analysis of the actual behavior, which is a hard problem in general. As we move from Type-3 to Type-4 clone categories, there lies a spectrum of clones, which, although are within the reach of automatic clone detection, are increasingly difficult to detect. Reflecting the vastness of this spectrum, the popular clone benchmark BigCloneBench [12] includes subcategories between Type-3 and Type-4, namely Very Strongly Type-3, Strongly Type-3, Moderately Type-3, and Weakly Type-3, which merge with Type-4.

Listing 1.1 Different Clone Categories [7]

```
1
2   // Original method
3   String sequence(int start, int stop) {
4       StringBuilder builder = new StringBuilder();
5       int i = start;
6       while (i <= stop) {
7           if (i > start) builder.append(',');
8           builder.append(i);
9           i++;
10      }
11      return builder.toString();
12  }
13
14  -----------------------------------------------------------
15  // Type-2 clone of Original method
16  String sequence(int begin, int end) {
17      StringBuilder builder = new StringBuilder();
18      int n = begin;
19      while (n <= end) {
20          if (n > begin) builder.append(',');
21          builder.append(n);
22          n++;
23      }
24      return builder.toString();
25  }
26
27  -----------------------------------------------------------
28  // Very strongly Type-3 clone of Original method
29  String sequence(short start, short stop) {
30      StringBuilder builder = new StringBuilder();
31      for (short i = start; i <= stop; i++) {
```

```
32        if (i > start) builder.append(',');
33        builder.append(i);
34      }
35      return builder.toString();
36  }
37
38  ---------------------------------------------------------------
39  // Moderately Type-3 clone of Original method
40  String seq(int start, int stop){
41      String sep = ",";
42      String result = Integer.toString(start);
43      for (int i = start + 1; ; i++) {
44          if (i > stop) break;
45          result = String.join(sep, result, Integer.toString(i));
46      }
47      return result;
48  }
49
50  ---------------------------------------------------------------
51  // Weakly Type-3 clone of Original method
52  String seq(int begin, int end, String sep){
53      String result = Integer.toString(begin);
54      for (int n = begin + 1; ;n++) {
55          if (end < n) break;
56          result = String.join(sep, result, Integer.toString(n));
57      }
58      return result;
59  }
60
61  ---------------------------------------------------------------
62  // Type-4 clone of Original method
63  String range(short n, short m){
64      if (n == m)
65          return Short.toString(n);
66      return Short.toString(n)+ "," + range(n+1, m);
67  }
```

In order to illustrate the spectrum of clone detection and its challenges, Listing 1.1 shows one example method followed by several of its clones, from Type-2 to Type-4. The original method takes two integers as parameters *start* and *end* and returns a comma-separated sequence of integers in between the two numbers, as a string. The Type-2 clone (starting in line #15) is syntactically identical to the original method but differs only in the identifiers used (e.g. the parameter *start* has been replaced by begin). It is easy for clone detectors to identify such clones. The very strong

Type-3 clone of the original method (starting in line #28) has some lexical as well as syntactic differences. It uses a for-loop instead of a while-loop. Although harder than Type-2, modern clone detectors can detect this subcategory of Type-3 relatively easily. The moderate Type-3 clone (starting in line #39) differs even more from the original method. Here, the method's name is different (seq vs. sequence), the comma is placed in its own local variable named *sep*, and instead of using the type StringBuilder, this method uses the type String. Modern clone detectors find it much harder to detect this subcategory of Type-3 clones than the previous ones. The weak Type-3 clone (starting in line#51) differs from the original method by a combination of lexical, syntactic, and semantic changes. The differences here include String versus StringBuilder, a conditional whose logic has changed, and the use of an additional input parameter, which lets the caller of the method decide what separator to use. The similarities here are weak and very hard to detect. Finally, the Type-4 clone (starting in line #62) implements a similar but not the exact same functionality in a completely different manner. This clone variant uses recursion instead of iteration, and it has almost no lexical or syntactic similarities to the original method. Detecting Type-4 clones, in general, requires a deep understanding of the intent of a piece of code, especially because the goal of clone detection is similarity, and not exact equivalence in structure and semantics.

Clones that are moderately Type-3 and onward fall in the *Twilight Zone* of clone detection. The reported precision and recall of existing clone detectors drop dramatically in this spectrum. Oreo aims to improve the performance of clone detection for these hard-to-detect clones.

The goals driving the design of Oreo [7] are twofold: (1) Oreo wants to detect clones in the Twilight Zone without hurting precision and (2) Oreo should be able to process very large datasets consisting of hundreds of millions of methods. To accomplish the first goal, Oreo introduces the concept of semantic signature based on actions performed by that method. To analyze structural similarity, Oreo uses machine learning based on features generated from methods' software metrics. By comparing semantic signature and structural similarities of methods, Oreo ensures the detection of complex clones which are in the Twilight Zone. In order to accomplish the second goal, Oreo uses a simple size-based heuristic that eliminates a large number of unlikely clone pairs. Additionally, the use of semantic signatures also allows it to eliminate unlikely clone pairs early on, leaving the machine learning-based metrics analysis to only the most likely clone pairs.

Table 1 shows the reported recall and precision numbers for Oreo. It has near-perfect recall in T1, T2, VST3, and ST3 clone categories. In the harder to detect clone categories (the Twilight Zone), namely MT3 and WT3, Oreo pushes the boundaries of clone detection as it detects a large number of clones while maintaining a healthy precision of 89.5%. To give some perspective, SourcererCC, which is not designed to detect clones in the Twilight Zone, detects 5% clones in MT3 and almost 0% in WT3 categories. Oreo is a scalable clone detector which was reported to scale the entire IJaDataset, a large inter-project Java repository containing 25,000 open-source projects [1]. There are around 3 million source files and around 250 million lines

Table 1 Oreo's reported recall and precision measurements on BigCloneBench

Recall						Precision
T1	T2	VST3	ST3	MT3	WT3	Sample size = 400
100	99	100	89	30	0.7	89.5

of code in this dataset. At the time of publication of Oreo, only two other clone detectors, SourcererCC and CloneWorks, have been shown to scale to this dataset.

2 Overview

Figure 1 gives an overview of Oreo. To find out if a method M_1 is a clone of another method M_2, Oreo first applies a size filter where it compares the size of both methods. If one method is significantly smaller than the other method, Oreo rejects the pair. The intuition is that two methods with considerably different sizes are very unlikely to implement the same, or even similar, functionality. It is important to note that this heuristic can lead to some false negatives, specifically in the case of Type-4 clones.

Oreo uses the number of tokens in the method as a metric of size where tokens are language keywords, literals (strings literals are split on whitespace), types, and identifiers. This is the same definition used in other clone detection work (e.g. [9]). Given a similarity threshold T between 0 and 1, and a method M_1 with x tokens, if a method M_2 is a clone of M_1, then its number of tokens, y, should satisfy the inequation $x \times T \leq y \leq \dfrac{x}{T}$.

If a method pair satisfies the size filter, the semantic signatures of the two methods are then compared. Oreo captures the semantics of methods using semantic signature consisting of Action tokens. The Action tokens of a method are the tokens corresponding to methods called and fields accessed by that method. Additionally, Oreo captures array accesses (e.g. student[i] and student[i+1]) as ArrayAccess and

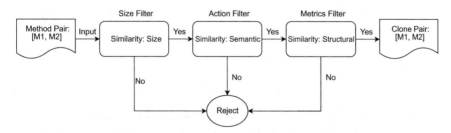

Fig. 1 Overview of Oreo

ArrayAccessBinary actions, respectively. This is to capture this important semantic information that the Java programming language encodes in its syntax.

As an example of *Action tokens* found in a method, consider the code in Listing 1.2, which converts its input argument to an encrypted format. The resulting *Action tokens* are *getBytes()*, *getInstance()*, *update()*, *digest()*, *length*, *append()*, *toString()*, *translate()*, *ArrayAccess*, and *toString()*. The *ArrayAccess action token* stands for *hashedPassword[i]*. The *Action tokens* contains semantic information which is robust against changes in variable names or types used by developers. *Action tokens* exploit the intuition that if two methods perform the same function, they likely call the same library methods and refer to the same object attributes, even if the methods are syntactically and lexically different. The use of libraries is common in modern software and these libraries provide basic semantic abstractions. Oreo assumes the use of these abstractions by developers. Hence, Oreo utilizes these tokens to compare semantic similarity between methods. This is done in the *Action filter*, as shown in Fig. 1. Oreo uses overlap-similarity, calculated as $Sim(A_1, A_2) = |A_1 \cap A_2|$, to measure the similarity between the *Action tokens* of two methods. Here, A_1 and A_2 are sets of Action Tokens in methods M_1 and M_2, respectively. Each element in these sets is defined as $<t, freq>$, where t is the Action Token and $freq$ is the number of times this token appears in the method.

Listing 1.2 Action Filter Example [7]

```
 1  public static String getEncryptedPassword(String password,
        String algorithm) throws InfoException {
 2    StringBuffer buffer = new StringBuffer();
 3    try {
 4      byte[] encrypt = password.getBytes("UTF-8");
 5      MessageDigest md = MessageDigest.getInstance(algorithm);
 6      md.update(encrypt);
 7      byte[] hashedPassword = md.digest();
 8      for (int i = 0; i < hashedPassword.length; i++) {
 9        buffer.append(Byte.toString(hashedPassword[i]));
10      }
11    } catch (Exception e) {
12      throw new
            InfoException(LanguageTranslator.translate("474"),
            e);
13    }
14    return buffer.toString();
15  }
```

Clones in the Twilight Zone have low syntactic and lexical similarity, but they still perform similar functions. To detect clones in this zone, a semantic comparison is necessary. Oreo uses Action Filter to measure the semantic similarity between the two methods. If the two methods satisfy the Action Filter, they are then passed on to the next stage, where their structural similarity is compared. This stage is labeled as "Metrics similarity" in Fig. 1. To compare the structural similarity, Oreo compares 24 software metrics of the two methods. Table 2 shows these metrics. The method pairs that reach the metrics filter are already known to be similar in size and their actions. The intuition for using metrics as the final comparison is that methods that are of about the same size and that do similar actions, but have quite different software metrics characteristics, are unlikely to be clones. The use of metrics requires fine-tuning over a large number of configurations between the thresholds of each individual metric. This makes manually finding the right configuration of these thresholds a hard task. For example, it is not easy to decide manually if the "number of conditionals" should have more weight over the "number of arguments" while comparing the structural similarity of the two methods. To address this issue, Oreo uses a supervised machine learning approach. If the machine learning model finds the input methods to be structurally similar, then Oreo classifies the method pair as a clone pair because by

Table 2 Method-level software metrics

Name	Description
XMET	# external methods called
VREF	# variables referenced
VDEC	# variables declared
NOS	# statements
NOPR	# operators
NOA	# arguments
NEXP	# expressions
NAND	# operands
MDN	maximum depth of nesting
LOOP	# loops (for,while)
LMET	# local methods called
HVOC	Halstead vocabulary
HEFF	Halstead effort to implement
HDIF	Halstead difficulty to implement
EXCT	# exceptions thrown
EXCR	# exceptions referenced
CREF	# classes referenced
COMP	McCabes cyclomatic complexity
CAST	# class casts
NBLTRL	# Boolean literals
NCLTRL	# Character literals
NSLTRL	# String literals
NNLTRL	# Numerical literals
NNULLTRL	# Null literals

this time size, semantic, and structural similarities have been compared which gives Oreo enough confidence to declare a method pair as a clone pair.

3   Machine Learning Model

Oreo uses deep learning to detect clone pairs. Neural networks, or deep learning methods, are among the most prominent machine learning methods that utilize multiple layers of neurons (units) in a network to achieve automatic learning. Deep neural networks (DNN) provide effective solutions due to their powerful feature learning ability and universal approximation properties. DNNs scale well to large datasets and can take advantage of well-maintained software libraries and can compute on clusters of CPUs, GPUs, and on the cloud. DNNs have been successfully applied to many areas of science and technology [10], such as computer vision [4], natural language processing [11], and even biology [3].

Oreo uses a Siamese architecture neural network [2] to detect clone pairs. Siamese architectures are best suited for problems where two objects are compared to assess their similarity. An example of such problems is comparing fingerprints. Another important characteristic of this architecture is that it can handle the symmetry [5] of its input vector, therefore, an input pair $(m1, m2)$ to the model will be the same as the input pair $(m2, m1)$. This ability is achieved by applying the same operation to each component of the pair by using two identical sub-neural networks. The other benefit brought by Siamese architectures is a reduction in the number of parameters; the weight parameters are shared within two identical sub-neural networks making it require fewer number of parameters than a plain architecture with the same number of layers.

Figure 2 shows the Siamese architecture model used by Oreo. The input to the model is a 48-dimensional vector created using the 24 metrics. The input vector is split into two input instances corresponding to the two feature vectors associated with the two methods for which we want to assess structural similarity. The two identical subnetworks then apply the same transformations on both of these input vectors. These two subnetworks have the same configuration and share the same parameter values while the parameters are getting updated. Both have 4 hidden layers of size 200 neurons, with full connectivity, which means that each neuron's output in layer $n - 1$ is the input to neurons in layer n.

The outputs of the two subnetworks are then concatenated and fed to the comparator network which has 4 layers of sizes 200, 100, 50, and 25 neurons with full connectivity between the layers. The comparator network's output is then fed to the Classification Unit which outputs a value between 0 and 1. Oreo claims that a clone pair is detected if this value is above 0.5.

To train a model, Oreo used a training dataset of clone and non-clone pairs which was generated using SourcererCC clone detector. Oreo used SourcererCC because

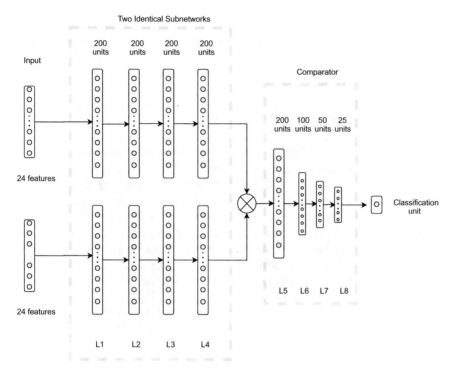

Fig. 2 Siamese architecture model

it has been shown to have a high recall in Type-1, Type-2, and Type-3 clone types [9]. Oreo's approach is not tied to SourcererCC. Any other clone detector which has a good Recall and Precision can be used to create this training dataset.

4 Power of Action Filter: Detecting Complex Clones at Scale

Previous clone detection techniques using software metrics and machine learning were found to be not scalable to large datasets. In previous metric-based clone detection approaches, the software metrics of each piece of code are required to be compared against the software metrics of every other piece of code in a given dataset. This leads to a large number of metric comparisons, which causes scalability issues, also known as the "candidate explosion problem". Moreover, metrics-based clone detection captures the structural properties of code snippets but is unable to capture semantic properties, which results in incorrectly reporting many similar-looking code pairs as clones that have different functionalities. This leads to a higher false positive rate, which is an undesirable outcome of such approaches. *Action filter* addresses both of these problems and enables Oreo to scale large datasets while maintaining acceptable precision.

4.1 Scalability Using Action Tokens

Similar to SourcererCC, Oreo also uses a bag of words model where instead of using all of the language tokens, Oreo focuses only on the *Action tokens*. Using *Action filter*, Oreo compares *Action tokens* of two methods to determine if they share a semantic similarity. In order to speed up comparisons, Oreo uses an inverted index of all the methods in the dataset using *Action tokens*. To detect clones for any method, say M, Oreo queries this inverted index for the *Action tokens* of M. Any method, say N, returned by this query becomes a candidate clone of M provided the overlap-similarity between M and N is greater than a preset threshold. We call M the query method, N a candidate of M, and the pair $<M, N>$ is called a candidate pair. The inverted index makes it possible to retrieve, in a time linearly proportional to the number of *Action tokens* in M, all semantically similar candidate clone methods of M. *Action filter* removes a large number of false candidates thereby addressing the candidate explosion issue.

Table 3 shows the impact of *Action filter* on the number of candidates which are needed to be compared by the machine learning model in order to report clones. These are the reported numbers where Oreo used 1,000 methods as a query to find their clones in the entire IJaDataset. The threshold for *Action filter* was set to 55%. The numbers demonstrate that the Action filter has a strong impact on reducing the number of candidate pairs.

4.2 Semantics Captured by Action Tokens

The *Action tokens* contains semantic information which is robust against changes in variable names or types used by developers. Consider a case where a developer clones a method because they wanted to implement similar functionality. In order to fit the copied code in their context, the developer will most probably modify the identifiers and remove or add a few statements. Unless the developer doesn't need a particular library function, none of these changes will impact the library calls this method depends upon. This makes *Action tokens* robust against Type-3 modifications.

Table 3 Impact of action filter

Action filter	Num-candidates
No filter	2,398,525,500
55%	260,655

Moreover, since the library methods encapsulate some functionalities, the *Action tokens* of a method captures the actions this method needs to take in order to encode a functionality.

Action tokens exploit the intuition that if two methods perform the same function, they likely call the same library methods and refer to the same object attributes, even if the methods are syntactically and lexically different.

5 Successful Applications of Oreo

Oreo introduced a powerful semantic filter which is robust against Type-3 modifications. Oreo also demonstrated how a Siamese DNN model can be used to detect structural similarities between two methods. When used together, these two enable Oreo to identify complex clones in the Twilight Zone. Nafi et al. used these concepts to detect cross-language clones [6]. In their technique to detect clones across different programming languages, they use the *Action filter* and the feature vectors from the machine learning model introduced in Oreo. The *Action filter* identified the cross-language clone-candidates with semantic similarities. These candidates were then validated by the machine learning model to report cross-language clones with high precision.

In another work, Saini et al. introduced InspectorClone, a novel semi-automatic technique to evaluate the precision of clone detection tools [8]. Calculating the precision of clone detection tools is important to compare the detection capabilities of different clone detectors. Automatic calculation of precision is still an open research problem and therefore, researchers spend many hours manually calculating the precision of their techniques. InspectorClone builds upon the concepts such as *Action tokens* and Siamese DNN introduced in Oreo and is shown to be very precise in identifying true clone pairs. They used InspectorClone to calculate the precision of 8 different state-of-the-art clone detectors and demonstrated that on an average, there is a 39% reduction in the manual work needed to calculate the precision of these clone detectors. In some cases, InspectorClone was able to reduce the manual work needed by more than 70%.

6 Adapting Oreo Architecture to Different Scenarios

Oreo presents a clever approach to generalize the detection capabilities of other clone detectors. It makes it possible to use slower and precise clone detectors for training purposes and presents a clever approach to generalize their detection capabilities while addressing scalability and speed of execution. Oreo used SourcererCC to train the DNN used in the metrics comparison stage. However, Oreo is not tied to SourcererCC. Any other clone detector can be used based on what kind of clones a user is interested in. Because SourcererCC has a low recall on ST3 and MT3 clone pairs, one can choose a clone detector with better performance on these clone categories to create a training dataset for Oreo's DNN model. Moreover, one can lower the threshold of SourcererCC while creating the training dataset if one is interested in creating a dataset with more examples of ST3 clone pairs. Another approach might be to use a manually tagged dataset for training purposes. It should also be possible to improve the precision of Oreo by training it with a more precise clone detector than SourcererCC.

References

1. Ambient Software Evoluton Group, IJaDataset 2.0 (2013), http://secold.org/projects/seclone
2. P. Baldi, Y. Chauvin, Neural networks for fingerprint recognition. Neural Comput. **5**(3), 402–418 (1993)
3. P. Di Lena, K. Nagata, P. Baldi, Deep architectures for protein contact map prediction. Bioinformatics **28**(19), 2449–2457 (2012)
4. A. Krizhevsky, I. Sutskever, G.E. Hinton, Imagenet classification with deep convolutional neural networks. Adv. Neural Inf. Process. Syst. **25**, 1097–1105 (2012)
5. G. Montavon, K.R. Müller, Better representations: invariant, disentangled and reusable, in *Neural Networks: Tricks of the Trade* (Springer, 2012), pp. 559–560
6. K.W. Nafi, T.S. Kar, B. Roy, C.K. Roy, K.A. Schneider, CLCDSA: cross language code clone detection using syntactical features and API documentation, in *2019 34th IEEE/ACM International Conference on Automated Software Engineering (ASE)* (IEEE, 2019), pp. 1026–1037
7. V. Saini, F. Farmahinifarahani, Y. Lu, P. Baldi, C.V. Lopes, Oreo: detection of clones in the twilight zone, in *Proceedings of the 2018 26th ACM Joint Meeting on European Software Engineering Conference and Symposium on the Foundations of Software Engineering* (2018), pp. 354–365
8. V. Saini, F. Farmahinifarahani, Y. Lu, D. Yang, P. Martins, H. Sajnani, P. Baldi, C.V. Lopes, Towards automating precision studies of clone detectors, in *2019 IEEE/ACM 41st International Conference on Software Engineering (ICSE)* (IEEE, 2019), pp. 49–59
9. H. Sajnani, V. Saini, J. Svajlenko, C.K. Roy, C.V. Lopes, SourcererCC: scaling code clone detection to big-code, in *Proceedings of the 38th International Conference on Software Engineering (ICSE16)* (IEEE, 2016), pp 1157–1168
10. J. Schmidhuber, Deep learning in neural networks: an overview. Neural Netw. **61**, 85–117 (2015)
11. R. Socher, Y. Bengio, C.D. Manning, Deep learning for NLP (without magic), in *Tutorial Abstracts of ACL 2012* (Association for Computational Linguistics, 2012), pp. 5–5
12. J. Svajlenko, C.K. Roy, BigCloneEval: a clone detection tool evaluation framework with BigCloneBench, in *Proceedings of 2016 IEEE International Conference on Software Maintenance and Evolution (ICSME)* (IEEE, 2016), pp. 596–600

CCLearner: Clone Detection via Deep Learning

Liuqing Li, He Feng, Na Meng, and Barbara Ryder

Abstract To facilitate clone maintenance, various automated tools were proposed to detect code clones by identifying similar token sequences or similar program syntactic structures in source code. They achieved different trade-offs between precision and recall. Inspired by prior work, we developed a new approach CCLEARNER, *a solely token-based clone detection approach using deep learning.* Given known clone pairs and non-clone pairs, CCLEARNER extracts features from each code pair and leverages the features to train a classifier. The classifier is then used to compare methods pair-by-pair in a given codebase to detect clones. We evaluated CCLEARNER by reusing an existing benchmark of real clone code—BigCloneBench. We split the benchmark such that some data was used for classifier training, and some data was used for testing. With the testing data, we evaluated CCLEARNER's effectiveness of clone detection, and also assessed three existing popular clone detection tools: SourcererCC, NiCad, and Deckard. CCLEARNER outperformed existing tools by achieving a better trade-off between precision and recall. To further investigate whether other machine learning algorithms can perform comparatively as deep learning, we replaced deep learning with five alternative machine learning algorithms in CCLEARNER, and observed that CCLEARNER worked best when using deep learning.

L. Li (✉) · H. Feng · N. Meng
Virginia Tech, Blacksburg, VA 24061, US
e-mail: liuqing@vt.edu

H. Feng
e-mail: fenghe@vt.edu

N. Meng
e-mail: nm8247@vt.edu

B. Ryder
Virginia Tech (Emeritus), Blacksburg, VA 24061, US
e-mail: ryder@cs.vt.edu

© The Author(s), under exclusive license to Springer Nature Singapore Pte Ltd. 2021
K. Inoue and C. K. Roy (eds.), *Code Clone Analysis*,
https://doi.org/10.1007/978-981-16-1927-4_6

1 Introduction

In software development, developers copy and paste code to quickly reuse already implemented functionalities in multiple program contexts. However, the produced code clones may be challenging to track and maintain. To overcome the challenge, researchers built various automated clone detection tools [1–6]. For instance, SoucererCC indexes code blocks with the least frequent tokens they use, in order to quickly retrieve potential clones of a given code block [5]. NiCad leverages TXL [7] to parse source code, and to convert the parsed syntax trees to a user-specified normalized code representation [3]. NiCad then detects clones by comparing the token sequences of normalized representations of different code. Both SourcererCC and NiCad mostly identify Type-1 (T1) and Type-2 (T2) clones. Deckard parses syntax trees from code, characterizes subtrees with numerical vectors, and detects similar code by comparing numerical vectors [2]. Different from SourcererCC and NiCard, Deckard detects more Type-3 (T3) clones [5].

Inspired by prior work, we designed and implemented CCLEARNER [8][1], a novel deep learning-based approach to detect clones solely based on tokens. Our insight is that *tokens (e.g., reserved words, type identifiers, method identifiers, and variable identifiers) provide good indicators of program implementation*. If two code blocks use the same tokens in identical or similar ways, the blocks are likely to be clones and may realize identical or similar features. Furthermore, by treating the clone detection problem analogous to a classification problem that decides whether two blocks are clones or not, we can leverage machine learning (including deep learning) to identify clones. In comparison with former approaches whose clone detection algorithms were manually designed, CCLEARNER exploits deep learning to train a classifier based on known clones and non-clones. With the classifier automatically characterizing any commonality and variation between clone peers, CCLEARNER detects clones by enumerating all method pairs in a given codebase and determining which pair has the cloning relationship.

In our evaluation, we experimented with CCLEARNER and three existing clone detection tools: Deckard [2], NiCad [3], and SourcererCC [5]. We constructed the evaluation dataset based on BigCloneBench [9]. CCLEARNER achieved the best trade-off between precision and recall among all tools. To further evaluate CCLEARNER's effectiveness when it uses machine learning (ML) algorithms other than deep learning, we also experimented with five alternative ML algorithms in addition to deep learning: AdaBoost [10], Decision Tree [11], Naïve Bayes [12], Random Forest [13], and Support Vector Machine (SVM) [14]. We observed that CCLEARNER's clone detection effectiveness varied a lot between the adopted ML algorithms.

This chapter extends our recent research publication on CCLEARNER [8]. In the following sections, we will first overview the published work (Sects. 2–4), and then introduce our new experiment and observations after the publication (Sect. 5). Finally, we will discuss the lessons learned from our investigation and share our thoughts on future research directions.

---

[1] Download link: https://github.com/liuqingli/CCLearner.

Fig. 1 The DNN
architecture

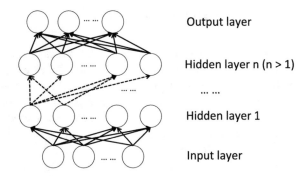

Output layer

Hidden layer n (n > 1)

... ...

Hidden layer 1

Input layer

2 Background

This section first introduces deep neural network (DNN)—the deep learning algorithm used in CCLEARNER, and then clarifies our terminology.

Deep Learning (DL) includes a set of algorithms that can be used to model high-level abstractions in data. Among various DL algorithms, the **deep neural network (DNN)** [15] is a representative algorithm that demonstrated impressive performance in a variety of classification tasks. DNN is an **artificial neural network (ANN)** that has one input layer, one output layer, and two or more hidden layers between the input and output layers (see Fig. 1). Each layer has multiple nodes (i.e., artificial neurons). Every node combines its inputs with the corresponding *weights* or *coefficients* to either amplify or dampen those inputs. During the learning process, all *weights* of nodes in DNN are optimized through backpropagation to minimize the loss between predicted labels and true labels. In this way, each node infers which inputs are more helpful for the overall learning task, and how each input progresses through the network to affect the ultimate outcome, say, an act of classification [16].

In our research, a **clone method pair** or **true clone pair** represents two methods or functions that have similar code. Each method in a true clone pair is denoted as a **clone peer** of the other. Similarly, we define **non-clone method pair** or **false clone pair** to represent any two methods that have very different code from each other. Each method in the false clone pair is called a **non-clone peer** of the other method.

3 Approach

As shown in Fig. 2, CCLEARNER consists of two phases: training (Sect. 3.2) and testing (Sect. 3.3). The Feature Extraction procedure (Sect. 3.1), performed in both phases, extracts eight features from token sequences. In the training phase, CCLEARNER takes in both clone and non-clone method pairs to train a deep learning-based classifier. In the testing phase, given any codebase, CCLEARNER uses the trained classifier to detect clones.

3.1 Feature Extraction

CCLEARNER extracts features that characterize the clone (or non-clone) relationship of any method pair ($method_A$, $method_B$). For each method, CCLEARNER first tokenizes the code to identify all tokens, and uses a *token-frequency list* to record the occurrence count of each token. In Fig. 2, $token\_freq\_list_A$ and $token\_freq\_list_B$ separately represent such token information of $method_A$ and $method_B$. We believe that different kinds of tokens provide distinct signals to indicate code (dis)similarity, so we classified tokens into eight categories, and CCLEARNER splits each method's token-frequency list into eight sublists accordingly. Next, CCLEARNER computes a similarity score for each pair of token sublists between $method_A$ and $method_B$. The resulting eight similarity scores are then used as features to represent the relationship between methods.

Token Categorization and Extraction. *Different types of tokens may have different capabilities to characterize clones.* For instance, clone peers are more likely to share reserved words (e.g., "`for`" and "`if`") rather than operators (e.g., "+" and "`&`"), because they usually have identical program structures but may use slightly different arithmetic or logic operations. Therefore, we classified tokens into eight categories based on their syntactic or semantic meanings. Table 1 presents all token categories and the related exemplar token-frequency sublists.

To create token-frequency (sub)lists based on source code, CCLEARNER uses both the ANTLR lexer [17] and Eclipse ASTParser [18]. Given a code block, the ANTLR lexer extracts all tokens in sequence. As the token sets of reserved words, operators, and markers are well defined, CCLEARNER recognizes C1–C3 tokens purely based on the lexer's outputs. The token sets of literals, type identifiers, method identifiers, qualifier names, and variable identifiers vary with codebases, so the ANTLR lexer cannot identify C4–C8 tokens precisely. To overcome the lexer's limitation, we used Eclipse ASTParser to generate an Abstract Syntax Tree (AST) for each method, and implemented several ASTVisitors to traverse trees and to retrieve tokens contained

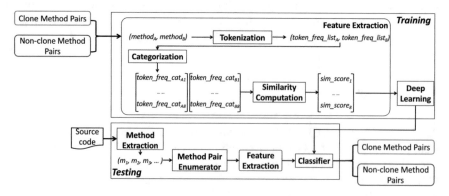

Fig. 2 The overview of CCLEARNER

Table 1 Token categories and related token-frequency sublists

Index	Category name	An exemplar token-frequency sublist
C1	Reserved words	<if, 2>, <new, 3>, <try 2>, …
C2	Operators	<+=, 2>, <!=, 3>, …
C3	Markers	<;, 2>, <[, 2>, <], 2>, …
C4	Literals	<1.3, 2> , <false, 3>, <null, 5>, …
C5	Type identifiers	<byte, 2>, <URLConnection, 1>,…
C6	Method identifiers	<read, 2>, <openConnection, 1>, …
C7	Qualified names	<System.out, 6>, <arr.length, 1>, …
C8	Variable identifiers	<conn, 2>, <numRead, 4>, …

by certain types of AST nodes. For instance, one of the ASTVisitors extracts method identifiers (C6 tokens) by locating and processing all method-relevant AST nodes, including MethodDeclaration and MethodInvocation. Notice that ASTParser complements instead of replacing the ANTLR lexer, because the parser is unable to reveal all tokens that the lexer detects (e.g., reserved words).

Similarity Computation. When two methods are characterized with vectors of token-frequency sublists, we rely on *vector-wise similarities to capture the similarity of method bodies*. Intuitively, the more similar vectors there are between two methods, the more likely those methods are clones to each other. Specifically for each token category $C_i(1 \leq i \leq 8)$, CCLEARNER computes a similarity score sim_score_i between methods' corresponding token-frequency sublists L_{Ai} and L_{Bi} as follows:

$$sim\_score_i = 1 - \frac{\sum_x |freq(L_{Ai}, x) - freq(L_{Bi}, x)|}{\sum_x (freq(L_{Ai}, x) + freq(L_{Bi}, x))}. \tag{1}$$

Here x is a token contained by L_{Ai} or L_{Bi}, $freq(L_{Ai}, x)$ represents the occurrence count of x in $method_A$, and $freq(L_{Bi}, x)$ denotes x's frequency in $method_B$. The computed similarity score varies within $[0, 1]$. In general, the more tokens shared between lists and the less frequency difference there is for each token, the higher the similarity score becomes. In particular, when the token-frequency sublists of a certain category share no token in common, we set the corresponding similarity score to 0.5 by default. We tried to set the default value as 0 or 1, but none of these values worked as well as 0.5 during the experiment. This may be because when no token is commonly shared between sublists, the frequency distributions may be similar or not; 0.5 does not suggest any bias toward either similarity or dissimilarity.

3.2 Training

We need both positive and negative examples to train a classifier for binary classification. CCLEARNER takes feature vectors extracted from clone method pairs as positive examples and feature vectors derived from non-clone pairs as negative examples. Each data point for training is represented as $< similarity\_vector, label >$, where $similarity\_vector$ is an eight-dimensional vector of similarity scores, and $label$ is either 1 ("*CLONE*") or 0 ("*NON_CLONE*"). To avoid any confusion caused by small clone methods, we refined our training data with methods that contained at least six lines of code. As our approach is built on the token-frequency list comparison between methods, when method bodies are small, any minor variation of token usage can cause significant degradation of similarity scores, making the training data noisy. We used DeepLearning4j [19] to train a DNN classifier. The input layer contains eight nodes, with each node taking one feature value in $similarity\_vector$. The output layer predicts whether a method pair is "*CLONE*" or "*NON_CLONE*". CCLEARNER configures DNN to include 2 hidden layers and to run 300 iterations for training, as CCLEARNER worked best with these parameter settings in our experiment. Each hidden layer is configured to have 10 nodes, as suggested by the literature [20].

3.3 Testing

Given a codebase, CCLEARNER first detects methods from source files with Eclipse ASTParser, and then enumerates all possible method pairs. CCLEARNER feeds each enumerated method pair to the trained classifier for clone detection. Theoretically, when n methods are extracted from a codebase, the clone detection algorithm complexity should be $O(n^2)$. To reduce the comparison runtime overhead, we developed two heuristics to filter out some unnecessary comparisons. One filter was applied to examine two methods' lines of code (LOC). If one method's LOC is more than three times the other method's LOC, it is very unlikely that the methods are clones, so we simply conclude that they compose a non-clone method pair and skip any further processing. Another filter removes any candidate method having less than six LOC for two reasons. First, small methods may contain so few tokens that CCLEARNER cannot effectively perform clone detection. Second, the six-line minimum is common in clone detection benchmarks mentioned in prior research [5, 21]. In CCLEARNER, the output layer has two nodes to separately predict the likelihood of clones and non-clones: l_c and l_{nc}, where $l_c + l_{nc} = 1$. We set $l_c \geq 0.98$ to detect clones as precisely as possible without producing many false alarms.

4 Empirical Comparison with Existing Tools

To assess how CCLEARNER compares with existing tools, we created training and testing sets based on a large-scale clone benchmark (Sect. 4.1). We also defined metrics to measure the effectiveness of automatic clone detection (Sect. 4.2). By applying CCLEARNER and three alternative tools on the datasets, we quantitatively evaluated different tools' capabilities of clone detection (Sect. 4.3).

4.1 Dataset Generation

BigCloneBench [9] is a large-scale code clone benchmark. It consists of two parts: a codebase and a database. Table 2 summarizes the clone data contained by our downloaded reduced version of BigCloneBench [22]. As shown in the table, Big-CloneBench's codebase has 10 source folders. Each folder has multiple Java files, and each file contains various Java methods. Every method independently implements one functionality (e.g., sorting). BigCloneBench's database stores clone information related to the codebase. It records over 6 million recognized true clone pairs and 260 thousand false clone pairs in the codebase. For each method pair, the database records their code locations and clone type information. Specifically, **VST3**, **ST3**, **MT3**, and **WT3/4**, respectively, represent "Very Strong T3", "Strong T3", "Medium T3", "Weak T3 or T4" clones.

Compared with other folders, **Folder #4** has the largest number of both true and false clone pairs. Therefore, we leveraged the data in this folder for training and the data in all other folders for testing. As MT3 and WT3/4 clones can contain totally different implementations of the same functionality, training a classifier with such

Table 2 Data in the downloaded BigCloneBench

Folder Id.	# of Files	LOC	# of True Clone Pairs						# of False Clone Pairs
			T1	T2	VST3	ST3	MT3	WT3/4	
#2	10,372	1,984,327	1,553	9	22	1,412	2,689	404,277	38,139
#3	4,600	812,629	632	587	525	2,760	24,621	862,652	4,499
#4	22,113	4,676,552	13,802	3,116	1,210	4,666	23,693	4,618,462	197,394
#5	56	3,527	0	0	0	0	1	34	12
#6	472	83,068	4	0	14	50	124	24,338	4,147
#7	1,037	299,525	39	4	21	212	1,658	11,927	15,162
#8	131	18,527	3	7	5	0	2	259	78
#9	669	107,832	0	0	0	0	0	55	1,272
#10	1,014	286,416	152	64	285	925	2,318	236,726	1,762
#11	64	6,736	0	0	1	6	0	245	0
Total	40,528	8,279,139	16,185	3,787	2,083	10,031	55,106	6,158,975	262,465

Table 3 Datasets for training and testing

Dataset	# of True Clone Pairs						# of False Clone Pairs
	T1	T2	VST3	ST3	MT3	WT3/4	
Training	13,750	3,104	1,207	4,602	0	0	22,663
Testing	2,383	671	873	5,365	31,413	1,540,513	0

noisy data can cause the resulting classifier to wrongly report a lot of clones and produce many false alarms. Therefore, we excluded MT3 and WT3/4 clones from the training data. We also removed all methods that have five or fewer LOC to reduce data noise. As **Folder #4** has a lot more false clone pairs than true clone pairs, we randomly sampled a subset of false clone pairs to achieve a count balance between the positive examples and negative examples used in training. Table 3 presents the resulting datasets we created based on BigCloneBench.

4.2   Evaluation Metrics

We defined three metrics to evaluate the effectiveness of automatic clone detection:

Recall measures a tool's ability to retrieve true clones; it is the fraction or percentage of known true clone pairs that are detected by any clone detection approach. Taking the labeled clones in BigCloneBench as known true clones, we could automatically evaluate an approach's recall for individual clone types. Since many tools cannot effectively retrieve MT3 and WT3/4 clones, as with prior work [5], we evaluated the overall recall for T1, T2, VST3, and ST3 clones as follows:

$$R_{T1-ST3} = \frac{\text{\# of true clone pairs (of T1-ST3)}}{\text{Total \# of known true clone (of T1-ST3)}}. \tag{2}$$

Precision measures a tool's ability to correctly report true clones; it is the fraction of true positives among all clone pairs reported by a tool. The labeled clones in BigCloneBench cannot be used to automatically compute precision, because based on our experience, the labeled dataset misses some true clones actually existing in the codebase. Instead, we need to manually inspect all clones reported by any tool to decide the precision rates. When a clone detection tool reports thousands of clone pairs, we cannot afford the manual effort to inspect every pair. Therefore, in our evaluation, we manually examined a sample set of clones reported by each tool. To ensure that our sampled data is representative, we chose 385 reported clones among all clone types for each approach. The number 385 is a statistically significant sample size with a 95% confidence level and ±5% confidence interval, when the population size is larger than 200,000. With the manual inspection of 385 sampled clone pairs, we estimated precision as follows:

$$P_{estimated} = \frac{\text{\# of true clone pairs}}{385 \text{ detected clone pair samples}}. \tag{3}$$

C score combines precision and recall to measure the overall accuracy of clone detection. It is calculated as the harmonic mean of R_{T1-ST3} and $P_{estimated}$:

$$C = \frac{2 * P_{estimated} * R_{T1-ST3}}{P_{estimated} + R_{T1-ST3}}. \tag{4}$$

4.3 Effectiveness Comparison of Clone Detection Approaches

To evaluate CCLEARNER's capability of clone detection, we compared it with three popular tools: SourcererCC [5], NiCad [3], and Deckard [2]. We applied all three existing tools to CCLEARNER's testing data with their default tool configurations.

Recall. As shown in Table 4, CCLEARNER achieved the highest recall among all tools when detecting T1-ST3 clones; it was unable to detect as many MT3 and WT3/4 clones as Deckard did. Specifically, CCLEARNER identified all T1 clones, 98% of T2 and ST3 clones, and 89% of ST3 clones. From T1 to WT3/4, as clone peers become less similar, CCLEARNER's recall decreased. The same trend was also observed for other tools, which could be explained by the increased difficulty of clone detection as clone peers become more dissimilar to each other. CCLEARNER was unable to achieve 100% recall for all clone types, mainly because it relies on the exactly same terms used in method pairs to compute similarity vectors. When two clone methods share few identifiers and contain significantly divergent program structures, CCLEARNER cannot reveal the clone relationship. In the future, we plan to devise supplementary techniques for these specialist clones.

Precision. Table 5 shows the $P_{estimated}$, the number of reported clone pairs, and the number of estimated *true* clone pairs for all tools. Notice that the number of *true* clones was calculated as the product of $P_{estimated}$ and the total number of reported clones. Compared with SourcererCC and NiCad, CCLEARNER reported more true clone pairs. Deckard had a lower $P_{estimated}$ of 71% but reported more clones than

Table 4 Recall comparison among tools (%)

Tool	T1	T2	VST3	ST3	MT3	WT3/4	Average (R_{T1-ST3})
CCLearner	100	98	98	89	28	1	93
SourcererCC	100	97	92	67	5	0	80
NiCad	100	85	98	77	0	0	85
Deckard	96	82	78	78	69	53	83

Table 5 Comparison among tools for the sampled precision, and the number of reported and true clone pairs

Tool	$P_{estimated}$ (%)	# of reported clone pairs	# of estimated true clone pairs
CCLearner	93	548,987	510,558
SourcererCC	98	265,611	260,299
NiCad	68	646,058	439,319
Deckard	71	2,301,526	1,634,083

Table 6 Tool comparison for C scores and runtime costs

Tool	C (%)	Runtime Cost (min)
CCLearner	93	47
SourcererCC	88	13
NiCad	76	34
Deckard	77	4h 24

any other tool. These numbers indicate that Deckard retrieved more true clones and produced more false alarms (wrongly reported clones). This may be because Deckard's flexibly matches code snippets by tolerating more differences in the token usage and program structures.

C Score and Time Cost. Table 6 lists different tools' C scores and execution time. CCLEARNER obtained the highest C score, which implies that CCLEARNER detected clones more accurately by achieving both high estimated precision and high T1-ST3 recall. Regarding tools' runtime overhead, SoucererCC ran the fastest (spending 13 min). NiCad was slower than SourcererCC (spending 34 min). Deckard worked the most slowly (spending 4 h and 24 min), because it used an expensive tree matching algorithm. Our observations on the above results align with the findings in prior work [5]. CCLEARNER took 47 min to detect clones. Similar to SourcererCC and NiCad, CCLEARNER worked faster than Deckard since it did not reason about program structures. However, CCLEARNER was slower than NiCad and SourcererCC, because it calculated *similarity_vector* and compared methods pair-by-pair to find clones. In addition, CCLEARNER spent another 5 minutes on training, which could be considered as one-time cost and ignored. Due to the pair-wise comparison mechanism, CCLEARNER's clone detection is an embarrassingly parallel task [23], indicating that we can easily parallelize the task to further reduce CCLEARNER's time cost in the future.

5 CCLEARNER Sensitivity to Machine Learning Algorithm Used

By default, CCLEARNER uses DNN to train a classifier for clone detection. To explore how well CCLEARNER works when it adopts different machine learning (ML) algorithms, after the published work [8], we also experimented with five alternative ML algorithms: AdaBoost [10], Decision Tree [11], Naïve Bayes [12], Random Forest [13], and Support Vector Machine (SVM) [14]. Specifically for algorithm implementation, we used Weka [24] because it is a software library implementing a collection of ML algorithms (including all five algorithms mentioned above). By replacing DNN with each alternative, we trained five distinct learners and thus obtained five tool variants: CCLEARNER$_a$, CCLEARNER$_d$, CCLEARNER$_n$, CCLEARNER$_r$, and CCLEARNER$_s$. For fair tool comparison, when exploiting each alternative ML algorithm, we reused the training and testing data shown in Table 3 to train a classifier and to evaluate the resulting clone detection effectiveness.

Effectiveness Comparison between CCLEARNER *and Its Variants.* Table 7 presents the evaluation results by CCLEARNER and its five variants. For instance, row **CCLEARNER** corresponds to the results by the default implementation using DNN, and row **CCLEARNER$_a$** shows results by the AdaBoost-based implementation. We observed an interesting phenomenon in Table 7. *Compared with* CCLEARNER, *all variant approaches obtained higher recall rates, lower precision rates, and lower C scores.* Specifically, all variants' overall recall rates are surprisingly identical: 97%. This number is higher than CCLEARNER's recall: 93%. All variants retrieved MT3 and WT3/4 clones much more effectively than CCLEARNER. For instance, both Random Forest and SVM led to the same highest MT3 and WT3/4 recall rates (i.e., 62 and 5%). Meanwhile, the variants' precision rates are much lower than CCLEARNER's, ranging from 46 to 70%. Overall, CCLEARNER acquired the highest C score—93%, while CCLEARNER$_n$ obtained the second highest C score: 81%. SVM produced the lowest C score: 63%. Although different ML algorithms were applied to the same data, they presented distinct trade-offs between precision and recall. The variants often found more true clones, but those true clones were always mixed in with a larger number of false clones than would be reported by CCLEARNER.

Table 7 The effectiveness of CCLEARNER and its variants (%)

Tool	ML Algorithm	Recall Per Type						R_{T1-ST3}	$P_{estimated}$	C
		T1	T2	VST3	ST3	MT3	WT3/4			
CCLEARNER	DNN	100	98	98	89	28	1	93	93	93
CCLEARNER $_a$	AdaBoost	100	98	98	95	58	4	97	63	76
CCLEARNER $_d$	Decision Tree	100	98	98	96	61	4	97	59	74
CCLEARNER $_n$	Naïve Bayes	100	98	98	95	59	4	97	70	81
CCLEARNER $_r$	Random Forest	100	98	98	96	62	5	97	56	71
CCLEARNER $_s$	SVM	100	98	98	96	62	5	97	46	63

(a) Folder #2, 1937566.java	(b) Folder #2, 2571726.java
| ```java
private JSONObject executeHttpGet(
    String uri) throws Exception{
  HttpGet req=new HttpGet(uri);
  HttpClient client=new
      DefaultHttpClient();
  HttpResponse resLogin=client.execute(
      req);
  BufferedReader r=new BufferedReader(
      new InputStreamReader(resLogin.
      getEntity().getContent()));
  StringBuilder sb=new StringBuilder();
  String s=null;
  while((s=r.readLine())!=null) {
    sb.append(s);
  }
  return new JSONObject(sb.toString());
}
``` | ```java
public static String getStringResponse
    (String urlString) throws
    Exception{
  URL url=new URL(urlString);
  BufferedReader in=new BufferedReader
      (new InputStreamReader(url.
      openStream()));
  String inputLine;
  StringBuilder buffer=new
      StringBuilder();
  while((inputLine=in.readLine())!=
      null) {
    buffer.append(inputLine);
  }
  in.close();
  return buffer.toString();
}
``` |

Fig. 3 An MT3 clone pair detected by all variants but missed by CCLEARNER

A Case Study. To understand how CCLEARNER's variants detect clones differently from CCLEARNER, we sampled 10 reported clone pairs for manual inspection. Among the 10 pairs, 5 pairs were identified by CCLEARNER but missed by some of its variants, while the other 5 pairs were revealed by all variants but missed by CCLEARNER. We observed that each of the variants achieved higher recall and lower precision because they tolerated more differences between clones. Figure 3 presents a clone pair detected by all variants but missed by CCLEARNER. The clone peers invoke different methods (*e.g.*, `HttpGet()` and `URL()`) and use different types (*e.g.*, `HttpClient` and `InputStreamReader`). The tool variants reported this clone pair by matching code more flexibly than CCLEARNER. They achieved different trade-offs between precision and recall, and all outperformed CCLEARNER in terms of recall at the cost of sacrificing precision.

Effectiveness Comparison between Learning-Based and Non-Learning-Based Approaches. We compared the effectiveness of variant approaches with the results of non-learning-based tools shown in Tables 4, 5, and 6. We found that the learning-based approaches obtained higher recalls but lower precisions. Specifically, all CCLEARNER's variants achieved the same R_{T1-ST3}: 97%. This number is much higher than the recall rates of non-learning-based approaches (i.e., SourcereCC, NiCad, and Deckard), which were 80–85%. All variants' MT3 and WT3/4 recall rates are lower than Deckard's but higher than those rates of SoucererCC and NiCad. On the other hand, the learning-based variants obtained relatively lower precision rates (46–70%) than non-learning-based approaches (68–98%). Although the Naïve Bayes-based approach (CCLEARNER$_n$) achieved the highest precision rate (70%) among all variants, the rate is only comparable to that of NiCad (68%) or Deckard's (71%). Overall, CCLEARNER$_n$ worked better than the other variants, but its C score (81%) is much lower than SourcereCC's 88%—the highest C score obtained by the explored non-learning-based approaches.

Table 8 Time cost comparison

Tool	Time Cost (min)
CCLEARNER	47
CCLEARNER$_a$	49
CCLEARNER$_d$	49
CCLEARNER$_n$	50
CCLEARNER$_r$	49
CCLEARNER$_s$	52

Table 8 presents the time cost comparison between CCLEARNER and its variants. All variants have similar time costs to CCLEARNER, with slightly higher runtime overhead. According to Table 6, all these variants are slower than SourcererCC and NiCad, but faster than Deckard.

6 Conclusion

We designed and implemented a deep learning-based clone detection approach—CCLEARNER. Different from traditional clone detection tools, CCLEARNER does not contain manually defined rules or algorithms to specially characterize clones. Instead, it computes token-level similarity vectors between given code blocks, and relies on DNN to characterize the similarity vectors for both clone pairs and non-clone pairs. More learning-based clone detection tools have been recently proposed [25–29]. These tools process source code to extract tokens, ASTs, control flows, and/or data flows, and to create vectorized program representations accordingly; they also adopt more complex neural networks (e.g., recurrent neural network [30], recursive neural network [31], and convolutional neural networks [32]) to take in the vector representations and to better learn the characteristics of clone pairs. All these approaches demonstrate the nice fusion of static program analysis and deep learning. They also evidence that to better interpret the syntax or semantics of programs, we need to improve both program representations and machine learning architectures.

We foresee that more and more learning-based approaches will be proposed in the future to detect clones, analyze code, locate bugs, and repair code. As the future research directions, we plan to conduct an empirical comparison between similar tools and understand which learning-based approach design is superior to others. Additionally, we are also curious about the limitation of deep learning (DL)-based approaches. It seems that DL is good at performing certain tasks and perhaps bad at doing other things. Although it is still unclear what is the domain where DL does not quite fit, we will explore more usage of DL in Software Engineering research to better characterize its application scope.

References

1. T. Kamiya, S. Kusumoto, K. Inoue, CCFinder: a multilinguistic token-based code clone detection system for large scale source code, in *TSE*, pp. 654–670 (2002)
2. L. Jiang, G. Misherghi, Z. Su, S. Glondu, DECKARD: scalable and accurate tree-based detection of code clones, in *ICSE* (2007), pp. 96–105. http://dx.doi.org/10.1109/ICSE.2007.30
3. C.K. Roy, J.R. Cordy, NICAD: accurate detection of near-miss intentional clones using flexible pretty-printing and code normalization, in *ICPC 2008. The 16th IEEE International Conference on Program Comprehension, 2008*, vol. 0. (Los Alamitos, CA, USA: IEEE, June 2008), pp. 172–181. http://dx.doi.org/10.1109/icpc.2008.41
4. N. Göde, R. Koschke, Incremental clone detection, in *CSMR '09. 13th European Conference on Software Maintenance and Reengineering, 2009* (2009)
5. H. Sajnani, V. Saini, J. Svajlenko, C.K. Roy, C.V. Lopes, SourcererCC: scaling code clone detection to big code, in *CoRR*, vol. abs/1512.06448 (2015)
6. T. Apiwattanapong, A. Orso, M.J. Harrold, A differencing algorithm for object-oriented programs, in *Proceedings of the 19th IEEE International Conference on Automated Software Engineering* (2004)
7. J.R. Cordy, The txl source transformation language. Sci. Comput. Program. **61**(3), 190–210 (2006)
8. L. Li, H. Feng, W. Zhuang, N. Meng, B. Ryder, Cclearner: A deep learning-based clone detection approach, in *IEEE International Conference on Software Maintenance and Evolution (ICSME)*, pp. 249–260 (2017)
9. J. Svajlenko, J.F. Islam, I. Keivanloo, C.K. Roy, M.M. Mia, Towards a big data curated benchmark of inter-project code clones, in *30th IEEE International Conference on Software Maintenance and Evolution, Victoria, BC, Canada, September 29–October 3, 2014* (2014)
10. B. Kégl, The return of adaboost.mh: multi-class hamming trees, in *CoRR*, vol. abs/1312.6086 (2013). http://arxiv.org/abs/1312.6086
11. J.R. Quinlan, Induction of decision trees. Mach. Learn. (1986)
12. S.J. Russell, P. Norvig, *Artificial Intelligence: A Modern Approach*, 2nd ed. (Pearson Education, 2003)
13. T.K. Ho, Random decision forests, in *Proceedings of the Third International Conference on Document Analysis and Recognition (Volume 1)* (vol. 1) (1995)
14. C. Cortes, V. Vapnik, Support-vector networks. Mach. Learn. (1995)
15. K. Fukushima, Neocognitron: a self-organizing neural network model for a mechanism of pattern recognition unaffected by shift in position, in *Biological Cybernetics*, vol. 36, no. 4 (1980), pp. 193–202. http://dx.doi.org/10.1007/BF00344251
16. "Introduction to deep neural networks," https://deeplearning4j.org/neuralnet-overview. Accessed 15 Feb 2017
17. "ANTLR" http://www.antlr.org/. Accessed 03 Dec 2020
18. "Use JDT ASTParser to Parse Single .java files. http://www.programcreek.com/2011/11/use-jdt-astparser-to-parse-java-file/. Accessed 03 Dec 2020
19. Deeplearning4j. http://deeplearning4j.org/. Accessed 03 Dec 2020
20. *Data Mining Techniques: For Marketing, Sales, and Customer Relationship Management.* (Wiley Publishing, 2011)
21. S. Bellon, R. Koschke, G. Antoniol, J. Krinke, E. Merlo, Comparison and evaluation of clone detection tools. IEEE Trans. Softw. Eng. **33**(9), 577–591 (2007)
22. BigCloneBench. https://github.com/clonebench/BigCloneBench#era-updated. Accessed 03 Dec 2020
23. M. Herlihy, N. Shavit, *The Art of Multiprocessor Programming.* (Morgan Kaufmann Publishers Inc., 2008)
24. Weka 3—data mining with open source machine learning software in java. https://www.cs.waikato.ac.nz/ml/weka/. Accessed 03 Dec 2020

25. M. White, M. Tufano, C. Vendome, D. Poshyvanyk, Deep learning code fragments for code clone detection, in *Proceedings of the 31st IEEE/ACM International Conference on Automated Software Engineering* (2016)
26. G. Zhao, J. Huang, Deepsim: deep learning code functional similarity, in *Proceedings of the 2018 26th ACM Joint Meeting on European Software Engineering Conference and Symposium on the Foundations of Software Engineering*, ser. ESEC/FSE 2018. New York, NY, USA: Association for Computing Machinery (2018), pp. 141–151. https://doi.org/10.1145/3236024.3236068
27. L. Büch, A. Andrzejak, Learning-based recursive aggregation of abstract syntax trees for code clone detection, in *2019 IEEE 26th International Conference on Software Analysis, Evolution and Reengineering (SANER)* (2019), pp. 95–104
28. H. Yu, W. Lam, L. Chen, G. Li, T. Xie, Q. Wang, Neural detection of semantic code clones via tree-based convolution, in *2019 IEEE/ACM 27th International Conference on Program Comprehension (ICPC)* (2019), pp. 70–80
29. Z. Gao, V. Jayasundara, L. Jiang, X. Xia, D. Lo, J. Grundy, Smartembed: A tool for clone and bug detection in smart contracts through structural code embedding, in *IEEE International Conference on Software Maintenance and Evolution (ICSME)*, pp. 394–397 (2019)
30. L.C. Jain, L.R. Medsker, *Recurrent Neural Networks: Design and Applications*, 1st edn. (CRC Press Inc, USA, 1999)
31. C. Goller, A. Kuchler, Learning task-dependent distributed representations by backpropagation through structure, in *Proceedings of International Conference on Neural Networks (ICNN'96)*, vol. 1 (1996), pp. 347–352
32. K. O'Shea, R. Nash, An introduction to convolutional neural networks, in *CoRR*, vol. abs/1511.08458 (2015). http://arxiv.org/abs/1511.08458

Research Basis of Code Clone

BigCloneBench

Jeffrey Svajlenko and Chanchal K. Roy

Abstract Many clone detection tools and techniques have been created to tackle various use-cases, including syntactical clone detection, semantic clone detection, inter-project clone detection, large-scale clone detection and search, and so on. While a few clone benchmarks are available, none target this breadth of usage. Big-CloneBench is a clone benchmark designed to evaluate clone detection tools across a variety of use-cases. It was built by mining a large inter-project source repository for functions implementing known functionalities. This produced a large benchmark of inter-project and intra-project semantic clones across the full spectrum of syntactical similarity. The benchmark is augmented with an evaluation framework named Big-CloneEval which simplifies tool evaluation studies and allows the user to slice the benchmark based on the clone properties in order to evaluate for a particular use-case. We have used BigCloneBench in a number of studies that demonstrate its value, as well as show where it has been used by the research community. In this chapter, we discuss the clone benchmarking theory and the existing benchmarks, describe the BigCloneBench creation process, and overview the BigCloneEval evaluation procedure. We conclude by summarizing BigCloneBench's usage in the literature, and present ideas for future improvements and expansion of the benchmark.

1 Introduction

BigCloneBench is a dataset of nearly nine million clone pairs found within an inter-project Java source code dataset named IJaDataset [1] (2.5M source files, 25K projects, 250M lines of code). It contains both intra- and inter-project clones of the first four clone types, and all of the clones it contains have been manually validated to be similar by an implemented functionality. BigCloneBench is publicly available [2], including an implementation of an evaluation framework called BigCloneEval [3].

J. Svajlenko (✉)
GitHub, Seattle, USA

C. K. Roy
University of Saskatchewan, Saskatoon, Canada
e-mail: chanchal.roy@usask.ca

© The Author(s), under exclusive license to Springer Nature Singapore Pte Ltd. 2021
K. Inoue and C. K. Roy (eds.), *Code Clone Analysis*,
https://doi.org/10.1007/978-981-16-1927-4_7

We were motivated to build BigCloneBench after building our synthetic clone benchmark, the Mutation and Injection Framework [4]. We had found success with this benchmarking strategy [5, 6], but knew we needed to complement it with a real-world benchmark to overcome the limitations of synthetic benchmarking. We had investigated the use of Bellon's benchmark for this purpose but had found it to not be reusable [6]. While a number of alternate benchmarks have been introduced [4, 7–9], none could evaluate tools for the large-scale inter-project clone detection and code search scenario for which interest was emerging [10–12].

There has been a lack of clone benchmarks due to the difficulty in building one. Any source code dataset large enough to contain a large and diverse set of clones is far too large to manually inspect for clones. A mining approach is needed to reduce the validation space to make benchmark construction feasible. Classically, the clone detectors themselves have been used for this after manual validation [13], however, this leads to a benchmark biased toward the clone detectors used to build it [6, 14], while research has shown that clone-pair validation is unreliable for building benchmarks [7, 15, 16].

BigCloneBench was built by mining IJaDataset for functions implementing specific functionalities using automated techniques with manual validation. This process efficiently creates large clone classes of functions similar by functionality, which generates a large number of reference clone pairs for the benchmark. Since functions are validated for target functionalities to build the reference clones, it avoids the manual clone pair validation that is known to be subjective and error-prone.

2   Clone Benchmark Theory

Clone detection tools are evaluated using information retrieval metrics such as recall and precision. While time-consuming, precision is not too challenging to measure, and typically involves executing the tool for a variety of software systems and manually validating a random sample of the detected clones. Recall has been very challenging to measure as it requires foreknowledge of the clones that exist within a subject source code dataset independently of the clone detector under evaluation.

A clone benchmark is simply a reference set of known (true) clones within a dataset of source code. The clone detector is executed for the dataset, and its recall is measured as the ratio of the benchmark clones that are sufficiently detected by the tool, accounting for reasonable differences in how the tool and benchmark may report the clone (e.g. line boundaries). While a benchmark may help in measuring precision, this is not typically the goal as precision can be measured independently.

2.1 Idealized Benchmark

Given a collection of source code files S, where U is the universe of all potential clones in the source code, an (idealized) clone benchmark is the set of true clones C, where $C \subset U$. This implies a set N of all non-clones defined as $N = U - C$. Sets U, C, and N may be expressed in terms of clone pairs or clone classes for standard clone detection benchmarking, or even as a mapping of search code fragment to result set in the case of code clone search.

A clone detection tool outputs a collection D as its detected clones, which using the benchmark can be decomposed into it's set of true positives—$T_P = D \cap C$, true negatives—$T_N = (U - D) \cap (U - C)$, false positives—$F_P = D \cap (U - C)$, and false negatives—$F_N = C - D$. The tool's recall, r, and precision, p, are then defined as follows:

$$r = \frac{|T_P|}{|T_P| + |F_N|} \qquad (1) \qquad p = \frac{|T_P|}{|T_P| + |F_P|} \qquad (2)$$

2.2 Practical Benchmarking

There are two major obstacles preventing the creation and use of an idealized benchmark. Firstly, for a subject source dataset large and varied enough to produce a quality benchmark, it is not practical to manually identify all clones within it [17]. Even if this were not the case, experts often disagree on what is a true clone [14–16], which may be user-case specific [18].

A (practical) clone benchmark is therefore a collection C_B of known true clones and F_B of known false clones in a subject source dataset. C_B is a subset of C, and should be built in such a way that C_B is a convincing approximation of C and can thereby be used to estimate recall.

A limitation in most clone benchmarks is C_B and F_B are not sufficient to estimate precision. Typically the benchmark creation process aims to create a high-quality C_B as recall cannot be measured without a benchmark, while the F_B produced is too small and unvaried to estimate precision. While C_B can be used to measure an upper and lower bound on precision, the range is typically too broad to be useful. However, this is not a major obstacle as precision can be estimated by manually validating a statistically significant random sample of a tool's output for the benchmark subject dataset, which is why the focus of benchmarks has been to measure recall.

The second obstacle is that clone detection tools often do not report clones perfectly, or there may be different (but equally legitimate) reporting styles for the detection of a given clone [14]. The consequence is it is not as simple to compute the intersection of the benchmark and the detection clone sets to measure recall. To use a benchmark, a clone-matching algorithm must be defined that converts the set of reported clones, R, into the set of detected clones, D, as defined in the benchmark: $D = m(R, C_B)$. A common and simple matching algorithm is to consider a benchmark clone in C_B as detected if R contains a reported clone that *covers* a minimum ratio of the benchmark clone by source line or token.

Therefore, with a (practical) clone benchmark, we can estimate recall and precision as follows, where R_s is a statistically significant random sample of R, and $v(R_s)$ is the clones in this sample manually validated as true positives:

$$r \approx \frac{|m(R, C_B)|}{|C_B|} \qquad (3) \qquad p \approx \frac{|m(R, C_B)|}{|m(R, C_B \cup F_B)|} \qquad (4)$$

While the bounds on precision can be measured solely with the benchmark as follows:

$$\lfloor p \rfloor = \frac{|m(R, C_B)|}{|R|} \qquad (5) \qquad \lceil p \rceil = 1 - \frac{|m(R, F_B)|}{|R|} \qquad (6)$$

3 Previous Benchmarks

One of the fundamental works in clone detection benchmarking was a tool evaluation and comparison study conducted by Bellon et al. [13, 19, 20] in 2002. This study challenged the creators of six contemporary clone detection tools to detect clones in four C and four Java software systems. A total of 325,935 detected clones were submitted to Bellon who performed a random blind validation of 2% of these clones (a total of 6,528 clones requiring 77 h of manual inspection) to produce a benchmark containing 4,319 true clones. This dataset, along with a tool evaluation framework implementing multiple clone-matching algorithms, was released to the community and referred to as Bellon's Benchmark. Multiple extensions of this benchmark have been proposed, including Murakami's [21] extension for gap-clone detectors, and our extension [6] with tweaked clone-matching algorithms.

However, as a generalized benchmark there has been some criticism of Bellon's Benchmark. Baker [14] found inconsistencies in the clone types and validation procedure. Svajlenko et al. [6] found significant anomalies in recall measurements for tools that did not participate in the original experiment, suggesting the need for an updated benchmark dataset. The primary cause is that the benchmark only contains clones the originating tools could detect, which differs from what the modern tools can detect, and their style of clone reporting. Charpentier et al. [15] re-validated the clones using multiple judges and found significant disagreement. In another work, Chapentier et al. [16] show that non-experts in a particular software system are not reliable in validating its clones. Studies have shown that manual clone validation is unreliable in building benchmarks [15, 16, 18]. While Bellon's Benchmark may not be suitable as a general benchmark outside of its original tool comparison study, it laid the groundwork for clone benchmarking studies.

Kurtz and Le [9] also built a benchmark based on manual clone validation. They randomly sampled 1536 function pairs from three C software systems for manual validation by multiple expert judges. This yielded a benchmark of 66 true clones. While this benchmark has high confidence and was built independently of any clone detection tool or methods, it is too small to provide generalized results.

Lavoie and Merlo [8] present an approach for automatically building idealized benchmarks. They use Levenshtein distance as a ground truth for discerning true versus false clones, and implement an algorithm for computing a clone benchmark given a configuration of the metric. The advantage of this approach is an ideal benchmark that can measure both recall and precision with no manual validation effort and no introduced subjectivity. The disadvantage of this approach is it can only measure the performance of a clone detector in comparison to Levenshtein distance, so it may be best for approaches aiming to efficiently approximate this approach.

Our Mutation and Injection Framework [4, 17] is a synthetic clone benchmarking framework based on mutation-analysis. Clone-producing mutation operators are used to introduce a copy and paste (with edits) clone to a subject system, and the clone detectors are evaluated for the detection of this clone. This is repeated many thousands of times across operators implemented based on a taxonomy [22] of the kinds of edits developers make on cloned code. The advantage of this benchmark is it allows the capabilities of a tool to be explored for each kind of clone edit [6, 23], evaluated in a controlled environment that prevents experimental biases and is particularity effective in debugging clone detectors [24–26]. Its disadvantage is its results may not reflect real-world performance, as the framework only produces simple clones, and has an even distribution across the clone types. We have shown that combining synthetic and real-world benchmarks reveals more about clone detection performance [23], and have explored using high-level mutations to produce benchmarks for variant analysis [5].

Yuki et al. [7] build a benchmark by automatically searching the history of a source control system for changes that match clone refactoring patterns. Heuristics and metrics are used to decide if an editing pattern is a true clone refactoring change. The authors executed this approach for three Java projects (15K revisions), identifying 19 refactored clones. The advantage of this approach is it builds a benchmark validated (indirectly) by the developers of the software system, which is considered the most reliable [16]. It is a good example of a benchmark targeting a particular use-case, as it has clones developers found worth removing by refactoring. The disadvantage is the scalability required to build a sizeable and diverse benchmark. A risk in this approach is that it may create a benchmark of the kinds of clones developers do not need clone detectors to detect, or ones that were detected by an existing clone detector. This is a promising work toward mining developer artifacts to indirectly locate and validated clones.

4   Building BigCloneBench

We built BigCloneBench by mining IJaDataset for functions implementing various target functionalities. We designed a semi-automatic approach that used search heuristics to identify candidate functions implementing functionality with manual validation to accept or reject the candidates. This yielded a large clone class of functions similar by their shared functionality, which yielded a large number of clone

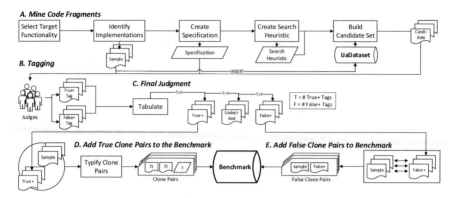

Fig. 1 Building BigCloneBench [27]

pairs across the first four clone types. We repeated this process for over 40 function-alities to build a diverse benchmark of nearly 9 million clone pairs. The procedure is shown in Fig. 1.

(A1) Select Target Functionality. We select a functionality we expect to appear frequently in open-source Java code, and which may yield many benchmark clones. Inspiration comes from the investigation of StackOverflow, online tutorials, popular third party libraries, and other Internet sources.

(A2) Identify Implementations. We research common ways of implementing the target functionality in Java. We consider our own experience in these functionalities, as well as explore common online sources such as StackOverflow and GitHub for implementations. We consider how an algorithm can be expressed in different ways (e.g. different control-flow statements), or how different first and third party libraries may be utilized. From this, we compose a handful of minimum working examples of the functionality that are then injected into IJaDataset as additional code.

(A3) Create Specification. We create a specification capturing the minimum steps or features of a function to be considered a true implementation of the func-tionality. The specification is designed to be permissive to any implementation of the functionality, even ones we had not identified.

(A4) Search Heuristic. From the exemplar implementations and specifications, we design a search heuristic that can be used to identify candidate functions that might implement the target functionality. The heuristic consists of a set of keywords and source-code patterns, which we expect to appear in implementation in various logical combinations. We design the heuristic to balance two requirements: (1) it should identify as many true positives as possible, but (2) it should not identify so many false positives that it is cumbersome to validate.

(A5) Build Candidate Set. The heuristic is then executed for every function in IJaDataset to identify the set of candidate functions.

(B) Tag Functions. The candidate functions are then manually validated by one or more judges. The judges are provided with the specification and exemplar implementations, and asked to mark a candidate as a true positive if it meets or exceeds the specification. The judges use an application designed to improve their accuracy by displaying the candidate with proper syntax highlighting, and by displaying the exemplar functions and specification beside the candidate for reference. The judge is able to example the candidate function in isolation as well as within the context of its original source file.

(C) Final Judgment. Once the functions are tagged by the judges, the final judgment is performed by summing the tags. When multiple judges have inspected a function, the final judgment is decided by the winning vote. In the case of a tie, the function is not included in the benchmark.

(D) True Clone Pairs. The set of exemplar functions and true positive functions for a target functionality are assembled into a large clone class from which the clone pairs are extracted and added to the benchmark. Automatic processing labels the clones with their syntactic clone type (Type-1, Type-2, or Type-3). While all of the clone pairs have semantical similarity due to their shared functionality, we find no agreement in the literature on when Type-3 ends and Type-4 begins for this case. Instead, we augment the clones with measures of syntactical similarity (by line and by token after normalizations) which the benchmark users can use to separate Type-3 and Type-4 as per their preference.

(E) False Clone Pairs. The exemplar functions (implementing only the functionality) are paired with each of the mined functions judged as false positives and added to the benchmark as false clones. These false clones are not to share functionality, at least as defined by the specification.

In total, nearly 80 thousand functions were tagged for 43 target functionalities building a benchmark of nearly 9 million true clone pairs and nearly 29 thousand false (semantic) clone pairs. This includes 48 thousand Type-1 clones, 4.2 thousand Type-2 clones, and 8.9 million Type-3/Type-4 clones. If we split the Type-3 and Type-4 clones by their measured syntactical similarity, we find we have 34 thousand with 70–90% similarity, 329 thousand with 50–70% similarity, and 8.5 million with 0–50% syntactical similarity. In this case, we measure similarity as the minimum ratio of lines or tokens the code fragments of a clone pair share after Type-1 and Type-2 differences are removed by normalizations. This separation of the Type-3/Type-4 clones is not enforced in the benchmark, but we have found it to be good summarization categories in our studies [23, 25, 26, 28].

To create this benchmark, 78 thousand functions were manually tagged by 9 judges over 514 combined validation hours. In order to measure the subjectivity in our validation efforts, 9,533 of these functions were examined by multiple judges. For only 14.5% of these functions did at least one judge disagree with the others, either due to subjectivity or validation error. Disagreement was less likely for code fragments examined by only two judges (10.8%), but higher for validation performed by three (20.4%) and four (18.8%) judges. While more judges increase the chance to discover subjectivity, it also increases the likelihood one of the judges made a validation error. We extrapolate the average disagreement to estimate that at least 15% of the clones across the benchmark are subjective or have validation errors.

5   Using BigCloneBench

The clones in BigCloneBench have metadata including functionality, clone type, size, syntactical similarity, and whether the clone is an intra- or inter-project clone. Users of the benchmark can and should slice the benchmark by combinations of this metadata to evaluate clone detection tools for particular clone properties. We demonstrated the use of BigCloneBench in an experiment evaluating ten clone detectors [23].

In this experiment, we evaluated the tools using BigCloneBench sliced by a variety of properties and compared the results against our synthetic benchmark (the Mutation Framework) [4]. The Mutation Framework showed us the precise capabilities of these tools against the kinds of differences that can occur between clones, while Big-CloneBench showed us how these capabilities translate into real-world performance. Generally, we found that good performance in synthetic benchmarking translated into good real-world performance, with some exceptions.

The Mutation Framework correctly identified that the Type-2 clone detectors could not detect clones with Type-3 edits—its clone-matching algorithm rejects detected clones that do not contain the introduced edit. However, BigCloneBench identified that these tools are approximately able to detect very similar Type-3 clones that have large Type-1/Type-2 regions. However, this detection is not ideal as it requires manual efforts by the tool user to correct the clone boundaries. We found that tools may be missing some Type-2 normalizations which resulted in poorer performance with the Mutation Framework, but that these types of edits are less common in real-world clones and therefore had better Type-2 recall with BigCloneBench. Conversely, there were cases where the tools performed very well for synthetic clones in a controlled environment, but then performed much poorer with BigCloneBench where the tools experienced more challenges in parsing edge-cases. In summary, our finding was that both synthetic and real-world benchmarks are needed to fully understand the tools.

We were able to use BigCloneBench to measure Type-3 recall across the range of syntactical similarity, with a focus on those with 50–100% similarity. We observed that tools which use a similarity metric with a minimum threshold typically had a hard drop-off in Type-3 recall. In contrast, tools that used techniques that were more independent of straight syntactical comparison were able to maintain a small level of recall even when the Type-3 similarity was much lower.

Unique to BigCloneBench is the ability to evaluate tools for both intra-project and inter-project clones separately. The tools we evaluated were primarily designed for the intra-project use-case, but there is interest in re-using these tools and algorithms for inter-project use-cases. We were able to compare recall per clone type of the tools for both use-cases, and we found that most of the tools had significantly weaker recall performance for one of these use-cases for at least one clone type. However, this was not uniformly in favor of intra-project clones, and in a little over half the cases the tools were performing better for inter-project clones. We concluded that the difference in performance was likely due to other factors, and that the tools are appropriate for the inter-project use-case.

We extended this experiment in our tool publications, including SourcererCC [25], CloneWorks [24, 29], and CCAligner [26]. These tools are designed for large-scale clone detection, so we took random samples of IJaDataset of sizes at each order of magnitude from one thousand lines of code to 100 million lines of code (including the full dataset at 250MLOC). In this way, BigCloneBench can also be used to evaluate and compare the execution performance and scalability of clone detection tools for large datasets. As well, it is a good target for evaluating precision for the inter-project detection scenario.

6   BigCloneEval

We introduced BigCloneEval [3], a clone detection tool evaluation framework, which is based on our tool comparison studies [23–26]. The procedure enabled by Big-CloneEval is shown in Fig. 2, with each step implemented as a command-line tool. The user registers the tools to be evaluated, which creates entries for them in the tools database. They then execute the tools for IJaDataset and import the clones into the framework. Many tools are unable to scale to IJaDataset, so BigCloneEval includes a reduced and partitioned version of IJaDataset which is within the scalability limits of most tools. For tools with significant scalability challenges, BigCloneEval can dynamically further partition the datasets down to any size. Users can either execute their tool for these partitions manually, or implement a simple plugin to let BigCloneEval automate tool execution for each partition.

Once the detection results are imported, the user can run the evaluation which outputs a summary of the tools' recall performance. This is measured per clone type, per functionality, for ranges of syntactical similarity with summary aggregates across these dimensions. The evaluation step is highly configurable so that the user can measure recall for different slices of BigCloneBench by features such as clone size and similarity. BigCloneEval includes multiple common clone-matching algorithms, and supports a plugin system for custom clone matchers.

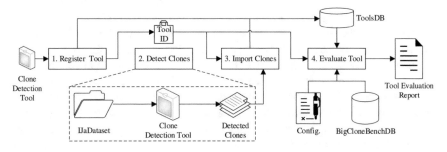

Fig. 2 BigCloneEval procedure [3]

BigCloneEval is publicly available[1] and open-sourced. It is written in Java and uses embedded file-based databases for portability.

7 BigCloneBench in the Literature

We have used BigCloneBench in a number of clone detection tool evaluation studies [4, 23]. It has been adopted by various authors for evaluating their clone detection [24–26, 30–32, 32–37] and code search techniques [38, 39]. It has been adopted as a training dataset for clone machine-learning studies. Keivanloo et al. [40] performed unsupervised clustering for threshold-free near-miss clone detection in order to overcome the configuration problem [41]. Li et al. [42] trained a token-based clone classifier. Zhou et al. [43] trained a real-time code example recommender system called Lancer. Guo et al. [44] trained a model that uses clone detection to perform review sharing across software projects.

8 Looking Forward

The first release of BigCloneBench included ten functionalities and demonstrated the methodology. The second release greatly expanded on the breadth of the benchmark by expanding to over 40 functionalities. It has been demonstrated that the benchmark is effective in measuring recall for near-miss clone detectors for intra- and inter-project clones [23], for the large-scale inter-project clone detectors [24–26] as well as for clone-search [38, 39]. BigCloneEval has made the benchmark more accessible and helped adoption in the literature. For future releases of BigCloneBench, our focus will be on improving validation accuracy and supporting additional use-cases.

We would like to expand the function validation to have multiple judges for each decision. Ideally, an even number of judges should be used so that high subjectivity (split vote) can be used to reject candidates from the benchmark.

During the function validation process, the judges mark a function as a true positive of a functionality if it meets the minimum specification of that functionality, regardless of if the function also performs other functionality. The implementation may be the primary purpose of the function, or a piece of a larger functionality. This can lead to clones that are similar by a shared piece of functionality, but on the whole may appear otherwise dissimilar. These clones are ideal for the semantic code search benchmark, as well as the use of clone detection for identifying cross-cutting concerns. However, these clones may be undesirable to detect in other clone detection use-cases. In order to identify these clones, we would augment the validation phase to also ask the judges to indicate whether the functionality is the primary purpose of the function or the part of a larger functionality. Users of the benchmark can then

---

[1] https://github.com/jeffsvajlenko/BigCloneEval.

include or omit these clones from their experiments as per their evaluation requirements. This has not impacted the near-miss clone detection benchmarking as we have focused on the clones that both share functionality as well as are at least 50% similar by syntax. This scenario is more likely with the simpler functionalities (e.g. "copy a file") and less-so with the more complex functionalities (e.g. "database update with rollback").

Other opportunities for expansion of BigCloneBench are to investigate other clone mining approaches to build additional benchmark datasets in IJaDataset, evolving BigCloneBench into a suite of benchmarks. Our previous studies have shown that a multi-benchmark evaluation experiment provides the most complete evaluation [6, 23]. For example, we could use our Mutation Framework [4] to seed synthetic clones into BigCloneBench. The clones identified by BigCloneBench could also be mined to classify them by different target use-cases for supporting more use-case-specific benchmarking scenarios.

References

1. Ambient Software Evolution Group. SECold IJaDataset 2.0. https://sites.google.com/site/asegsecold/projects/seclone, January 2013
2. J. Svajlenko, C. Roy. Bigclonebench. http://www.jeff.svajlenko.com/bigclonebench.html
3. J. Svajlenko, C.K. Roy, Bigcloneeval: a clone detection tool evaluation framework with bigclonebench, in *International Conference on Software Maintenance and Evolution* (2016)
4. J. Svajlenko, C. Roy, The mutation and injection framework: evaluating clone detection tools with mutation analysis. IEEE Trans. Softw. Eng. (01):1
5. J. Svajlenko, C.K. Roy, S. Duszynski, Forksim: generating software forks for evaluating cross-project similarity analysis tools. In *International Working Conference on Source Code Analysis and Manipulation (SCAM)* (2013), pp 37–42
6. J. Svajlenko, C.K. Roy, Evaluating modern clone detection tools, vol. 10 (2014)
7. Y. Yuki, Y. Higo, K. Hotta, S. Kusumoto, Generating clone references with less human subjectivity, in *2016 IEEE 24th International Conference on Program Comprehension (ICPC)* (2016), pp 1–4
8. T. Lavoie, E. Merlo, Automated type-3 clone oracle using levenshtein metric, in *Proceedings of the 5th International Workshop on Software Clones, IWSC '11* (ACM, New York, NY, USA, 2011), pp. 34–40
9. D.E. Krutz, W. Le, A code clone oracle, in *Proceedings of the 11th Working Conference on Mining Software Repositories, MSR 2014* (ACM, New York, NY, USA), pp. 388–391 (2014)
10. H. Sajnani, V. Saini, C. Lopes, A parallel and efficient approach to large scale clone detection. J. Softw. Evol. Process, **27**(6), 402–429 (2015). JSME-13-0129.R2
11. J. Svajlenko, I. Keivanloo, C.K. Roy, Scaling classical clone detection tools for ultra-large datasets: an exploratory study, in *International Workshop on Software Clones*, pp. 16–22 (2013)
12. I. Keivanloo, J. Rilling, P. Charland, Internet-scale real-time code clone search via multi-level indexing, in *Working Conference on Reverse Engineering*, pp. 23–27 (2011)
13. S. Bellon, R. Koschke, G. Antoniol, J. Krinke, E. Merlo, Comparison and evaluation of clone detection tools. IEEE Trans. Softw. Eng. **33**(9), 577–591 (2007)
14. B.S. Baker, Finding clones with dup: analysis of an experiment. IEEE Trans. Softw. Eng. **33**(9), 608–621 (2007)
15. A. Charpentier, J.-R. Falleri, D. Lo, L. Réveillère, An empirical assessment of Bellon's clone benchmark, in *International Conference on Evaluation and Assessment in Software Engineering, EASE '15* (ACM, New York, NY, USA), pp. 20:1–20:10 (2015)

16. A. Charpentier, J.-R. Falleri, F. Morandat, E.B.H. Yahia, L. Réveillère, Raters' reliability in clone benchmarks construction. Empirical Softw. Eng. **22**(1), 235–258 (2017)
17. C.K. Roy, J.R. Cordy, Towards a mutation-based automatic framework for evaluating code clone detection tools, in *Proceedings of the 2008 C3S2E Conference, C3S2E '08* (ACM, New York, NY, USA), pp. 137–140 (2008)
18. A. Walenstein, N. Jyoti, J. Li, Y. Yang, A. Lakhotia, Problems creating task-relevant clone detection reference data. WCRE, 285–294 (2003)
19. S. Bellon, Stefan Bellon's clone detector benchmark. http://www.softwareclones.org/research-data.php
20. S. Bellon, Vergleich von Techniken zur Erkennung duplizierten Quellcodes. Master's thesis, Universität Stuttgart, 2002. 156 pp
21. H. Murakami, Y. Higo, S. Kusumoto, A dataset of clone references with gaps. MSR'14, 412–415 (2014)
22. C.K. Roy, J.R. Cordy, R. Koschke, Comparison and evaluation of code clone detection techniques and tools: a qualitative approach. Sci. Comput. Program. **74**(7), 470–495 (2009). May
23. J. Svajlenko, C.K. Roy, Evaluating clone detection tools with bigclonebench, in *International Conference on Software Maintenance and Evolution*, pp. 131–140 (2015)
24. J. Svajlenko, C.K. Roy, Fast and flexible large-scale clone detection with cloneworks, in *Proceedings of the 39th International Conference on Software Engineering Companion, ICSE-C '17* (IEEE Press, Piscataway, NJ, USA), pp. 27–30 (2017)
25. H. Sajnani, V. Saini, J. Svajlenko, C.K. Roy, C.V. Lopes, Sourcerercc: scaling code clone detection to big-code, in *Proceedings of the 38th International Conference on Software Engineering* (ACM), pp. 1157–1168 (2016)
26. P. Wang, J. Svajlenko, Y. Wu, Y. Xu, C. K. Roy, Ccaligner: a token based large-gap clone detector, in *2018 IEEE/ACM 40th International Conference on Software Engineering (ICSE)*, pp. 1066–1077 (2018)
27. J. Svajlenko, J.F. Islam, I. Keivanloo, C.K. Roy, M.M. Mia, Towards a big data curated benchmark of inter-project code clones, in *Proceedings of the 2014 IEEE International Conference on Software Maintenance and Evolution, ICSME '14* (IEEE Computer Society, Washington, DC, USA), pp. 476–480 (2014)
28. J. Svajlenko, Large-scale clone detection and benchmarking. Ph.D. thesis, University of Saskatchewan, Saskatoon, Canada, 2 2018
29. J. Svajlenko, C.K. Roy, Cloneworks: a fast and flexible large-scale near-miss clone detection tool, in *2017 IEEE/ACM 39th International Conference on Software Engineering Companion (ICSE-C)*, pp. 177–179 (2017)
30. Y. Gao, Z. Wang, S. Liu, L. Yang, W. Sang, Y. Cai, Teccd: a tree embedding approach for code clone detection, in *2019 IEEE International Conference on Software Maintenance and Evolution (ICSME)*, pp. 145–156 (2019)
31. J. Liu, T. Wang, C. Feng, H. Wang, D. Li, A large-gap clone detection approach using sequence alignment via dynamic parameter optimization. IEEE Access **7** (2019)
32. S. Zhou, H. Zhong, B. Shen, Slampa: Recommending code snippets with statistical language model, in *2018 25th Asia-Pacific Software Engineering Conference (APSEC)*, pp. 79–88 (2018)
33. J. Zhang, X. Wang, H. Zhang, H. Sun, K. Wang, X. Liu, A novel neural source code representation based on abstract syntax tree, in *2019 IEEE/ACM 41st International Conference on Software Engineering (ICSE)*, pp. 783–794 (2019)
34. H. Yu, W. Lam, L. Chen, G. Li, T. Xie, Q. Wang, Neural detection of semantic code clones via tree-based convolution, in *2019 IEEE/ACM 27th International Conference on Program Comprehension (ICPC)*, pp. 70–80 (2019)
35. J. Zeng, K. Ben, X. Li, X. Zhang, Fast code clone detection based on weighted recursive autoencoders. IEEE Access **7**, 125062–125078 (2019)
36. D.K. Kim. A deep neural network-based approach to finding similar code segments. IEICE Trans. Inf. Syst. **E103.D**(4):874–878 (2020)
37. M. Hammad, Ö. Babur, H.A. Basit, M. van den Brand, Deepclone: modeling clones to generate code predictions, in *Reuse in Emerging Software Engineering Practices* (Springer International Publishing), pp 135–151 (2020)

38. F. Zhang, H. Niu, I. Keivanloo, Y. Zou, Expanding queries for code search using semantically related API class-names. Trans. Softw. Eng. **44**(11), 1070–1082 (2018)
39. Y. Fujiwara, N. Yoshida, E. Choi, K. Inoue, Code-to-code search based on deep neural network and code mutation, in *2019 IEEE 13th International Workshop on Software Clones (IWSC)*, pp. 1–7 (2019)
40. I. Keivanloo, F. Zhang, Y. Zou, Threshold-free code clone detection for a large-scale heterogeneous java repository, in *2015 IEEE 22nd International Conference on Software Analysis, Evolution, and Reengineering (SANER)*, pp. 201–210 (2015)
41. T. Wang, M. Harman, Y. Jia, J. Krinke, Searching for better configurations: a rigorous approach to clone evaluation, in *Joint Meeting on Foundations of Software Engineering, ESEC/FSE 2013* (ACM, New York, NY, USA), pp. 455–465 (2013)
42. L. Li, H. Feng, W. Zhuang, N. Meng, B. Ryder, Cclearner: a deep learning-based clone detection approach, in *International Conference on Software Maintenance and Evolution*, pp. 249–260 (2017)
43. S. Zhou, B. Shen, H. Zhong, Lancer: your code tell me what you need, in *International Conference on Automated Software Engineering (ASE)*, pp. 1202–1205 (2019)
44. C. Guo, D. Huang, N. Dong, Q. Ye, J. Xu, Y. Fan, H. Yang, Y. Xu. Deep review sharing, in *2019 IEEE 26th International Conference on Software Analysis, Evolution and Reengineering (SANER)*, pp. 61–72 (2019)

Visualization of Clones

Muhammad Hammad, Hamid Abdul Basit, Stan Jarzabek,
and Rainer Koschke

Abstract Identifying similar code fragments, referred to as code clones, is beneficial in software re-engineering and maintenance. Various visualization techniques have been developed to present cloning information for programmers in a more useful and comprehensible manner. This chapter provides a summary of state of the art in visualizing software clones, along with a classification of visualizations according to the supported user goals, and the relevant information needs to achieve the user goals. Moreover, it further presents an assessment of clone visualizations on the basis of clone relations and clone granularity.

1 Introduction

Similar code fragments known as software clones frequently exist in software applications. Cloning rates of 5–50% have been reported in the literature [13]. Many clone detection and analysis tools have been developed, supporting different visualizations to help developers in comprehending various aspects of cloning data. In our previous publications [1, 2, 7], we presented a systematic mapping study [3, 11] on clone visualizations. We classified those visualizations according to different criteria such as clone data, data facets, and human-vision characteristics, following the guidelines of Card and Mackinlay [4] and Shneiderman [15]. We presented

M. Hammad (✉)
Eindhoven University of Technology, Eindhoven, Netherlands
e-mail: m.hammad@tue.nl

H. Abdul Basit
Prince Sultan University, Riyadh, Saudi Arabia
e-mail: hbasit@psu.edu.sa

S. Jarzabek
Bialystok University of Technology, Bialystok, Poland
e-mail: s.jarzabek@pb.edu.pl

R. Koschke
University of Bremen, Bremen, Germany
e-mail: koschke@uni-bremen.de

© The Author(s), under exclusive license to Springer Nature Singapore Pte Ltd. 2021   107
K. Inoue and C. K. Roy (eds.), *Code Clone Analysis*,
https://doi.org/10.1007/978-981-16-1927-4_8

a framework relating user goals with information needs and clone visualizations. We also provided statistics on clone visualization research publications, identified gaps in visualizations, information needs, and user goals, presented the state of empirical evaluations in this field, and described the status quo and challenges in industrial adoption. In this chapter, we summarize all our previous contributions, together with an assessment of clone visualizations, on the basis of clone granularity and clone relations.

2 User Goals and Information Needs

Clone detection tools identify clones and present cloning data with different visualizations to assist developers in completing software development tasks—referred to as *user goals* in this chapter—such as bug detection, refactoring, and program comprehension. Each user goal requires some specific clone-related information—called *information needs*—that can assist developers to attain that goal. We have identified a list of information needs from the literature, as shown in Table 1. The process of searching for user goals and information needs is documented in our previous publications [1, 2, 7]. We have made the list as comprehensive as possible, but new user goals or information needs can be discovered and added to it. We have identified a total of 24 user goals and 38 information needs from the literature. Figure 1 maps user goal with information needs as a Dot plot. A colored cell indicates that the user goal in that column requires the information listed in that row. The color gradient above and on the left side of the matrix represents the extent to which a user goal is supported by existing visualizations and how many alternative visualizations exist for the listed information needs.

3 Facets of Visualization

We have introduced a taxonomy or classification of clone visualizations as per the guidelines of Card and Mackinlay [4] and Shneiderman [15]. The objective is to describe the visualizations more coherently and group them on the basis of similarities. To differentiate what is visualized from how it is visualized, we considered two types of similarities: similarities in the aspects of human vision (*human-vision facets*) and similarities in the structure of the data (*data facets*) shown in the visualizations. Figure 2a, b show the two taxonomies, respectively. Further details can be found in the original publication [7].

Table 1 Information needs

N1	Where are clones in a given program unit located?
N2	Where are the instances of a given clone class located?
N3	Which clones exist across programs or program variants?
N4	How many instances are in a clone class?
N5	How large is a cloned fragment?
N6	How much is cloned in a given program unit?
N7	How much code is contained in a clone class (volume: the total sum over the size of all instances of a clone class)?
N8	What types of syntactic structures are contained in a clone?
N9	What are the differences among the instances of a clone class?
N10	How different are the clones?
N11	What is the relevance ranking of clones for a particular task at hand?
N12	What are the differences in the context of clones (e.g., the units containing the clone instances)?
N13	How much code of one program unit is cloned in another program unit?
N14	How much code of one program unit is cloned across a particular given group of program units?
N15	What is the size of the program unit containing clones?
N16	Is there a clone in the current scope of the program?
N17	Which clones are present across versions of the evolving system and which clones disappeared?
N18	How has the location of a clone changed in different system versions?
N19	How has a clone changed from one version to another?
N20	What is the overall trend of cloning across versions?
N21	What is the spread of cloning across versions?
N22	What are the effects of a clone onto quality and maintenance costs?
N23	Who is the owner of original and copied code?
N24	What is the license of the clone?
N25	Is the code private?
N26	How much code can be eliminated when clones are removed?
N27	How much code can be eliminated when a clone class is removed?
N28	What is the reduction of maintenance effort?
N29	Which clones can be removed?
N30	How can a given clone be removed?
N31	What are the costs and risks of removing a given clone?
N32	How are the clone classes related to each other (e.g., are their instances contained in the same files)?
N33	How are clones related to formal and non-formal system artifacts other than code?
N34	What is the higher level abstraction/concept behind the clones or clone classes?
N35	What is the reason for the clones?
N36	Which other instances of a clone class need to be updated?
N37	How to update other instances of a clone class?
N38	Which (inconsistent) type-2 or type-3 clones must be re-synchronized?

Fig. 1 Relation of
information needs and user
goals

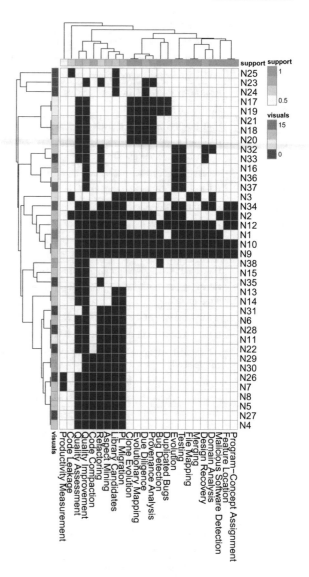

4 Clone-Visualization Techniques

In this section, we briefly summarize the existing categories of visualizations along
the facets described in Sect. 3. We also summarize the description of all the identified
visualizations in Table 2. More details including the references to the original papers
can be found in our previous publications [2, 7].

Table 2 Visualization descriptions and their evaluation on the basis of clone granularity and clone relations (S = subsystem or sub-directory, F = file, C = code segment, P = clone pair, G = clone class, Sc = super-clone)

	Visualization	Clone granularity	Clone relations	Description
Textual	bm	F, C	P, G	It is a visual component of code inspection view that presents the relative positions and sizes of specific code sections with bars
	tmv	F, C	G	It uses triangles to decorate regions with code clones, and displays the frequency of a clone in those regions
	ss	F, C	G	It is used to visualize code clones in a large volume of source code, where files are shown as vertical bars and code lines as thin horizontal rows within bar segments (stripes) representing clones
	tcv	F, C	P	It is used to display the set of identifier names in the cloned source code to help a user to more quickly grasp the semantics of a clone, where size and color may denote the frequency of those words
	civ	F, C	P, G	It is similar to the visual diff [18] tools and used to distinguish and highlight cloned and non-cloned code in the source code of two or more files
Attribute measure	pc	S, F, C	P, G, Sc	It is a circle partitioned into typically distinctly colored segments reflecting the proportions of clone information such as clone pairs, clone classes, and super-clones at various levels of granularity such as subsystems, files, code segments, and clone types
	bc	S, F, C	P, G, Sc	It consists of rectangular bars, which are used to represent and compare clones according to the selected metrics
	lc	S, F, C	P, G, Sc	It displays the relationship between two variables to display a trend in clones over intervals of time. It is plotted along the x and y axes of a grid, as a series of data points connected by straight line segments
	pcv	C	G	It is used to analyze n-dimensional data such as various clone-class metrics. The n-dimensional space is drawn by n parallel and evenly spaced vertical axes—one axis for each variable
	rsp	S, F, C	P, G	It graphically depicts the similarity of clone instances relative to a given instance called the leading node, which is determined by using some similarity criteria
	hm	C	P	It is a mini-map representing whole clone instances, where a color gradient is used to encode the number of copies of clone instances
Temporal	ts	S, F, C	G	It is a special case of line chart which is used to display the evolution of single or multiple clone metrics over time
	cev	C	P, G	It displays clone classes for each version of the software and links the clones across versions through edges to display their evolution as clone genealogies
Bipartite	ccfe	F	G	It is used to display the bipartite relation among clone-class families and source files, where smaller nodes represent clone-class families, whereas larger nodes represent source files
	cccg	S	S, C, G	It provides a summary about the extent of clone coupling and cohesion in a software system at a higher level of cloning through super-clones

(continued)

Table 2 (continued)

	Visualization	Clone granularity	Clone relations	Description
Tree	ntv	S, F	P, G, Sc	It is used to present a hierarchical view of various clone-related elements, up to the level of files and subsystems. The hierarchy is shown as a list with increasing indentation at each level of the tree
	htv	S, F	P, G	It is used to display cloning as well as the evolution of clones over time at various levels of granularity as a node-link diagram where a link represents containment
	tm	S, F	P, G	It typically represents clone information at various granularity levels such as files and subsystems in the form of a tree. The tree contains a group of nested rectangles, where their sizes and colors can depict certain clone information
	es	S, F	P	It is used to visualize cloning at the system level in virtual reality as road junctions. The streets represent the subsystem hierarchy in terms of directories and the buildings depict files
Acyclic	hd	F	G	It is used to display cloning relationships between clusters of files as a partially ordered set in the form of a directed acyclic graph
	ccd	C	G	It is a graph-based visualization of clones that describes both the content and the context of a single given clone class
Cyclic	dp	S, F, C	P	It shows cloning as a matrix, where rows and columns are the entities (lines, files, directories, etc.), while a dot indicates cloning between the corresponding entities. The rows may present entities different from those in the columns
	wv	S, F	P	It is used to display internal and external clones along with their relationship in the form of a tree as nested circle segments. These segments represent an entity, which are placed in concentric rings representing the hierarchy
	db	S	P	It is a node-link diagram showing relations between cloned code fragments and code entities such as methods, classes, and packages
	dwv	F	P	It is used to display all files in the system as nodes arranged in a circle and connected with each other as edges based on shared clones
	cs	F	P	It consists of nodes and edges representing files and clone connections
	sg	S	P, G	It is a node-link diagram, in which the nodes represent clones, and their distances depend upon their similarity
	ng	S	P	It is a node-link diagram with composite nodes in which edges are annotated by the extent of cloning
	crvw	C	G	It visualizes refactoring edits and anomalies in the history of a clone class as a node-link diagram

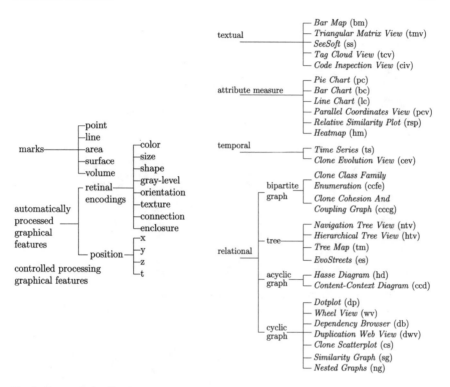

Fig. 2 Facets of visualization

4.1 Visualization of Attribute Measures

Visual attributes such as shape, color, and pattern are used to represent quantified attributes of cloning, such as the degree of redundancy. Visualizations of attribute measures include *Pie Charts*, *Bar Charts*, *Line Charts*, *Parallel-coordinate Charts*, *Relative Similarity Plot View*, and *Heatmap*. Figure 3 shows an example *Heatmap*, where the number of clones of a code segment is encoded with a color gradient.

4.2 Textual Visualizations

Textual visualizations are used to display the source text, which helps developers to analyze what is cloned and what changes have been made at the textual level and can also show other characteristics of the text. Visualizations of text include *Bar Maps*, *Seesoft*, *Tag Cloud View*, and *Code Inspection View*. Figure 4 displays an example *Tag Cloud View* to represent the relative significance of key identifiers contained in cloned (in red) and non-cloned code (in black).

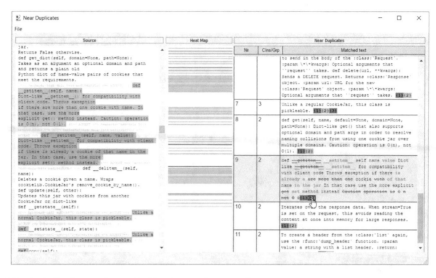

Fig. 3 Left: *Source* view with highlighted duplicate lines; middle: *Heatmap*; right: differences between code snippets selected in the *Source* view [10] (Example of Attribute Measure)

Fig. 4 Tag cloud view [14] (Example of Textual Visualization)

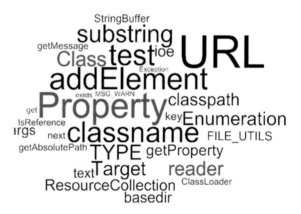

4.3 Temporal Data Visualizations

Temporal data visualizations are used to display how software clones are evolved from one version of the software to another. A *Time Series* is a classic example of temporal data visualization which displays the change of one or more variables of at least ordinal scale over time, represented as a chart where the x-axis is time and the y-axis are the evolving data of interest. *Clone Evolution View* is another visualization that can be used to visualize the evolution of clone classes by linking the various evolved versions of a clone as clone genealogies (Fig. 5a).[1]

---

[1] http://softwareclones.org/cyclone.php Last accessed January 17, 2021.

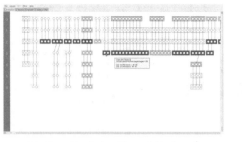
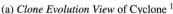

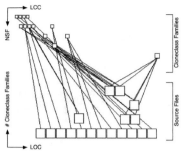

(a) *Clone Evolution View* of Cyclone [1]

(b) Clone-Class Family Enumeration [12]

Fig. 5 Example of temporal and bipartite visualizations

4.4 Bipartite Graph Visualization

Binary relations can be modeled as graphs with nodes representing entities and edges representing relationships between entities. Bipartite graphs are a special kind of graphs in which the set of nodes form two disjoint sets, such that there is no edge connecting two nodes of the same set. These graphs are used to model situations when there are two different concepts in a domain and it is required to model only the relations between those two concepts. In the cloning domain, these graphs can be used to display the containment of clones in various containers like files and directories. *Clone Cohesion and Coupling Graph* and *Clone-Class Family Enumeration* are examples of bipartite graphs applied to cloning data. Figure 5b shows a *Clone-Class Family Enumeration*, where smaller nodes represent clone class families and larger nodes represent source files. The edges express containment between the two. The location of the nodes in the two stacked two-dimensional charts (one for clone-class families and one for source files) depict two metrics for each of those nodes.

4.5 Tree Data Visualization

Hierarchies are frequently found in modeling software data and clone data is no exception: clone instances are contained in files, which are contained in directories, which may be contained in other directories. Trees are a natural visualization for hierarchies. *Navigation Tree View*, *Hierarchical Tree View* (Fig. 6a), *Tree Map*, and *EvoStreets* are different types of tree-data visualization. Figure 6a displays an example *Hierarchical Tree View* [12], with leaf nodes representing files and internal nodes representing directories. As in polymetric views, the width, height, and color of nodes can describe different metrics. As one can see in this example, the tree formed by the containment relation may be overlaid with other kinds of edges. In

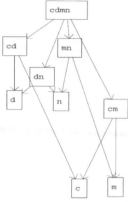

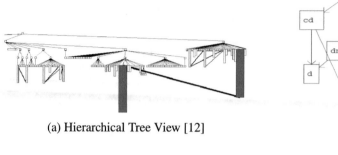

(a) Hierarchical Tree View [12]

(b) *Hasse Diagram* [9]

Fig. 6 Example of tree and acyclic visualizations

the example, those edges connect files sharing code. The thickness of those edges is proportional to the amount of shared code.

4.6 Acyclic Graph Data Visualization

An acyclic graph represents a parent-child hierarchy between items such that each item has exactly one parent item (except for root items that do not have any parent and at least one root must exist in the graph). In other words, the graph is directed and has no cycles. The total or partial containment (overlap) between cloned code fragments is an example of such an acyclic relation. Visualizations for acyclic graphs include *Content-Context Diagram* and *Hasse Diagram*. Figure 6b displays a *Hasse Diagram* [9], where a parent node (*cm*) represents the cloned code shared between its children (files *c* and *m*). The width and height of the nodes can be used to depict two different metrics, one of which, for instance, could be the number of cloned lines.

4.7 Cyclic Graph Visualization

Visualization of type-2 clones results in cyclic graphs because the relation is reflexive, commutative, and transitive. Hence, the resulting graph representing three code fragments that are all type-2 clones of each other is a fully connected graph with cycles. Cycles can also arise when clone data is enriched with additional static dependency edges (e.g., method calls, which can be cyclic). There are various kinds

Fig. 7 Clusters of similar
files (Example of Cyclic
Visualization) [16]

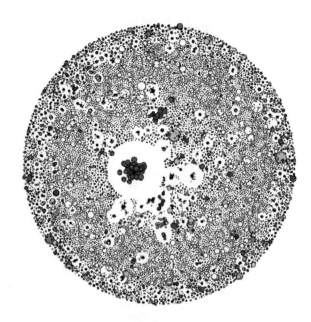

of visualizations of arbitrary graphs such as *Dot Plot,Wheel View, Duplication Web
View, Dependency Browser, Clone Scatterplot, Similarity Graph, Exploration Graph,
Nested Graph*, and *Clone Refactoring Visualization View.* Figure 7 displays an example *Similarity Graph* in which nodes represent files, such that the area of the nodes is
proportional to their sizes and the edges indicate cloning across files. Interestingly,
the edges are not actually shown. Instead, they are used by a force-directed layout
algorithm to form clusters of connected nodes. Nodes in the same fully connected
components in the graph receive the same color and are placed next to each other
by the layouter (colors may be re-used for other clusters farther away). This way,
drawing the edges can be avoided.

5 Evaluation on the Basis of Clone Granularity and Relations

Jiang et al. [8] and Zibran [17] have categorized clone visualizations based on clone
granularity and clone relationships. *Clone granularity* refers to a type of cloned entity
a particular visualization can display such as a code segment, file, and a subsystem.
Visualizations showing a higher granularity are particularly useful in visualizing
clones in large software systems. *Clone relations* refer to clone pairs, clone classes, or
super-clones. A super-clone or clone class family is a group of multiple clone classes
which exist in the same code entity (e.g., file) [13]. All these cloning situations can
be viewed from multiple perspectives, depending on the specific goal of the clone

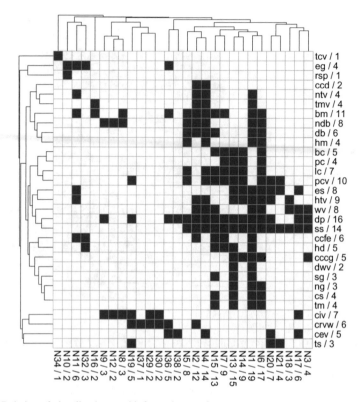

Fig. 8 Relation of visualizations and information needs

analysis at hand. Typically, a user will initially want to get a global view of cloned modules or subsystems and then zoom in to the detailed views of specific regions of the system. There is a rich set of visualization techniques that can help users analyze clones from global and detailed perspectives.

We enhanced the proposed list, as shown in Table 2. The second column describes the level of granularity. The third column describes the type of clone relationship a particular visualization can address. The last column gives a brief description of each visualization. In order to interpret Table 2, we are mentioning some examples. The hierarchical tree view can visualize clones at the subsystem level, which allows dealing with huge software systems. Similarly, navigation tree view can visualize clones not only at the clone pair level but also at clone class or super-clone level. Dot plot and code inspection view are good in visualizing clones at the clone pair level. We further notice that there are only a few visualizations such as navigation tree view, designed to display clones at the super-clone class level. New visualizations or user interface features are required in the future.

6 Discussion

We have related clone visualizations with their supported user goals through the information needs addressed by them. This allows us to analyze the availability of visualizations for each information need and user goal, and to identify the gaps in terms of the information needs of user goals that are currently not addressed by any visualizations. Figure 8 provides a mapping between information needs and visualizations in the form of a grid. The rows of the grid represent the visualizations while the columns represent information needs in abbreviated form. Colored cells of the grid indicate that the given visualizations support the corresponding information need. We analyze the gaps present in Fig. 8 which can lead to three cases: (i) the information describes abstract concepts for which we do not find visualizations in the literature (e.g., N25 and N33), (ii) the information can be addressed with simple extensions into existing visualizations (e.g., N26 and N27), or (iii) the information requires exploration of new visualizations (e.g., N35). Similarly, Fig. 1 provides a mapping of user goals onto information needs. By combining the two mappings, we can assess the extent to which user goals are supported by existing visualizations [7].

Clone detection and analysis has steadily moved from research to practice, although not all proposed work in the scientific literature has been adopted by the software industry. There can be many reasons for the slow adoption. Most of the clone analysis tools are not yet an integral part of software development tool suites. Developers may not be aware of available clone tools or problems associated with cloning. Cordy [5] stated several other reasons for industrial resistance in adopting software maintenance automation in general. Despite these obstacles, some of the clone visualizations are now actually part of industrial tools. For instance, XIAO [6] is part of Microsoft Visual Studio where users can perform clone-management tasks with the help of various visualizations. We hope that our classification framework of clone visualizations will help to further close the gaps between practical needs in the industry and the state of the art in clone-visualization research.

7 Conclusions

In this chapter, we have summarized our contributions of previous publications [1, 2, 7]. We have described our classification of clone visualizations in terms of visual attributes (*how* data is presented) and the information needs that they address (*what* data is presented). We have shown a mapping of visualizations with information needs and also a mapping of information needs with user goals. These mappings allow us to identify information needs and user goals with multiple alternative visualizations and those with currently insufficient support. We believe our classification of visualizations will be useful for programmers, clone-analysis tool users, tool vendors, and clone researchers. Users can evaluate the capabilities of clone tools in light of their needs for clone detection and analysis. Based on the goals of tool users, tool vendors can decide which visualizations to include in their tools. Researchers can use this work as a reference point for exploring open problems that are worth further investigation. We do not claim that our list of clone visualizations, user goals, and information needs presented in this work is complete, but at least it provides a solid starting point and a useful framework for conducting further studies on clone visualizations.

References

1. H.A. Basit, M. Hammad, S. Jarzabek, R. Koschke, What do we need to know about clones? deriving information needs from user goals, in *IEEE International Workshop on Software Clones (IWSC)* (2015)
2. H.A. Basit, M. Hammad, R. Koschke, A survey on goal-oriented visualization of clone data, in *IEEE Working Conference on Software Visualization (VISSOFT)* (2015)
3. P. Brereton, B. Kitchenham, D. Budgen, M. Turner, M. Khalil, Lessons from applying the systematic literature review process within the software engineering domain. J. Syst. Softw. (JSS) (2007)
4. S.K. Card, J. Mackinlay, The structure of the information visualization design space, in *Proceedings of VIZ'97: Visualization Conference, Information Visualization Symposium and Parallel Rendering Symposium* (1997)
5. J.R. Cordy, Comprehending reality-practical barriers to industrial adoption of software maintenance automation, in *IEEE 11th International Workshop on Program Comprehension* (2003)
6. Y. Dang, D. Zhang, S. Ge, R. Huang, C. Chu, T. Xie, Transferring code-clone detection and analysis to practice, in *IEEE/ACM 39th International Conference on Software Engineering: Software Engineering in Practice Track (ICSE-SEIP)* (2017)
7. M. Hammad, H.A. Basit, S. Jarzabek, R. Koschke, A systematic mapping study of clone visualization. Comput. Sci. Rev. (2020)
8. Z.M. Jiang, A.E. Hassan, R.C. Holt, Visualizing clone cohesion and coupling, in *IEEE 13th Asia Pacific Software Engineering Conference (APSEC'06)* (2006)
9. J.H. Johnson, Visualizing textual redundancy in legacy source, in *Conference of the Centre for Advanced Studies on Collaborative Research (CASCON)* (1994)
10. D. Luciv, D. Koznov, G. Chernishev, H.A. Basit, K. Romanovsky, A. Terekhov, Duplicate finder toolkit, in *Proceedings of the 40th International Conference on Software Engineering: Companion Proceeedings* (2018)
11. K. Petersen, S. Vakkalanka, L. Kuzniarz, Guidelines for conducting systematic mapping studies in software engineering: an update. Inf. Softw. Technol. (2015)
12. M. Rieger, S. Ducasse, M. Lanza, Insights into system-wide code duplication, in *IEEE 11th Working Conference on Reverse Engineering* (2004)
13. C.K. Roy, J.R. Cordy, A survey on software clone detection research. Technical Report, School of Computing, Queen's University (2007)
14. M. Sano, E. Choi, N. Yoshida, Y. Yamanaka, K. Inoue, Supporting clone analysis with tag cloud visualization, in *Proceedings of the International Workshop on Innovative Software Development Methodologies and Practices* (2014)
15. B. Shneiderman, The eyes have it: a task by data type taxonomy for information visualizations. *The Craft of Information Visualization* (Elsevier, 2003)
16. K. Yoshimura, R. Mibe, Visualizing code clone outbreak: an industrial case study, in *IEEE 6th International Workshop on Software Clones (IWSC)* (2012)
17. M.F. Zibran, Analysis and visualization for clone refactoring, in *IEEE 9th International Workshop on Software Clones (IWSC)* (2015)
18. https://w3.cs.jmu.edu/bernstdh/web/common/tools/diff.php

Source Code Clone Search

Iman Keivanloo and Juergen Rilling

Abstract Identifying similarities in source code is the main challenge for reuse, plagiarism, and code clone detection. Code clone search has emerged as a new research branch in clone detection, aiming to provide similarity search functionality for code snippets. While clone search shares its fundamentals with clone detection, both its objective and requirements differ significantly. Clone search focuses on search engines that are designed to find clones of a single input code snippet (i.e., query) from a large set of code snippets (i.e., corpus). Scalability, short response time, and the ability to rank result sets among the major challenges have to be dealt with by a clone search engine. In this chapter, we identify and define major concepts related to clone search. We then present a framework that summarizes the architecture of a clone search engine and enables us to provide a systematic view of the internals of such an engine. Finally, we discuss how to benchmark and evaluate the performance of clone search engines. The discussion includes a set of measures that are helpful in evaluating clone search engines.

1 Introduction

The term clone dates back to 1903, referring to the outcome of a derivation activity in living species [1]. In computer science, derivation and reuse are unavoidable parts of programming and are known as cloning. The potential harms caused by cloning in software development became a major motivation for computer scientists to investigate this problem further, and a research discipline—clone detection—has emerged.

Iman Keivanloo—this work was done prior to joining Amazon.

I. Keivanloo (✉)
Amazon, Seattle, USA
e-mail: imankei@amazon.com

J. Rilling
Concordia University, Montreal, Canada
e-mail: juergen.rilling@concordia.ca

"Source Code Clone Search", also known as just-in-time [2] or "clone search" [3], has emerged in the last decade as a sub-branch of the traditional clone detection. While clone search shares its fundamentals with clone detection, both its objective and requirements differ significantly from clone detection. Clone detection focuses on offline processes to find all possible clone pairs within a static source code repository. In contrast, clone search focuses on search engines that are designed to find clones of a single code snippet (i.e., query) from a large set of code snippets (i.e., corpus).

There are a few common requirements for clone search engines. Responsiveness is one of these common aspects of clone search engines. In the literature, several terms have been used to emphasize the importance of response time in this area, e.g., just-in-time [2] search. Ranking result sets is another major functionality of clone search engines. Similar to other search domains (e.g., Web search), clone search engines are dealing with large search spaces [3]. As a result, for a given query (i.e., code snippet), a clone search engine may return hundreds of matches (i.e., clones) [4]. The ability to provide a meaningful ranking of result sets (prior to showing it to the end-user) is yet another common functionality provided by clone search engines.

A clone search engine requires several components and algorithms that work together to provide its end-to-end functionality. In this chapter, first, we will start by defining major concepts related to clone search. Then, we present a framework that provides an overview of the architecture of a clone search engine, and its major internal components.

Benchmarking and evaluation of clone search engines is challenging, e.g., [4]. First, we discuss the requirements prior to evaluation. Then, we present a set of measures that can be used for evaluating clone search engines. We provide guidelines for when and how to use each measure to avoid common pitfalls.

The remainder of the chapter is organized as follows. In Sect. 2, concepts and components of a clone search engine are defined. Section 3 describes how to evaluate clone search engines and avoid common pitfalls. Finally, in Sects. 4 and 5, we review the past, present, and future of clone search research.

2   A Framework for Code Clone Search

In this section, we introduce the details of a search engine that supports *source code clone search*. First, we review major concepts related to code search engine which is followed by an overview of the major logical components of such search engines. The goal of this section is to provide a general framework that can be adopted and extended in the future by the research community.

2.1   Key Concepts

A *source code clone search engine* is responsible for finding similar code snippets (e.g., code clones) matching a given code snippet. The engine searches through a collection of code snippets for finding the matches. We refer to this collection as *corpus*. We also refer to the input code snippet as *query*. The output of the search process is a *ranked list of code snippets*. This list is sorted based on a relevancy measure.

To serve a query, the engine has two responsibilities: (1) retrieval and (2) ranking. The retrieval stage is responsible for returning as many relevant code snippets as possible from the corpus. We refer to the output of the retrieval stage as *candidate list*. The ranking stage sorts the candidate list based on specified relevancy measures. The goal of the ranking stage is to identify and place the most relevant code snippets at the top of the ranked list. As part of this ranking process, certain code snippets might be removed from the candidate list before returning the final ranked list to the end-user.

Figure 1 shows a sample query. This query is a code snippet written in Java. The intent of the code snippet, used in the search query, is to print the size of a list of files. Using a clone search engine, our goal is to find code snippets in the corpus that are similar to the search query. Figure 2 shows a sample output returned by a code search engine. In this example, the first code snippet in the result set corresponds to a Type-1 clone, whereas all other items in the result set can be considered only Type-3 clones. For example, the second item is identical to the original search query, except it deletes files (instead of printing the content size). In this example, the ranking of the Type-3 clone results is based on their degree of dissimilarity with the search query.

2.2   Framework Overview

In this section, we introduce the main components of a typical code clone search engine. These components enable the engine to perform its two main responsibilities (i.e., retrieval and ranking) of code snippets. Figure 3 provides an overview of the architecture of code clone search engines and their major components. We can split these components into two groups: (1) offline and (2) online. The offline components

Fig. 1 An example of a query for a source code clone search engine. The main part of the query is a computer program, e.g., a code snippet

```
List<String> files;
files=db.loadFiles('/usr');
for(String f : files))
{
    String content=readFile(f);
    System.our.println(content.size());
}
```

Fig. 2 A ranked list of code
snippets generated by a code
clone search engine for a
given query, i.e., query
shown in Fig. 1

```
                    Top K (Ranked Result Set)
HIT# 1
      List<String> files;
      files=db.loadFiles('/the_other_user');
      for(String f : files))
      {
          String content=readFile(f);
          System.our.println(content.size());
      }

HIT# 2
      Iterator<String> files;
      files=db.loadFiles('/usr');
      for(String f : files))
      {
          boolean status=deleteFile(f);
      }

HIT# 3
      file=db.loadFile('/usr/uid');
      String content=readFile(f);
      System.our.println(content);

HIT# 4
      List<String> files;
      files=db.loadFiles('/usr');
      ArrayList<String> contents=new ArrayList<String>();
      for(String f : files))
      {
          String content=readFile(f);
          contents.add(content);
      }

HIT# 5
      List<String> files;
      files=db.loadFiles('/usr');
      ArrayList<String> contents=new ArrayList<String>();
      for(String f : files))
      {
          try{
              String content=readFile(f);
              contents.add(content);
          catch(Exception ex){
              System.our.println(f);
```

refer to processes that are required to prepare and initialize the search engine, before it
can process any incoming search queries. Among the offline components are crawling
and preprocessing as well as an indexing component. The online components are
processes that are triggered and executed once a search query is received and include
a retrieval and a ranking component. In the following, we discuss these components
with some examples.

2.2.1 Crawling and Preprocessing

Crawling the Internet (or internal resources) is the first step of offline processing. The
crawling step creates a comprehensive corpus of source code. This can be achieved by
direct access to source code repositories or by crawling off-the-shelf datasets. After
crawling, some form of source code preprocessing is required. For example, source
code normalization and style unification via abstract syntax tree (AST) construction
are common methods of preprocessing. The crawled source code in the corpus is the
content that can be searched by the clone search engine.

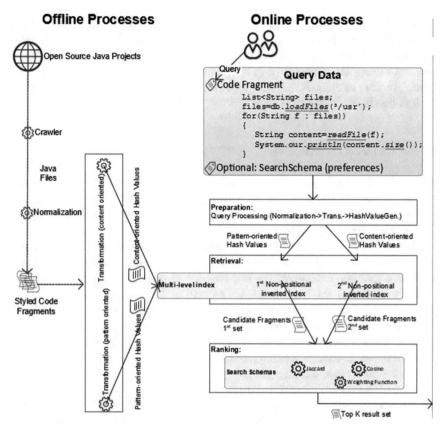

Fig. 3 Components of a source code clone search engine. For each component, some examples are provided. For example, code normalization and style unification are sample methods of preprocessing in this figure

During preprocessing, a uniform representation of source code is generated by transforming code tokens (e.g., from AST) using transformation rules. This includes annotating token types and data cleaning by removing unnecessary information from the content. In Fig. 3, two sample transformation rules are shown: Pattern-oriented and Content-oriented.

2.2.2 Indexing

The indexing component is responsible for preparing the code corpus for fast and efficient retrieval. Without this indexing, the search engine would have to iterate through the complete corpus of code snippets in order to find matching query results. An indexing method is therefore key for generating query results effectively.

A multi-level indexing approach is recommended for large-scale code search [3]. Using a multi-level index, the source code is fingerprinted and indexed from different angles and granularity. For example, one might consider both pattern- and content-oriented fingerprints (introduced in the preprocessing stage) to create a multi-level index. Another example is to create fingerprints at two or more levels of granularity, such as line level and function level.

2.2.3 Retrieval and Ranking

At run-time, the given query is passed to the retrieval component to find and retrieve all indexed code fragments in the corpus that are similar to the encoded code pattern or fingerprint of the search query. The union of all candidate lists retrieved across all indexes forms the final candidate list.

However, not all of the retrieved result candidates are equally similar to the search query. Also, in a large Internet-scale corpus, most of the candidates are false positives. Without a ranking component, the end-user has to manually inspect thousands of matches to identify the true positives. The goal of the ranking step is to sort and return the most relevant results, based on their degree of similarity (e.g., Fig. 2) with the search query, at the top of the result set. The position of each candidate in the ranked list is determined by its similarity degree to the query. Jaccard similarity coefficient and the vector space model with cosine similarity are two scalable ranking models for code clone search engines.

Jaccard coefficient. Jaccard similarity coefficient is a widely used set theory function for content matching. In the context of clone search, it quantifies the similarity between a code snippet and a given search query based on their shared encoded patterns (e.g., lines). The similarity scores generated for each code snippet (in the candidate list) can be used to rank the items in the candidate list. In $J(q, s)$, q refers to a set of encoded patterns that are extracted from the given query. Similarly s refers to the set of encoded patterns from the target code snippet.

$$J(q, s) = |s \cap q| / |s \cup q| \tag{1}$$

Vector space model (VSM). VSM is an alternative method for ranking. A key benefit of VSM is that it provides additional flexibility during ranking compared to the Jaccard coefficient. Using VSM, code snippets are represented as vectors of frequency values. Entity frequency can be used to discriminate among entities' contributions by considering both their local and global popularity (occurrences). The relevance of an entity is expressed as the similarity between a pair of vectors. Similarity is calculated using the cosine similarity function that measures the angle between participating vectors.

$$Cosine_{similarity}(q, s) = \vec{q} \cdot \vec{s} / |\vec{q}| |\vec{s}| \tag{2}$$

3   Evaluation Framework for Code Clone Search Engines

Evaluating the ranking quality is typically not part of the performance assessment of classic code clone detection research (e.g., [5]). This is in contrast to code clone search, which shares many features with information retrieval, including the need for evaluating the ranking quality of result sets.

In this section, we review a set of performance measures that support the evaluation of code clone search engines. These performance measures can be classified into three main categories: (1) common metrics for evaluating ranked result sets, (2) metrics for ranked results sets with certain properties, and (3) non-functional performance measures. We also review the concept of labeled datasets, which are an essential part of any search engine evaluation framework.

3.1   Labeled Dataset

In information retrieval, evaluating the quality of search engines is based on the relevancy of the reported results. That is, a search is considered to be successful if it locates documents that are not only lexically similar to the query but also meet end-user expectations [6]. Therefore, only hits (results) that are relevant from an end-user perspective are considered to be correct answers (i.e., true positives). For example, a result returned by the query "Java" might only be relevant when one considers the user's expectation, which might be referring either to the concept coffee or the programming language concept. In its simplest form, such relevancy can be measured on a binary scale (relevant vs. non-relevant). In more advanced methods, a more refined scale, using different degrees of relevancy, is considered. For example, we can use a scale with 4 labels: highly relevant, relevant, marginal, and non-relevant. Benchmarks (with labeled datasets) are required to measure the quality of result sets reflecting the feedback of either users or experts. The benchmark has a labeled dataset which constitutes the "gold standard" or "ground truth". The labeled dataset includes three major parts: (1) the input data, i.e., search space, (2) some queries, and (3) a set of relevant items per query. The dataset also typically contains relevance scores for each query and relevant answers. These scores are subjective to the human experts creating the benchmark, e.g., BigCloneBench [7]. In cases when no benchmarks are available, user studies might be performed or researchers may have to complete the labeling process, e.g., [4].

3.2   Measure Suite—Measures for Evaluation Ranked Clones

Recall and precision are common measures for evaluating the quality of unranked result sets in clone detection. For clone search, we need measures for evaluating ranked result sets. In this section, we review four measures that are in particular useful for evaluating code clone search engines.

3.2.1 First False Positive Measure

The location of the First False Positive (FFP) in the displayed result list can be used as a measure for evaluating the performance of clone search engines. For example, R1 and R2 are two sorted results with both result sets containing 5 hits: R1 = fp_1, h_2, h_3, h_4, h_5 and R2 = h_1, h_2, h_3, h_4, fp_5. In this example, h_i refers to a correct answer at rank i. fp_i refers to an incorrect answer at rank i, also known as False Positive. While both R1 and R2 have four correct answers, end-user perceived quality for R2 would be considered higher, since the FFP occurs later in the ranked result set (position 5 in R2 versus position 1 in R1).

Discussion. In clone search, one typically deals with a corpus that contains a large amount of noise (irrelevant code snippets). For example, a case study conducted on Internet-scale intra-project code clone search reports that for some queries, only 6 out of over 1 million code snippets in the corpus were relevant [4]. This example highlights two major challenges in evaluating clone search engines: (1) being able to detect the few relevant snippets and (2) assigning these true positive results a higher priority than the false positives in the result sets. The FFP measure is easy to use and interpret.

Weakness. Given that the FFP is highly dependent on the data and query characteristics, its applicability to evaluate system performance is often limited. For example, if a corpus contains a skewed dataset with only x true positives for a given query, the best achievable result using this measure is $x + 1$. This becomes an issue particularly in cases where the number (true positives) varies across queries. Consequently, FFP cannot be generalized well in the presence of such variance.

3.2.2 Precision@K Measure

Precision at k (P@K) is a measure that reports the number of true positives within the top items of a ranked result set. This measure captures closely the end-user's perceived quality assuming the result set is presented to the end-user on a computer screen. This measure is in particular applicable when (1) the total number of relevant results is unknown and therefore no recall can be computed, and (2) the number of returned items is too large to be fully validated, making the calculation of standard precision measures impossible.

$$Precision@K = tp_k/(tp_k + fp_k) \tag{3}$$

Weakness. The major drawback of P@K is its dependency on the query and data availability. For example, in order to provide a fair evaluation for "Precision at 10", at least 10 actual relevant items must exist in the corpus for all executed queries. Furthermore, similar to the FFP measure, results from this measure cannot be generalized (averaged) across queries if variance in the labeled dataset exists.

3.2.3   Normalized Discounted Cumulative Gain Measure

The Normalized Discounted Cumulative Gain (NDCG) measure assesses the quality of search engines and their ranking algorithms in terms of being able to assign higher ranks to more relevant true positive answers. NDCG takes into consideration not only the relevance of hits but also the order of the results. To calculate NDCG, each answer in the labeled dataset must be assigned a relevance score that presents its relevancy to the query. Then we need to calculate Discounted Cumulative Gain or DCG. To calculate DCG, we need to obtain the relevancy score of each item in the ranked result for a given query in the labeled dataset. $r(q, i)$ refers to the relevancy score of ith item in the ranked result set for the given query q.

$$DCG(q, n) = r(q, 1) + \sum_{i=2}^{n} r(q, i)/log_2(i) \tag{4}$$

The output of DCG depends on the query and available data within the corpus. It is not possible to compare directly DCG results of different queries with each other, since the number of positive hits is dependent on the data characteristics of the corpus. To overcome this limitation and to be able to compare results, we use NDCG, which is a normalized value of DCG. We first calculate the Ideal DCG (IDCG), which is the highest achievable DCG given the available relevance scores in the oracle. Using DCG and IDCG, we can then calculate the final NDCG value as follows: $DCG(q, n)/IDCG(q, n)$.

Weakness. The measure allows for a fine-grained evaluation of the quality and ordering of result sets, by providing a single value assessment for comparing different options or configurations of a clone search engine. However, the measure is only applicable when fine-grained ordering is important, otherwise, measures such as Precision@K are preferred. Measuring NDCG is also expensive, since not only all possible answers for each query have to be evaluated manually but also a similarity score for each matching code snippet is to be provided. This is non-trivial since manually assessing code snippets requires expertise and time.

3.2.4   Mean Average Precision Measure

Mean Average Precision (MAP) is a single value measure similar to NDCG. To compute MAP for a single query, we need to measure the average of all precision at ks, where k refers to the position of all relevant retrieved items in the result set. We refer to the list of relevant answers in the result set as R. For experiments involving more than one query, MAP is simply the average of all APs across queries.

$$AP = Average\ Precision = 1/|R| \sum_{k \in R} p@k \tag{5}$$

Weakness. MAP is an essential and low-cost measure that does not require the creation of relevance scores (unlike NDCG) and only considers the positions of true positives. However, since MAP does not include relevance scores, it lacks the ability to distinguish high-quality true positives from the rest of the relevant answers. Moreover, it is generally only suitable for queries where a reasonable number of true positives are available; otherwise, its output might be biased.

3.3 Measures for Highly Positive Ranked Results

Sometimes, no or only a few false positives appear at the top of the ranked result set. In other situations, all hits might be true positives. Assessing in such context the type of ranking requires more precise measures that take also into account the exact order of results in a ranked result set and compare them against the labeled dataset. Such measures differ from earlier measures introduced in this section (e.g., NDCG), as they evaluate the relative or exact position of all items within the ordered list. For such scenarios, we can consider the Normalized Kendall's τ distance and Spearman's rank correlation coefficient measure.

Normalized Kendall's τ distance. Kendall's τ measures the dissimilarity of the items' order against the ideal order. Suppose π and σ denote the ordering of two item sets containing the same items, N. $S(\pi, \sigma)$ is the minimum number of switches required between adjacent items to make the first ordered list identical to the second ordered list. Finally, we can compute the measure as follows:

$$\tau = 1 - \frac{2 \times S(\pi, \sigma)}{N(N-1)/2} \tag{6}$$

Spearman's rank correlation coefficient. This measure compares the rank of each shared retrieved item among two subject ranked lists, which are denoted by π and σ with the number of items being equal to N, and i refer to the rank of an item in the ranked list.

$$spearman = 1 - \frac{6 \sum_{i=1}^{N} (\pi(i) - \sigma(i))^2}{N(N^2-1)/2} \tag{7}$$

3.4 Non-functional Performance Measures

In addition to the quality of the result set, one has also to consider additional measures to evaluate non-functional aspects of a code clone search engine that can potentially impact end-user satisfaction. The following three non-functional measures can be automatically calculated and used to compare different code clone search engines: (1) indexing time, (2) querying latency time, and (3) corpus size.

4 Past, Present, and Future

In this section, we review past, present, and future of source code similarity and source code clone search. First, we review early research on code similarity search and clone detection. Then, we review the current approaches for code clone search. Finally, we highlight a few directions for future research in the domain of code clone search.

One of the earliest similarity detection approaches dates back to the work by Ottenstein [8] in 1976. Ottenstein introduced a metric-based approach for finding plagiarism in student programming assignments. Later on, Grier [9] in 1981 extended Ottenstein's work to Pascal code. However, the first reference to the term "clone" (in the domain of source code and programming domain) dates back to the work by Abrams and Myrna [10] in 1979. Abrams and Myrna used the term clone in a Programming Language (APL) context describing it as "... creates an output file and starts a 'clone' of itself". The concept of a "clone" in source code was later used by Jacobsen [11] to describe pre-defined commands. Caudill and Wirfs-Brock [12] also refer to "clone" as a reproduction of executable files in Smalltalk. Tanenbaum [13] used clone to describe the variations of a software system. During the 1980s, "clone" as a concept was further popularized mostly through its use as a reference to computer hardware, such as compatible computer (hardware), an IBM compatible (or short IBMclone) computer [14] or, in [15], as "...can't tell what is on my disk without a clone of my computer". Among the first researchers who actually used the term clone detection at the source code level were Carter et al. in 1993 [16]. They described clone detection as the process of finding similar telecommunications systems using neural networks.

Over the last three decades, source code clone detection, the process of finding duplicated contents in software artifacts, has matured as a research discipline. Common to this body of work is that they rely on a complete offline detection process to find all possible clone pairs within a static source code repository. We refer to this line of work as clone detection (e.g., [17]).

"Source code clone search", a research area also known as just-in-time [2], instant [18, 19], or simply clone search [3], has emerged in the last decade. SHINOBI [20] supports clone search via a suffix array built on transformed tokens using CCFinder. Barbour et al. [2] introduce a result sampling approach that uses results obtained from other clone detection tools to find candidate clones. The collected candidates are indexed and then compared by the Knuth-Morris-Pratt string searching algorithm. Bazrafshan and Koschke [21] exploit Chang and Lawler's search algorithm, which was originally proposed for the bioinformatics domain to find approximate source code patterns. Clone search is also studied for compiled code (e.g., Java bytecode) by Keivanloo et al. [22]. Further, Keivanloo conducted one of the first large-scale studies on code clone ranking using the Jaccard coefficient and vector space model via cosine similarity [4].

Indexing is one of the major parts of a clone search engine. Various techniques have been explored in this area. Hummel et al. [23] use inverted index for scalable Type-2 clone search. A multidimensional token-level indexing approach is introduced by Lee et al. [18] using an R*tree on DECKARD's approximate vector matching. The language elements (e.g., assignment) constitute the dimensions of the search space. Zibran and Roy [24] introduced an IDE-support for Type-3 clone search based on Rabin's fingerprinting algorithm and suffix trees.

Searching for Type-3 code clones within the source code published on the Internet is a challenging task. We refer to this line of work as "Internet-scale clone search". Keivanloo et al. show hash-based multi-level inverted indexing [3, 25] is a viable solution for Internet-scale Type-3 clone search. Recent studies provide evidence that incremental indexing is also possible for Type-3 clone search [26].

There are many unsolved problems in code clone search specifically in the context of Internet-scale clone search. Current code clone search engines provide no support for Type-4 clones. Furthermore, more work is needed in studying how deep learning can contribute to real-time Type-4 clone search. Another major area to explore is how to integrate and take advantage of code clone search in downstream applications (e.g., code example search [27]).

Benchmarking clone search engines is a research area that still requires more attention. A major challenge in this area is the lack of large-scale labeled datasets. Due to the lack of such datasets, Keivanloo had to manually label 32,000 query and code snippet pairs to complete his early research on Internet-scale code clone search [4]. Later, he initiated the BigCloneBench [7] to create a dataset that can be used for clone detection, clone search, and code search community. Larger and more diverse datasets are now needed specifically to provide better support for research in deep learning. Finally, automatic filtering and pruning of the result set of a clone search engine is an area that has yet to be explored. For example, the threshold-free clone detection method [28] can be extended to clone search engines.

5   Conclusion

A clone search engine requires several components and algorithms that work together to provide useful end-to-end functionality. In this chapter, we provide a blueprint for designing and evaluating clone search engines. First, we define major concepts related to clone search. Then, we present a framework that summarizes the architecture of a clone search engine. This enables us to provide a systematic view of the internals of a clone search engine, including reference techniques that can be used for future research. We also discuss requirements for evaluating clone search and present a set of measures that can be used to evaluate and compare clone search engines.

We also include a discussion on future directions for code clone search, such as (1) support of clone search beyond Type-3 clones, including the use of deep learning, (2) the creation of more diverse datasets for evaluating and training clone search models, (3) and multi-purpose clone search engines.

References

1. H.J. Webber, New horticultural and agricultural terms. Science **18**(459), 501–503 (1903)
2. L. Barbour, H. Yuan, Y. Zou, A technique for just-in-time clone detection in large scale systems, in *International Conference on Program Comprehension* (2010)
3. I. Keivanloo, J. Rilling, P. Charland, Internet-scale real-time code clone search via multi-level indexing, in *Working Conference on Reverse Engineering* (2011)
4. I. Keivanloo, Source code similarity and clone search. Ph.D. thesis, Concordia University (2013)
5. A. Walenstein, A. Lakhotia, Clone detector evaluation can be improved: ideas from information retrieval, in *International Workshop on Detection of Software Clones* (2003)
6. C. D. Manning, P. Raghavan, H. Schütze, *Introduction to Information Retrieval* (Cambridge University Press, 2008)
7. J. Svajlenko, J.F. Islam, I. Keivanloo, C.K. Roy, M.M. Mia, Towards a big data curated benchmark of InterProject code clones, in *30th International Conference on Software Maintenance and Evolution* (2014)
8. K.J. Ottenstein, An algorithmic approach to the detection and prevention of plagiarism. ACM SIGCSE Bull. (1976)
9. S. Grier, A tool that detects plagiarism in Pascal programs, in *SIGCSE Technical Symposium on Computer Science Education* (1981)
10. P.S. Abrams, J.W. Myrna, Automatic control of execution: an overview, in *International Conference on APL* (1979)
11. J. Jacobsen, An automated management system for applications software, in *ACM SIGUCCS Conference on User Services* (1984)
12. P.J. Caudill, A. Wirfs-Brock, A third generation Smalltalk-80 implementation, in *Conference on Object-Oriented Programming Systems, Languages and Applications* (1986)
13. A.S. Tanenbaum, A UNIX clone with source code for operating systems courses. ACM SIGOPS Operating Systems Review (1987)
14. M.I. Kellner, Ten years of software maintenance: progress or promises?, in *Conference on Software Maintenance* (1993)
15. J.V. Lombardi, *Computer Literacy: The Basic Concepts and Language* (Indiana University Press, 1983)
16. S. Carter, R.J. Frank, D.S.W. Tansley, Clone detection in telecommunications software systems: a neural net approach, in *International Workshop on Applications of Neural Networks to Telecommunications* (1993)
17. T. Kamiya, S. Kusumoto, K. Inoue, CCFinder: a multilinguistic token-based code clone detection system for large scale source code. IEEE Trans. Softw. Eng. (2002)
18. M.W. Lee, J.W. Roh, S.W. Hwang, S. Kim, Instant code clone search, in *International Symposium on Foundations of Software Engineering* (2010)
19. V. Balachandran, Reducing accidental clones using instant clone search in automatic code review, in *IEEE International Conference on Software Maintenance and Evolution* (2020)
20. S. Kawaguchi, T. Yamashina, H. Uwano, K. Fushida, Y. Kamei, M. Nagura, H. Iida, SHINOBI: a tool for automatic code clone detection in the IDE, in *Working Conference on Reverse Engineering* (2009)
21. S. Bazrafshan, R. Koschke, N. Gode, Approximate code search in program histories, in *Working Conference on Reverse Engineering* (2011)
22. I. Keivanloo, C.K. Roy, J. Rilling, SeByte: scalable clone and similarity search for bytecode. Sci. Comput. Program. 426–444 (2014)
23. B. Hummel, E. Juergens, L. Heinemann, M. Conradt, Index-based code clone detection: incremental, distributed, scalable, in *International Conference on Software Maintenance* (2010)
24. M.F. Zibran, C.K. Roy, IDE-based real-time focused search for near-miss clones, in *ACM Symposium on Applied Computing* (2012)
25. I. Keivanloo, J. Rilling, P. Charland, SeClone-a hybrid approach to internet-scale real-time code clone search, in *International Conference on Program Comprehension* (2011)

26. C. Ragkhitwetsagul, J. Krinke, Siamese: scalable and incremental code clone search via multiple code representations. Empir. Softw. Eng. (2019)
27. I. Keivanloo, J. Rilling, Y. Zou, Spotting working code examples, in *36th International Conference on Software Engineering ICSE* (2014)
28. I. Keivanloo, J. Rilling, P. Charland, Threshold-free code clone detection for a large-scale heterogeneous Java repository, in *IEEE 22nd International Conference on Software Analysis, Evolution, and Reengineering (SANER)* (2015)

Code Similarity in Clone Detection

Jens Krinke and Chaiyong Ragkhitwetsagul

Abstract Clone detection is one application of measuring the similarity of code. However, clone and plagiarism detectors use very different representations of source code and different techniques to identify similar code fragments. This chapter investigates the impact of source code representation (i.e. tokenisation and renaming of identifiers and literals) and the impact of similarity measurements (e.g. Jaccard index or Kondrak's distance over n-grams) for measuring source code similarity on two known datasets. A comparison using average precision at k with dedicated clone and plagiarism detectors shows that simple similarity measurements like Kondrak's distance using n-grams over tokenised source code usually outperform specialised tools for the detection of similar, cloned, plagiarised or duplicated code.

1 Introduction

In our previous work [17, 21], we have compared the performance of clone detectors and plagiarism detectors to other measurements of source code similarity. The performance in terms of recall, precision, etc. was very different and varied depending on the dataset the detectors were applied to. The clone and plagiarism detectors were using very different approaches on how they transform the source code and how they match fragments to identify clones. They typically tokenise the source code before some kind of similarity measurement is applied and sometimes the tokenised or otherwise transformed fragments must even be identical, not just similar. Moreover, our previous work also showed that other similarity measurements, e.g. textual similarity, can outperform clone or plagiarism detectors. Despite previous work that has compared different clone detectors or plagiarism detectors, it is unknown how much different forms of tokenisation and different similarity measurements actually

J. Krinke
University College London, London, England
e-mail: j.krinke@ucl.ac.uk

C. Ragkhitwetsagul (✉)
Mahidol University, Salaya, Thailand
e-mail: chaiyong.rag@mahidol.edu

matter in clone or plagiarism detection. Therefore, we have investigated the impact
of tokenisation and varying similarity measurements on detection of similar code
fragments using the two datasets we used in our previous work.

In the next section, we summarise our previous work and present new results. The
following section presents the investigation on tokenisation and similarity measurements. A discussion section compares the results of the investigation to the results
from known clone, plagiarism and duplication detectors.

2 Background

In this chapter, we summarise the main elements of our previous work and present a
few extensions that have been made to it. In our previous work [21], we compare 30
code similarity analysers on Java source code with the presence of pervasive source
code modifications, created with tools for source code and bytecode obfuscation and
boiler-plate code. The code similarity analysers are compared using their optimal
configurations, i.e. the best parameter settings and similarity thresholds for the techniques to differentiate between similar and dissimilar code. From the experiment, we
found that highly specialised source code similarity tool, such as CCFinderX [13],
outperforms general textual similarity measures. However, there are some special
cases when the code is heavily modified that general string matching techniques can
outperform code clone and plagiarism detection tools. Our experimental results also
show that by applying compilation and decompilation to the source code before performing similarity detection can increase the performance of code similarity tools.
The extension of the work that apply compilation and decompilation before performing clone detection on open-source software projects also gives similar findings [19].
Furthermore, the study demonstrates that optimal configurations from one dataset
cannot be applied effectively on another dataset. The optimal configurations reported
in the previous work can be used as a guideline for tuning the tools in the situation
where Java source code contains pervasive modification and boiler-plate code.

2.1 Experimental Setup

In this chapter, we adopt the experimental framework that have been used in our
previous work [21]. The overview of the framework is shown in Fig. 1, which consists
of three main phases or steps.

In Step 1, the test data preparation, a collection of Java source code files are
prepared. In Step 2, the code similarity detection tools that are being evaluated are
executed inside the framework. The tools are executed on every file pair in the dataset
to generate a similarity report containing similarity values for all the pairs. In Step 3,
the similarity report is analysed. We extract a similarity value $sim(x, y)$ from the
report for every pair of files (x, y), and classify the pair as being similar (clones) or

Fig. 1 The code similarity
evaluation framework

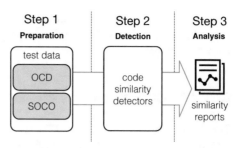

not similar based on a chosen threshold T. The set $\text{Sim}(F)$ of similar pairs out of all
the file pairs in F is

$$\text{Sim}(F) = \{(x, y) \in F \times F : \text{sim}(x, y) > T\} \tag{1}$$

After the classification, any performance score such as precision, recall, accuracy
or F1 score can be computed. The framework focuses on the F1 score as the main
criteria to rank the results and optimises the threshold so that the best F1 score is
achieved. Moreover, the framework varies the configuration of each tool to find the
configuration that achieves the best F1 score. The optimisation overfits the configuration and the threshold in order to find the best achievable performance of a tool
for a dataset.

2.2 Datasets

There are two main datasets that are used in the framework: the *SOCO* dataset and
the *OCD* dataset. We briefly explain them below.

2.2.1 The SOCO Dataset

The SOCO dataset is adopted from the Detection of SOurce COde Re-use competition
that aims for discovering monolingual re-used source code among a given set of
programs [5, 6]. The source code is originated from the Google Code Jam 2012
edition. We found that many of them share the same or very similar boiler-plate code
fragments which perform the same task. Some of the boiler-plate fragments have
been modified to adapt to the environment in which the fragments are re-used. Since
we re-used the dataset from another study [5, 6], we merely needed to format the
source code files by removing comments and applying pretty-printing to them in
Step 1 of our experimental framework (see Fig. 1). We selected the Java training set
containing 259 files for which the answer key of true clone pairs is provided. The
answer key contains 97 file pairs that share boiler-plate code. Using the provided

pairs, we are able to measure both false positives and negatives. For each tool, this dataset produced $259 \times 259 = 67,081$ pairwise comparisons, of which 453 pairs are true positives.

2.2.2 The OCD Dataset

The Obfuscation, Compilation and Decompilation (OCD) dataset is created (Step 1 in the experimental framework) by applying pervasive source code modifications to a set of original Java code files to create pervasively modified variants (clones). The details of the pervasive source code modifications can be found in our previous work [18, 21]. Multiple source code modification tools, including Java source code and bytecode obfuscators (Artifice [25], ProGuard [9]), Javac compiler, and decompilers (Krakatau [7] and Procyon [27]), are used to transform the source code in this step to generate different combinations of the variants. For example, if we have an original file F and we select one source code obfuscator O and one decompiler D, we retrieve three variants of F including F_O, F_D and F_{OD}. After that, the original and the variants are normalised by formatting the source code.

According to the way the dataset is generated, it offers a complete ground truth, i.e. we know exactly which pair is similar and which pair is not. The files that originated from the same Java file must be treated as similar, and vice versa. Thus, we can decide whether a code pair is correctly classified as a similar pair (true positive, *TP*), correctly classified as a dissimilar pair (true negative, *TN*), incorrectly classified as a similar pair while it is actually dissimilar (false positive, *FP*), and incorrectly classified as dissimilar pair while it is actually a similar pair (false negative, *FN*).

The dataset contains 100 Java files which originated from 10 Java files. After executing a code similarity detection tool on this dataset (Step 2), there are $100 \times 100 = 10,000$ file pairs, of which 1,000 pairs are true positives.

2.3 *Updated Results*

We have added five additional code similarity tool results to the existing results of the 30 tools for the SOCO and the OCD datasets from our previous work [18, 21]. The updated results are included in Table 1. The additional code similarity tools include SourcererCC [24], a scalable token-based code clone detector, Vincent [22], an image-based code clone detector and CCAligner [29], a token-based large-gap clone detector. Moreover, two Java implementations of n-gram-based similarities using Jaccard index and Cosine similarity[1] [4] are also included (with the default configuration using 3-grams).

---

[1] The cosine similarity presented in this chapter is an n-gram-based string similarity using cosine similarity and it differs from the cosine similarity used in our previous work [21].

Table 1 Performance and the optimal configuration of new code similarity tools and techniques on the SOCO and OCD datasets

Tool	Settings	T	FP	FN	Acc	Prec	Rec	F1
SOCO dataset								
Clone detection								
SourcererCC (T)*	similarity = 60	24	42	58	0.9985	0.9039	0.8720	0.8876
Vincent	sim = jaccard	25	38	127	0.7196	0.9975	0.8956	0.7980
	threshold = 0.25							
	GBRadius = 20							
CCAligner (T)*	q = 7, e = 0, sim = 0.5	16	13	46	0.9991	0.9690	0.8985	0.9324
String similarity								
Jaccard	3-grams	58	36	72	0.9984	0.9134	0.8411	0.8759
Cosine	3-grams	86	26	84	0.9984	0.9342	0.8146	0.8703
OCD dataset								
Clone detection								
SourcererCC (T)*	similarity = 40	21	232	205	0.9563	0.7741	0.7950	0.7844
Vincent	sim = jaccard	16	77	509	0.8647	0.4915	0.9426	0.6268
	Threshold = 0.15							
	GBRadius = 20							
CCAligner (T)*	q = 8, e = 2, sim = 0.4	8	66	322	0.9612	0.9113	0.6870	0.7775
String similarity								
Jaccard	3-grams	40	108	116	0.9776	0.8911	0.8840	0.8876
Cosine	3-grams	65	784	226	0.8990	0.4968	0.7740	0.6052

*—Tools that do not report similarity value directly. Similarity is measured at the granularity level of token (T)

For the SOCO dataset, we found that two clone detectors, SourcererCC (F1 score of 0.8876) and CCAligner (0.9324), outperform the 3 n-gram-based string similarity techniques. This is possibly due to the nature of the dataset that contains traditional clones with boiler-plate code, which can be easily handled by clone detectors. Also, some are gapped clones which makes CCAligner, a large-gap clone detector, performs very well on this dataset. The best performing tool overall for the SOCO dataset is still JPlag [16] (text version) from our previous work [21] with the F1 score of 0.9692.

The results show that for the OCD dataset, which contains pervasively modified code, the n-gram-based string similarity using Jaccard index outperforms the three code clone detectors with F1 score of 0.8876. Among the clone detectors, Sourcer-erCC performs best with F1 score of 0.7844, followed by CCAligner (0.7775) and Vincent (0.6268). The n-gram-based string similarity using cosine similarity performs worst in this dataset (0.6052). This still follows the observation we found in the previous work that some string similarity tools work well in pervasively modified code. Nonetheless, the best performing tool overall for the OCD dataset is still CCFinderX [13] from our previous work [21] with the F1 score of 0.9760.

Based on the results of our study which observed that textual similarity measurements often outperform dedicated code similarity measurements and are easier to apply and language independent, we have adopted textual similarity to measure source code similarity in other work, for example, for the recommendation of related tests [30] or for the recommendation of related code reviews [11] with great success. We have also built a highly scalable Clone Search engine on top of a document search engine which uses multiple code representations [20].

3   Tokenisation and Similarity

Given the results of our previous work and the experience we gained by adopting textual similarity measurements to measure code similarity and by varying the source code representation for code clone search, we had to investigate the effect of tokenisation and the impact of the similarity measurements.

To investigate the impact on tokenisation and the similarity measurements, we extended our framework in which we could easily vary the applied similarity measurement together with different representations of the source code. The extended framework is, therefore, independent of a specific implementation of a clone or plagiarism detector. For example, changing the tokenisation or the similarity measurement of an existing detector would bias the results.

3.1   Approach

For the investigation, we extended the framework presented in the previous section. In Step 1, the preparation step, the two datasets are tokenised in two additional representations. In Step 2, the detection step, various different similarity measurements are adopted. In Step 3, the analysis step, the similarity reports are analysed and different performance scores are used to compare and rank the results.

3.1.1   Similarity Measurement

Our framework simply measures the similarity of two strings that encode the two source code fragments. If the measured similarity is high (higher than a certain threshold), then the two fragments can be suggested as being cloned or plagiarised. However, instead of specifying an actual threshold, the extended framework will use the similarity measurements over a ground truth to evaluate the performance in a threshold-independent way, no longer using the F1 score.

At the core of our extended framework is a library that implements a number of string similarity measurements [4]. From the library, our extended framework uses the similarity measurements that provide a normalised distance which is then turned into a similarity measure in the range of 0 to 1. Three of the similarity measurements are normalised classic string distance of measurements:

- (Normalised) Levenshtein.
- Jaro–Winkler.
- (Metric) Longest Common Subsequence (LCS).

Some more distance measurements are based on n-grams where the original string is replaced by n-grams which are sequences of n characters. The following similarity measurements are using such n-grams:

- Jaccard index: The original string is replaced by a set of n-grams.
- Cosine similarity: The original string is replaced with a profile of n-grams.
- Kondrak's n-gram distance [14]: The original string is replaced with a sequence of n-grams.

With 1-grams, the Jaccard index and the Cosine similarity are measuring similarity based on the individual characters in the two string. In the used library, Kondrak's n-gram distance for 1-grams is equivalent to normalised Levenshtein and therefore we will not consider normalised Levenshtein separately in the following.

3.1.2 Tokenisation

To tokenise the fragments, our extended framework uses an existing tokenisation tool created by [26]. The extended framework produces two different tokenised representations:

1. A tokenised representation which ignores whitespace and replaces comments and strings by corresponding tokens.
2. A representation that, in addition to the tokenisation described above, also replaces all identifiers by a single token and replaces values with values on a logarithmic scale.

The token stream created by both representations is turned into a string by mapping each token onto a single character.[2] The strings created from the token stream can then be used in the same way as normal strings for similarity measurements as described above.

---

[2] Java's strings are encoded in UTF-16 so the range is large enough to encode tokens by characters.

3.1.3 Evaluation

With the described extended framework we can apply the three classic string similarities and the three n-gram-based similarities for n-grams varying n from 1 to 10 on three different representations, the actual source code and the two different stages of tokenisation. The extended framework then computes the similarity between each pair of fragments out of a set of source code fragments in our ground truth and measures the performance with the following three scores:

- AUC: Area under the receiver operating characteristic curve.
- AP: Average precision which summarises the precision–recall curve.
- AP@k: Average precision at k.

For average precision at k, the limit k is set to number of positives in the ground truth (i.e. fragments that are cloned, plagiarised or similar), $k = 453$ for SOCO and $k = 1000$ for OCD. The three scores are independent of a threshold and therefore are preferable over the scoring we used in the previous section.

3.2 SOCO

Table 2 shows the results for the SOCO dataset (the best results for a performance score are highlighted in bold and the best n-gram size is underlined). With the SOCO dataset it was not possible to compute the Metrics LCS distance measures.[3] Overall, the performance increases with higher n-gram sizes. For the 10-grams, the Jaccard index and Kondrak's distance measurements perform best, depending on the considered performance score (Jaccard index has the better AUC and Kondrak's distance has the better AP@k). As the SOCO dataset is skewed (few positives and many negatives), the AP@k score is the most important. Considering AP@k only, Kondrak's distance performs best in all three variations. Using tokenisation (AP@k = 95.9%) outperforms the plain text (AP@k = 93.5%) and the tokenisation plus renaming (AP@k = 92.7%) representations, while plain text is better than tokenisation + renaming. It is worth mentioning that Kondrak's distance performs better in terms of AP@k than the other similarity measurements also for lower n-gram sizes.

We limited the size of the n-grams to 10 as the computation becomes increasingly expensive for higher n-grams making larger sizes impractical. However, we performed additional experiments with higher values for n, up to 20. The Jaccard index AP@k increases for higher n, reaching a maximum of 0.9655 on the tokenised representation with 19-grams. The AP@k increases similarly for Kondrak's distance, reaching a maximum of 0.9676 on the tokenised representation with 19-grams. For Cosine similarity on the tokenised representations (with and without renaming), higher n values do not improve AP@k, only on plain source code up to 0.9058 for 20-grams.

---

[3] The library did run out of memory.

Table 2 String similarity results for the SOCO dataset

n	AUC	AP	AP@k	AUC	AP	AP@k	AUC	AP	AP@k
	Plain text			Tokenised			Tokenised + renaming		
Cosine									
1	0.942483	0.773646	0.725199	0.932090	0.796242	0.745543	0.893635	0.728507	0.690120
2	0.981917	0.863362	0.808510	0.965480	<u>0.865593</u>	<u>0.804177</u>	0.930470	0.766166	0.726384
3	0.990450	0.911526	0.847904	0.975602	0.851654	0.791692	0.961402	0.836159	0.783832
4	0.995115	0.936822	0.872453	0.982012	0.842019	0.788261	0.969102	0.865543	0.809498
5	0.998467	0.944394	0.873175	0.985886	0.837235	0.784644	0.974286	<u>0.865882</u>	0.806162
6	0.998649	0.943959	0.872477	0.988566	0.835805	0.784322	0.979847	0.863649	0.806029
7	0.998727	0.943372	0.872130	0.991242	0.835750	0.783936	0.985300	0.862780	0.811079
8	0.998850	0.944149	0.871738	0.993494	0.836374	0.783456	0.989584	0.862572	0.815123
9	0.999007	0.947530	0.875402	0.995022	0.836909	0.782589	0.992641	0.863169	0.815434
10	<u>0.999106</u>	<u>0.950632</u>	<u>0.879628</u>	<u>0.995953</u>	0.837633	0.782016	<u>0.994471</u>	0.864055	<u>0.815548</u>
Jaccard									
1	0.973822	0.727393	0.624999	0.997210	0.924175	0.844944	0.994897	0.864069	0.780071
2	0.996458	0.886330	0.791853	0.999707	0.967051	0.870565	0.999285	0.948140	0.865061
3	0.999160	0.943648	0.860523	0.999842	0.978399	0.887701	0.999679	0.966003	0.879583
4	0.999657	0.963879	0.882228	0.999873	0.981996	0.900734	0.999809	0.975233	0.888845
5	0.999804	0.975093	0.899884	0.999890	0.984241	0.909808	0.999838	0.977786	0.888240
6	0.999839	0.978406	0.904395	0.999905	0.986222	0.918900	0.999857	0.980025	0.896408
7	0.999857	0.980305	0.904665	0.999912	0.987423	0.923741	0.999871	0.981735	0.913018
8	0.999867	0.981375	<u>0.904798</u>	0.999913	0.987943	0.924415	0.999881	0.983109	0.913519
9	0.999871	0.981776	0.904726	0.999909	0.987986	0.936986	0.999888	0.984103	0.914262
10	**0.999876**	**0.982315**	0.904659	**0.999914**	0.988656	0.941492	**0.999890**	**0.984598**	0.914655
Kondrak									
1	0.997431	0.959880	0.922369	0.997814	0.987229	0.945020	0.994434	0.944480	0.911651
2	0.997745	0.963136	0.926471	0.997879	0.988162	0.949447	0.995686	0.951461	0.912297
3	0.997915	0.965479	0.926423	0.997967	0.989123	0.949730	0.996407	0.957683	0.913064
4	0.998033	0.967590	0.926447	0.998057	0.989771	0.954107	0.996881	0.962682	0.913704
5	0.998110	0.969441	0.926489	0.998144	0.990302	0.954212	0.997169	0.966794	0.922190
6	0.998179	0.970954	0.930626	0.998215	0.990569	0.954251	0.997368	0.969566	0.922338
7	0.998237	0.972389	0.930745	0.998294	0.990865	0.954393	0.997504	0.971969	0.922491
8	0.998283	0.973678	0.930912	0.998359	0.991085	0.954473	0.997617	0.974115	0.926758
9	0.998318	0.974528	0.935053	0.998420	0.991309	0.958714	0.997700	0.975775	0.926819
10	<u>0.998342</u>	<u>0.975301</u>	**0.935139**	0.998480	**0.991522**	**0.958773**	<u>0.997775</u>	<u>0.977222</u>	**0.926950**
Jaro-Winkler									
	0.956778	0.789582	0.727252	0.989106	0.931157	0.864918	0.964399	0.788191	0.725396

3.3   OCD

Table 3 shows the results for the OCD dataset (the best results for a performance score are highlighted in bold and the best *n*-gram size is underlined). The results are very different from the SOCO dataset. Overall, the best performing similarity measurement here is the Jaccard index with an *n*-gram size of two applied to the plain source code; however, Jaccard index performs poorly for the tokenised representation for any *n*-gram size. For the tokenised representations, Kondrak's distance is best with $n = 2$ and renaming makes the results slightly worse.

4   Discussion

To allow a general discussion about how tokenisation and renaming affect similarity measurements, we extracted the same scores for the clone and plagiarism detectors as discussed before. We picked a subset of tools and similarity measurements and extracted for each tool and similarity measurement the configuration that produced the best AP@k score. Table 4 shows on overview of the scores, ranked by AP@k score for the SOCO dataset.

As the SOCO dataset is targeting source code plagiarism, it is no surprise to see JPlag performing best; however, in the general setting, not the Java-specific one (which ranks fourth). simjava [8] is ranked second. It is interesting to see that a simple detector like Simian [12] outperforms more complex detectors. However, Kondrak's distance on the tokenised representation is ranked third and outperforms all clone detectors. With 18-grams or 19-grams using tokenisation, Kondrak's distance and Jaccard index would rank best. It is worth noting that well-known or modern tools like NiCAD, CCAligner or SourcererCC are not performing well with AP@k scores below 90%.

When looking at the three different representations, it seems that their impact is limited as the scores for Kondrak's distance are close to each other. Moreover, when considering the variation is tokenisation over all tools, there is no clear pattern. For JPlag, the text version outperforms the Java-specific version, but simjava outperforms its text variant simtext; Simian performs best when variable names are ignored; NiCAD performs best with consistent renaming; etc.

As the SOCO dataset is a simple dataset mainly using copied blocks of source code, all clone and plagiarism detectors should be able to perform well, in particular, as we search for optimal configurations.

Table 5 shows on overview of the scores, ranked by AP@k score for the OCD dataset. The first thing to note is that every tool or measurement achieves its optimal performance with a different configuration. For the OCD dataset, CCFinderX clearly outperforms every other tool or measure. However, the plain text Jaccard index over 2-grams is ranked second and the tokenised Kondrak's distance over 2-grams is ranked third. The relative ranking of the clone detectors Simian, Deckard,

Table 3 String similarity results for the OCD dataset

n	AUC	AP	AP@k	AUC	AP	AP@k	AUC	AP	AP@k
	Plain text			Tokenised			Tokenised + renaming		
Cosine									
1	0.8209	0.5420	0.4053	0.9022	0.6404	0.4833	0.9459	0.7804	0.6448
2	0.8632	0.5977	0.4314	0.9063	<u>0.7096</u>	<u>0.5899</u>	0.9457	0.7744	0.6579
3	0.9319	0.7022	0.5106	0.8979	0.7067	0.5767	0.9411	0.7413	0.6159
4	0.9428	0.7531	0.5791	0.8784	0.6818	0.5566	0.9451	0.7625	0.6323
5	<u>0.9511</u>	<u>0.7861</u>	0.6349	0.8666	0.6769	0.5639	0.9472	0.7809	0.6588
6	0.9443	0.7823	0.6449	0.8607	0.6723	0.5677	0.9500	0.7898	0.6580
7	0.9326	0.7734	0.6399	0.8765	0.6884	0.5726	<u>0.9559</u>	0.8070	0.6763
8	0.9292	0.7692	0.6470	0.8843	0.6901	0.5614	0.9554	0.8078	0.6715
9	0.9225	0.7611	0.6433	0.8898	0.6794	0.5390	0.9508	0.8179	0.6726
10	0.9166	0.7545	<u>0.6486</u>	<u>0.9064</u>	0.6968	0.5418	0.9550	<u>0.8335</u>	<u>0.6963</u>
Jaccard									
1	0.9832	0.9321	0.8467	0.9208	<u>0.7695</u>	<u>0.6569</u>	0.9452	0.8191	0.7099
2	**0.9949**	**0.9745**	**0.9233**	0.9122	0.6912	0.5378	<u>0.9799</u>	0.9103	0.8205
3	0.9936	0.9611	0.8777	<u>0.9226</u>	0.6976	0.5251	0.9772	0.8891	0.7694
4	0.9874	0.9320	0.8378	0.9178	0.6958	0.5433	0.9762	0.8785	0.7445
5	0.9789	0.9060	0.8136	0.9054	0.6863	0.5397	0.9776	0.8829	0.7447
6	0.9737	0.8954	0.8103	0.8969	0.6675	0.5135	0.9785	0.8897	0.7504
7	0.9726	0.8914	0.8008	0.8901	0.6537	0.4862	0.9770	0.8967	0.7745
8	0.9702	0.8850	0.8008	0.8944	0.6514	0.4687	0.9753	0.9072	0.8052
9	0.9679	0.8809	0.7991	0.9052	0.6606	0.4954	0.9752	0.9159	0.8345
10	0.9665	0.8772	0.7955	0.9065	0.6673	0.4982	0.9738	<u>0.9201</u>	<u>0.8449</u>
Kondrak									
1	0.9295	0.8531	0.7996	0.9886	0.9466	0.8798	0.9817	0.9377	0.8658
2	0.9327	0.8570	0.8044	**0.9887**	**0.9479**	**0.8802**	0.9823	0.9388	**0.8667**
3	0.9341	0.8584	0.8048	0.9884	0.9465	0.8797	**0.9824**	**0.9390**	0.8654
4	0.9353	0.8596	<u>0.8050</u>	0.9881	0.9448	0.8717	0.9822	0.9380	0.8653
5	0.9362	0.8600	0.8031	0.9878	0.9436	0.8680	0.9819	0.9368	0.8649
6	0.9370	<u>0.8601</u>	0.8011	0.9874	0.9419	0.8644	0.9812	0.9351	0.8612
7	0.9374	0.8598	0.7957	0.9870	0.9405	0.8642	0.9806	0.9334	0.8611
8	0.9378	0.8596	0.7936	0.9867	0.9394	0.8639	0.9801	0.9319	0.8609
9	0.9382	0.8594	0.7932	0.9864	0.9382	0.8581	0.9792	0.9299	0.8606
10	<u>0.9386</u>	0.8592	0.7928	0.9861	0.9369	0.8543	0.9784	0.9280	0.8587
Jaro-Winkler									
	0.8644	0.6228	0.4941	0.9679	0.8570	0.7240	0.9419	0.8318	0.7170
Metrics LCS									
	0.9073	0.8180	0.7484	0.9783	0.9247	0.8517	0.9547	0.8933	0.8451

Table 4 Overall scores for the SOCO dataset

Measurement	Configuration	AUC	AP	AP@k
JPlag-text	t = 4	0.9997	0.9887	0.9653
simjava	r = 25	0.9987	0.9891	0.9605
Kondrak	Tokenised, 10-grams	0.9985	0.9915	0.9588
JPlag-Java	t = 12	0.9895	0.9749	0.9513
Simian (L)	threshold = 4, ignoreVariableNames	0.9921	0.9753	0.9509
Deckard	mintoken = 50, stride = 2, similarity = 1.0	0.9823	0.9564	0.9438
Jaccard	tokenised, 10-grams	0.9999	0.9887	0.9415
Kondrak	plain text, 10-grams	0.9983	0.9753	0.9351
CCFX	b = 16, t = 12	0.9905	0.9705	0.9276
Kondrak	tokenised + renaming, 10-grams	0.9978	0.9772	0.9269
Jaccard	tokenised + renaming, 10-grams	0.9999	0.9846	0.9147
Jaccard	plain text, 10-grams	0.9999	0.9823	0.9047
Sherlock	N = 5, Z = 3	0.9983	0.9468	0.8986
NiCAD (C)	UPI = 0.30, minline = 5, rename = consistent, abstract = condition	0.9695	0.9198	0.8940
CCAligner (T)	windowsize = 7, editdistance = 0, similarity = 0.5	0.9503	0.8914	0.8908
iClones (T)	minblock = 40, minclone = 50	0.9469	0.8880	0.8873
Cosine	plain text, 10-grams	0.9991	0.9506	0.8796
simtext	r = 10	0.9931	0.9603	0.8617
NCD-zlib	N/A	0.9983	0.9187	0.8464
SourcererCC	similarity = 60%	0.9412	0.8232	0.8169
Cosine	tokenised + renaming, 10-grams	0.9945	0.8641	0.8155
Cosine	tokenised, 10-grams	0.9960	0.8376	0.7820
Vincent	threshold = 0.25, similarity = jaccard	0.8561	0.7292	0.7231

Table 5 Overall scores for the OCD dataset

Measurement	Configuration	AUC	AP	AP@k
CCFX (C)	b = 5, t = 11	0.9997	0.9975	0.9753
Jaccard	2-grams	0.9949	0.9745	0.9233
Kondrak	tokenised, 2-grams	0.9887	0.9479	0.8802
Kondrak	tokenised + renaming, 2-grams	0.9823	0.9388	0.8667
Jaccard	tokenised + renaming, 10-grams	0.9738	0.9201	0.8449
Simjava	r = 16	0.9714	0.9106	0.8421
JPlag-Java	t = 5	0.9728	0.9090	0.8230
Simian (C)	threshold = 4, ignoreVariableNames	0.9263	0.8500	0.8198
Deckard (T)	mintoken = 30, stride = inf, similarity = 0.95	0.9662	0.9019	0.8191
NCD-bzlib	N/A	0.9636	0.8961	0.8188
Kondrak	4-grams	0.9353	0.8596	0.8050
Plaggie	M = 7	0.9562	0.8808	0.7979
Sherlock	N = 4, Z = 2	0.9449	0.8560	0.7936
Jplag-text	t = 4	0.9677	0.8754	0.7814
NiCAD (T)	UPI = 0.50, minline = 10, renaming = blind, abstract = Declaration	0.9257	0.8273	0.7444
Cosine	tokenised + renaming, 10-grams	0.9550	0.8335	0.6963
CCAligner (T)	windowsize = 8, editdistance = 2, similarity = 0.4	0.8367	0.6993	0.6748
SourcererCC	similarity = 40%	0.9337	0.7720	0.6708
Jaccard	tokenised, 1-grams	0.9208	0.7695	0.6569
Cosine	10-grams	0.9166	0.7545	0.6486
simtext	r = 4	0.8075	0.6452	0.6103
Cosine	tokenised, 2-grams	0.9063	0.7096	0.5899
Vincent	threshold = 0.10, similarity = jaccard	0.7641	0.5089	0.4660
iClones (T)	minblock = 10, minclone = 50	0.7117	0.4792	0.4259

NiCAD, CCAligner and SourcererCC has not changed, with NiCAD, CCAligner and SourcererCC again not performing well with an AP@k below 80%. However, in the OCD dataset, the underlying tokenisation seems to have a stronger impact. Kondrak's distance is performing much worse on plain source code without tokenisation but Jaccard index is performing much better on plain source code. Again, we cannot identify a clear pattern but it seems that the similarity measurement itself has a stronger impact than the representation of the source code below.

For code clones that are created from copied fragments and may only contain renaming operations for identifies or literals (similar to the SOCO dataset), larger n-grams achieve better average precision at k scores (10-grams for the SOCO dataset). However, increasing the n-gram sizes will make the similarity measure more expensive. Moreover, measuring similarity with the Jaccard index is much faster than using Kondrak's distance ($O(m * n)$, m and n are the length of the strings) because the Jaccard index ($O(m + n)$) is using profiles over n-grams instead of sequences.

Overall, the main observation is that simple textual similarity measurements over n-grams usually outperform dedicated clone and plagiarism detectors when the AP@k score is considered. In both datasets, more recent clone detectors like SourcererCC or CCAligner were performing worse than textual similarity measurements and older detectors.

5   Related Work

There are a few studies on comparing performance of code similarity analysers. Most of the studies focus on comparing only code clone detectors [1, 3, 23, 28], source code plagiarism detectors [10], and a mix between dedicated techniques and general textual similarity measures [2]. Nonetheless, there is little work that investigates the effect of source code representation (i.e. tokenisation and renaming of identifiers and literals) and the impact of similarity measurements when performing code clone detection. The work that is close to our study is by Novak et al. [15] that studies of effect of several source code pre-processing techniques on plagiarism detection accuracy in student programming assignments. The study includes five pre-processing techniques (removing comments, template exclusion, removing common code, all techniques without normalisation and all techniques with normalisation), and their effects on three code plagiarism detectors: SIM, JPlag and Sherlock. The study also evaluates the tools on two modes: Java and text. The experiment was done on two datasets, SOCO (also used in this chapter) and RSS. The results show that pre-processing techniques can help boosting the performance of code plagiarism detection tools. Similar to our study, the experimental result from Novak's study also shows that, in some cases, by applying the right pre-processing techniques, text-based version of the tools can outperform their dedicated Java counterpart.

6 Conclusions

The comparison using average precision at k with dedicated clone and plagiarism detectors shows that simple similarity measurements like Kondrak's distance using n-grams over tokenised source code usually outperform specialised tools for the detection of cloned, plagiarised or duplicated code.

When one considers the complexity of setting up and configuring dedicated clone or plagiarism detectors which sometimes are unable to analyse source code that cannot be compiled or parsed, a simple measurement like Kondrak's distance or Jaccard index over a tokenised source code may be a better choice to measure code similarity. Moreover, future work on code similarity should compare with simple measurements like Kondrak's distance or Jaccard index as a baseline to establish whether a suggested new technique actually improves the state of the art.

References

1. S. Bellon, R. Koschke, G. Antoniol, J. Krinke, E. Merlo, Comparison and evaluation of clone detection tools. Trans. Softw. Eng. **33**(9), 577–591 (2007)
2. B. Biegel, Q.D. Soetens, W. Hornig, S. Diehl, S. Demeyer, Comparison of similarity metrics for refactoring detection, in *MSR '11* (2011)
3. E. Burd, J. Bailey, Evaluating clone detection tools for use during preventative maintenance, in *SCAM '02*, pp. 36–43 (2002)
4. T. Debatty, java-string-similarity: version 2.0.0 (2020). https://github.com/tdebatty/java-string-similarity
5. E. Flores, P. Rosso, L. Moreno, E. Villatoro-Tello, On the detection of source code re-use, in *Proceedings of the Forum for Information Retrieval Evaluation FIRE '14* (ACM Press, 2015), pp. 21–30
6. E. Flores, P. Rosso, L. Moreno, E. Villatoro-Tello. Detection of source code re-use. http://users.dsic.upv.es/grupos/nle/soco/ (2014). Accessed 14 Feb 2016
7. R. Grosse, Krakatau bytecode tools (2016). https://github.com/Storyyeller/Krakatau. Accessed 14 Feb 2016
8. D. Grune, The software and text similarity tester SIM (2014). https://dickgrune.com/Programs/similarity_tester/. Accessed 09 Jan 2019
9. GuardSquare, ProGuard: bytecode obfuscation tool (2015). http://proguard.sourceforge.net/. Accessed 24 Aug 2015
10. J. Hage, P. Rademaker, N. van Vugt, A comparison of plagiarism detection tools. Technical Report UU-CS-2010-015, Department of Information and Computing Sciences Utrecht University, Utrecht, The Netherlands (2010)
11. D.G. Han, *Supporting Modern Code Review*. Ph.D. thesis, UCL (University College London, 2019)
12. S. Harris, Simian—similarity analyser, version 2.4 (2015). http://www.harukizaemon.com/simian/. Accessed 14 Feb 2016
13. T. Kamiya, S. Kusumoto, K. Inoue, CCFinder: a multilinguistic token-based code clone detection system for large scale source code. Trans. Softw. Eng. **28**(7), 654–670 (2002)
14. G. Kondrak, N-gram similarity and distance, in Lecture Notes in Computer Science (including subseries Lecture Notes in Artificial Intelligence and Lecture Notes in Bioinformatics), vol. 2088 (2005), pp. 115–126

15. M. Novak, Effect of source-code preprocessing techniques on plagiarism detection accuracy in student programming assignments. Ph.D. thesis (University of Zagreb, 2020)
16. L. Prechelt, G. Malpohl, M. Philippsen, Finding plagiarisms among a set of programs with JPlag. J. Univers. Comput. Sci. **8**(11), 1016–1038 (2002)
17. C. Ragkhitwetsagul, J. Krinke, D. Clark, Similarity of source code in the presence of pervasive modifications, in *International Working Conference on Source Code Analysis and Manipulation (SCAM)* (2016), pp. 117–126
18. C. Ragkhitwetsagul. *Code Similarity and Clone Search in Large-Scale Source Code Data.* Ph.D. thesis (University College London, 2018)
19. C. Ragkhitwetsagul, J. Krinke, Using compilation/decompilation to enhance clone detection, in *Proceedings of the IEEE 11th International Workshop on Software Clones (IWSC '17)* (IEEE, 2017), pp. 1–7
20. C. Ragkhitwetsagul, J. Krinke, Siamese: scalable and incremental code clone search via multiple code representations. Empir. Softw. Eng. **24**(4), 2236–2284 (2019)
21. C. Ragkhitwetsagul, J. Krinke, D. Clark, A comparison of code similarity analysers. Empir. Softw. Eng. **23**(4), 2464–2519 (2018a)
22. C. Ragkhitwetsagul, J. Krinke, B. Marnette, A picture is worth a thousand words: code clone detection based on image similarity, in *Proceedings of the IEEE 12th International Workshop on Software Clones (IWSC '18)* (IEEE, 2018b), pp. 44–50
23. C.K. Roy, J.R. Cordy, R. Koschke, Comparison and evaluation of code clone detection techniques and tools: a qualitative approach. Sci. Comput. Program. **74**(7), 470–495 (2009)
24. H. Sajnani, V. Saini, J. Svajlenko, C.K. Roy, C.V. Lopes, SourcererCC: scaling code clone detection to big-code, in *Proceedings of the 38th International Conference on Software Engineering (ICSE '16)* (ACM Press, 2016), pp. 1157–1168
25. S. Schulze, D. Meyer, On the robustness of clone detection to code obfuscation, in *IWSC'13* (2013), pp. 62–68
26. D. Spinellis, Dspinellis/tokenizer: version 1.1. (2019). https://doi.org/10.5281/zenodo.2558420, https://github.com/dspinellis/tokenizer/
27. M. Strobel, Procyon/Java decompiler (2016). https://bitbucket.org/mstrobel/procyon/wiki/Java%20Decompiler. Accessed 14 Feb 2016
28. J. Svajlenko, C.K. Roy, Evaluating modern clone detection tools, in *ICSME '14* (2014), pp. 321–330
29. P. Wang, J. Svajlenko, Y. Wu, Y. Xu, C.K. Roy, CCAligner: a token based large-gap clone detector, in *Proceedings of the 40th International Conference on Software Engineering (ICSE '18)* (ACM Press, 2018), pp. 1066–1077
30. R. White, J. Krinke, E. Barr, F. Sarro, C. Ragkhitwetsagul, Artefact relation graphs for unit test reuse recommendation (2021). In IEEE International Conference on Software Testing (ICST)

Is Late Propagation a Harmful Code Clone Evolutionary Pattern? An Empirical Study

Osama Ehsan, Lillane Barbour, Foutse Khomh, and Ying Zou

Abstract Two similar code segments, or clones, form a clone pair within a software system. The changes to the clones over time create a clone evolution history. Late propagation is a specific pattern of clone evolution. In late propagation, one clone in the clone pair is modified, causing the clone pair to become inconsistent. The code segments are then re-synchronized in a later revision. Existing work has established late propagation as a clone evolution pattern, and suggested that the pattern is related to a high number of faults. In this chapter, we replicate and extend the work by Barbour et al. (2011 27th IEEE International Conference on Software Maintenance (ICSM). IEEE (2011) [1]) by examining the characteristics of late propagation in 10 long-lived open-source software systems using the iClones clone detection tool. We identify eight types of late propagation and investigate their fault-proneness. Our results confirm that late propagation is the more harmful clone evolution pattern and that some specific cases of late propagations are more harmful than others. We trained machine learning models using 18 clone evolution related features to predict the evolution of late propagation and achieved high precision within the range of 0.91–0.94 and AUC within the range of 0.87–0.91.

O. Ehsan (✉) · L. Barbour · Y. Zou
Queen's University, Kingston, Canada
e-mail: osama.ehsan@queensu.ca

L. Barbour
e-mail: l.barbour@queensu.ca

Y. Zou
e-mail: ying.zou@queensu.ca

F. Khomh
Polytechnique Montréal, Quebec City, Canada
e-mail: foutse.khomh@polymtl.ca

1 Introduction

A code segment is labeled as a code clone if it is identical or highly similar to another code segment. Similar code segments form a clone pair. Clone pairs can be introduced into systems deliberately (e.g., "copy-and-paste" actions) or inadvertently by a developer during development and maintenance activities. Like all code segments, code clones are not immune to change. Large software systems undergo thousands of revisions over their lifecycles. Each revision can involve modifications to code clones. As the clones in a clone pair are modified, a change evolution history, known as a clone genealogy [2], is generated.

In a previous study on clone genealogies, Kim et al. [2] define two types of evolutionary changes that can affect a clone pair: a consistent change or an inconsistent change. During a consistent change, both clones in a clone pair are modified in parallel, preserving the clone pair. In an inconsistent change, one or both of the clones evolve independently, destroying the clone pair relationship. Inconsistent changes can occur deliberately, such as when code is copied and pasted and then subsequently modified to fit the new context. For example, if a driver is required for a new printer model, a developer could copy the driver code from an older printer model and then modify it. Inconsistent changes can also occur accidentally. A developer may be unaware of a clone pair and cause an inconsistency by changing only one half of the clone pair. This inconsistency could cause a software fault. If a fault is found in one clone and fixed, but not propagated to the other clone in the clone pair, the fault remains in the system. For example, a fault might be found in the old printer driver code and fixed, but the fix is not propagated to the new printer driver. For these reasons, a previous study [2] has argued that accidental inconsistent changes make code clones more prone to faults.

Late propagation occurs when a clone pair undergoes one or more inconsistent changes followed by a re-synchronizing change [3]. The re-synchronization of the code clones indicates that the gap in consistency is accidental. Since accidental inconsistencies are considered risky [4], the presence of late propagation in clone genealogies can be an indicator of risky, fault-prone code.

Many studies have been performed on the evolution of clones. A few (e.g., [3, 4]) have studied late propagation and indicated that late propagation genealogies are more fault-prone than other clone genealogies. Thummalapenta et al. began the initial work in examining the characteristics of late propagation. The authors measured the delay between an inconsistent change and a re-synchronizing change and related the delay to software faults. In our chapter, we examine more characteristics of late propagation to determine if only a subset of late propagation genealogies are at risk of faults. Developers are interested in identifying which clones are most at risk of faults. Our goal is to support developers in their allocation of limited code testing and review resources toward the most risky late propagation genealogies. To achieve this goal, we first study the prevalence and fault-proneness of late propagation genealogies, and secondly we train multiple machine learning models to predict whether a clone pair would have late propagation. Early diagnosis of late propagation can help developers in addressing the clones with late propagation fast before they become buggy.

In this chapter, we replicate and extend the analysis of late propagation performed by Barbour et al. [1]. We study the characteristics of late propagation genealogies and estimate the likelihood of faults. We used 10 open-source projects from GitHub instead of only two projects as in the original study. We also include an additional research question aimed at predicting occurrences of late propagation genealogies.

2 Experimental Setup

The *goal* of our study is to investigate the fault-proneness of clone pairs that undergo late propagation. The *quality focus* is to lower the maintenance effort and cost due to the presence of late propagated clone pairs in software systems. The *perspective* is that of researchers interested in studying the effects of late propagation on clone pairs. The results may also be of interest to developers who perform development or maintenance activities. The results will provide insight in deciding which code segments are most at risk for faults and in prioritizing the code for testing.

The *context* of this study consists of the change history of open-source software projects, which have different sizes and belong to different domains. This section describes the setup used to perform our study which aims to address the following four research questions:

- RQ1: Are there different types of late propagation?,
- RQ2: Are some types of late propagation more fault-prone than others?,
- RQ3: Which type of late propagation experiences the highest proportion of faults?, and
- RQ4: Can we predict whether a clone pair would experience late propagation?.

2.1 Project Selection

We use GHTorrent on the Google Cloud[1] to extract all projects that have more than 1,000 commits, 1,000 issues, and 1,000 pull requests. We use such a high number of commits, pull requests, and issues to ensure that we have enough history of clone genealogies. We limit our study to Java projects. Our selection criteria provide us with 66 Java projects. Then, we discard the projects that are younger than 5 years (created after June 2015). If a project has more source lines of code (SLOC), the probability of having code clones increases. A recent study suggests [5] to include projects with more than 100K source lines of code. We remove the projects with less than 100K

---

[1] https://ghtorrent.org/gcloud.html.

Table 1 Description of selected projects

Project name	# of commits	# of issues	SLOC	% of java files (%)	# of clone genealogies
Druid	10,496	1,657	1.2m	94.50	61,718
Netty	9,910	4,174	476.2k	98.60	6,576
Muikku	16,970	2,696	318.4k	50.4	23,836
Framework	18,969	1,788	867.9k	95.50	11,961
Checkstyle	9,454	2,198	457.4k	97.80	7,705
Gatk	4,173	2,736	2.2m	93.70	22,651
Realm	8,318	3,358	199.9k	83.80	13,540
Nd4j	7,021	1,238	467.0k	99.80	45,413
Rxjava	5,762	1,950	474.9k	99.90	8,866
K	15,997	1,134	243.3k	83.50	6,026

SLOC by using the GitHub project SLOC calculator extension.[2] Furthermore, we remove the forked projects and the projects which have less than 70% of Java files. The percentage of Java files is calculated using GitHub's language information of each project. Finally, after applying all the selection criteria, we retain the top 10 projects used in this study. Table 1 provides the description of the selected projects.

2.2 Building Clone Genealogies

The selected projects are all Git-based projects. Git provides multiple functions to extract the history of the projects. The history includes the renamed files, changed files, and changes made to each file using the `blame` function. We perform the following steps on each of the projects in our dataset. After downloading the repositories, we use the following command to extract the identifier, committer email, commit date, and the message of each commit:

git log – pretty=format:"%h,%ae, %ai, %s"

2.2.1 Detecting Code Clones

We use the latest version of the iCLONES clone detection [6] to identify the clones from the projects. We select iCLONES because it is recommended by Svajlenko et al. [7] who evaluate the performance of 11 different clone detection tools. iCLONES uses a hybrid approach to detect clones. We use the settings used by Svajlenko et al. [7] as the recommended settings are reported to achieve higher precision and recall

---

[2] https://github.com/artem-solovev/gloc.

values. We use the `git checkout` command to extract a snapshot of a project at a specific commit. We sort all commits chronologically and run the clone detection on each commit.

2.2.2 Extracting Clone Genealogies

Code clones may experience changes during the development and maintenance phases of the project. Such changes can be consistent or inconsistent based on a relative similarity score. Inconsistent clones can be later synchronized to become consistent. The set of states and the history of changes to any clone pairs are known as clone pair genealogy. We identify clone genealogies of all the clones in the studied projects. Our approach for generating clone genealogies is similar to the approaches used in other studies [8, 9]. Both Göde and Krinke track clones over time by acquiring a list of changes from the source code repositories of the subject systems.

The iCLONES tool produces a list of clones that exist in a project at any specific commit. We link the clone pairs between each commit to create a set of genealogies. A change to a clone can affect its size while a change to a file containing the clone can shift the position of the clone (i.e., changes its line numbers). To address this issue, we use the `git diff` command to detect all the changes to a specific file. We track the clone positional changes affected by the changes to the non-clone part of the file. We include only the changes to the clone contents rather than the clone line number since a shift in the line numbers does not change the state of the clone.

We build a clone genealogy for each clone pair detected by the iCLONES tool. We start by extracting the commit sequence of each project under study. We use the commit sequence to identify the modifications in the clone pairs of each commit. If a commit C2 changes a file that contains code in the clone pair, we use the `diff` command to compare the changes to a previous commit C1. If a clone snippet is changed in C2, we update the start and end line numbers of the clone from C2. To generate the mapping and to check the modifications, we used a third-party Python patching parser called `whatthepatch` [10]. If the start or the end of the clone snippet is deleted, we move the clone line numbers accordingly to address the deleted lines. Krinke [9] made several assumptions when updating line numbers of clones between revisions. We use the same assumptions in our study:

1. If a change occurs before the start of the clone, or after the end of the clone, the clone is not modified.
2. If an addition occurs starting at the first line number of a clone, the clone shifts within the method but is not modified.
3. If a deletion occurs anywhere within the clone boundaries, the clone is modified and its size shrinks.
4. If a deletion followed by an addition overlaps the clone boundaries, we assume that the clone size shrinks because of the deletion, and the new lines do not makeup part of the clone.

In the last assumption, it is possible that there exists a clone containing both our updated reference clone and the newly added lines. We use the strictest assumption that the new lines are not included. When determining consistent and inconsistent changes, we look for clones in the clone list that *contain* our updated reference clone. Therefore, this scenario would still be considered a consistent change. In addition, we also track changes to the names of the clone files.

2.3 Classification of Genealogies

In the current state of the art, late propagation is defined as a clone pair that experiences one or more inconsistent changes followed by a re-synchronizing change [4]. For example, consider two clones that call a method. A developer modifies the call parameters of the method and updates one of the clones to reflect the change. This causes the clone pair to become inconsistent. Using all combinations of the inconsistent phases described by Barbour et al. [1], we identify eight possible types of late propagation (LP) genealogies. The detail of the eight types of late propagation are described in [1]. The eight types are organized in three groups based on the occurrence or not of a change propagation: (1) propagation always occurs (three types named LP1, LP2, and LP3), (2) propagation may or may not occur (four types named LP4, LP5, LP6, and LP7), and (3) propagation never occurs (one type named LP8). In this study, we examine if the cases that always involve propagation (i.e., LP1, LP2, and LP3) or never involve propagation (i.e., LP8) are more prone to faults than the other types of late propagation. We made a slight modification in the definition of LP7 to include cases where during divergence either A or B is changed, instead of considering only instances in which both A and B are changed during divergence.

2.4 Detecting Faulty Clones

We use the SZZ algorithm [11] to identify the changes that introduced faults. First, we use the Fischer et al. [12] heuristic to identify fault-fixing commits using a regular expression. The regular expression identifies the bug-ID in the commit messages. If a bug-ID appears in the commit message, we map the commit to the bug as a bug-fixing commit. Second, we mine the issue reports of each project from GitHub. For the issues that are closed, we identify if there are any pull requests associated with such issues. If there is a pull request associated with an issue, we identify all the commits included in the pull request and map the commits to the issue as a bug-fixing commit. Once we have a list of all bug-fixing commits, we use the following command to identify all the modified files in each commit.

git log [commit-id]-n 1—name-status

We consider only changes to Java files in a commit. A commit is a set of changes to the file(s) in the software repository. For all changes to a specific file of a bug-fixing commit, we use the `git blame` command to identify all the commits when the same snippet was changed. We consider such commits as the "candidate faulty changes." We exclude the changes that are blank lines or comments.

Finally, we filter the commits that are submitted before the creation date of the bugs. We then check whether the commits identified as bug-inducing commits include clone pairs. If a clone snippet is included in the bug-inducing commits, we label the clone change as "buggy."

3   Case Study Results

This section reports and discusses the results of our study.

3.1   RQ1: Are There Different Types of Late Propagation?

Motivation. This question is preliminary to questions RQ2 and RQ3. It provides quantitative data on the percentages with which different types of late propagation occur in our studied systems.

Approach. We address this question by classifying all instances of late propagation as described in Sect. 2.3. For each type of late propagation, we report the number of occurrences in the systems. Table 2 lists each of the categories and the proportion of occurrences in our dataset, both as a numerical value and a percentage of the overall number of late propagation instances for the systems.

Results. As summarized in Table 2, four types of late propagation are dominant across all systems when using the iClones clone detection tool (i.e., LP1, LP3, LP7, and LP8). The four dominant types represent the three late propagation categories. Only LP3 (instead of LP6) is more dominant as compared to the results of Barbour et al. [1]. As shown in Table 2, LP7 occurs in an average of 40.5% of instances of late propagation, so it is the most common form of late propagation across all systems. However, LP7 is also the least understood of the types of late propagation. Since both clones in LP7 clone pairs can be modified during all three steps of late propagation (i.e., experiencing a diverging change, a change during the period of divergence, a re-synchronizing change), it is unclear in which direction changes are propagated during the evolution of the clone pair. A few types of late propagation (i.e., LP2, LP4, and LP5) contribute minutely to the number of late propagation genealogies. Other than the one project (Muikku), all the other projects include almost all types of late propagation. Our further investigation shows that only 1% (297 out of 23,836)

Table 2 Summary of late propagation types for the studied open-source projects

Propagation category	LP type	Projects										Total	%
		Druid	Netty	Muikku	Framework	Checkstyle	Gatk	Realm	Nd4j	RxJava	K		
Propagation always occurs	LP1	102	15	78	46	3	102	39	74	10	21	490	13
	LP2	23	–	4	5	5	3	3	5	–	4	52	1.5
	LP3	195	22	–	24	14	11	57	67	3	58	451	12
Propagation may or may not occur	LP4	18	5	10	7	6	1	4	15	1	6	73	2
	LP5	49	3	–	3	10	3	19	24	3	6	120	3
	LP6	207	12	–	12	10	7	28	76	6	19	377	10
	LP7	714	62	–	29	81	21	143	297	78	102	1,527	40.5
Propagation never occurs	LP8	102	18	210	29	3	195	28	50	2	53	690	18
Total LPs		1,410	137	302	155	132	343	321	608	103	269	3,780	100

of the clone genealogies experience late propagation which is the lowest among all the projects and this might be the reason for the absence of half of LP types.

Overall, we conclude that there is representation from multiple types of late propagation and across all categories of late propagation. In the next two research questions, we examine the types in more detail to determine if some types are more risky than others.

Summary of RQ1

Late propagation types LP1, LP3, LP7, and LP8 are the most commonly occurring type of late propagation in the 10 studied open-source projects from GitHub. The results are consistent with the previous study except that LP3 is more frequent instead of LP6. Most of the projects include all types of late propagations.

3.2 RQ2: Are Some Types of Late Propagation More Fault-Prone than Others?

Motivation. Previous researchers have determined that late propagation is more prone to faults than other clone genealogies [3]. Using the classification of late propagation clone genealogies proposed by Barbour et al. [1], we evaluate late propagation in greater depth and examine if the risk of faults remains consistent across all types of late propagation.

Approach. We compute the number of fault-containing and fault-free genealogies in each late propagation category. We compute the same values for non-late propagation clone genealogies that experience at least one change. For the remainder of this chapter, we use the abbreviation "Non-LP" for clone pairs that experience at least one change but are not involved in any type of late propagation. We test the following null hypothesis[3] H_{02}: *Each type of late propagation genealogy has the same proportion of clone pairs that experience a fault fix.*

We use the Chi-square test [13] and compute the *odds ratio* (OR) [13]. The Chi-square test is a statistical test used to determine if there are non-random associations between two categorical variables. The odds ratio indicates the likelihood of an event to occur. It is defined as the ratio of the odds p of an event (i.e., fault-fixing change) occurring in one sample (i.e., experimental group), to the odds q of the event occurring in the other sample (i.e., control group): $OR = \frac{p/(1-p)}{q/(1-q)}$. An $OR = 1$ indicates that the event is equally likely in both samples; an $OR > 1$ shows that the event is more likely in the experimental group while an $OR < 1$ indicates that it is more likely in the control group. Specifically, we compute two sets of odds ratios. First,

---

[3] There is no H_{01} because RQ1 is exploratory.

Table 3 Contingency table, Chi-square tests results for clone genealogies with and without late propagation. The table shows the values for all the combinations of late propagations and faults

LP-faults	LP-no faults	No LP-faults	No LP-no faults	p-value	OR
1,851	1,929	42,526	48,928	<0.05	1.8

we select the clone pairs that underwent a late propagation as an experimental group. Second, we form one experimental group for each type LP_i of late propagation and re-compute the odds ratios. In both cases, we select the non-LP genealogies as the control group.

Results. Previous researchers [4] have studied the relationship between late propagation and faults. In this research question, we first replicate the earlier studies and then extend the study to include the different categories of late propagation.

(a) Fault-proneness of late propagation. Table 3 summarizes the results of the tests described above for instances of late propagation compared to non-late propagation (LP) genealogies. The first and second columns show the number of LP genealogies with and without faults. The third and fourth columns in the table list the number of non-LP genealogies that experience fault fixes and the number that is free of fault fixes. The last column of the table lists the odds ratio test results for each system. All of our results pass the Chi-square test with a p-value less than 0.05 and are therefore significant. Where there are few data points, we use Fisher's exact test to confirm the results from the Chi-Square test. Fisher's exact test is more accurate than the Chi-square test when sample sizes are small [13]. In this study, the Fisher test provides the same information as the Chi-square test, so we do not present the Fisher test results in the tables. Table 4 shows the percentage of fault-prone late propagation in each of the studied projects. In all the significant cases, the odds ratio is greater than 1, indicating that late propagation genealogies are more fault-prone than non-LP genealogies. Overall, our results agree with previous studies [4] that found that late propagation is more at risk of faults.

(b) Fault-proneness of late propagation types. We repeat the previous tests, dividing the instances of late propagation into their respective late propagation types. We compare each type of late propagation to genealogies with no late propagation. For each type of late propagation, Table 5 lists the number of instances that experience a fault fix, the number of instances with a no-fault fix, the result from the Chi-square test, and the odds ratio using the control group composed of non-LP genealogies.

An examination of the significant cases in Tables 5 reveals that the odds ratios are greater than 1, so each type of late propagation is more fault-prone than non-LP genealogies. There are two exceptions to this observation, LP2 and LP3 in Table 5. All exceptions belong to the "propagation always occurs" category. Thus, in general, these late propagation types are not more fault-prone than non-LP genealogies. Our observation is consistent with the previous findings by Barbour et al. [1].

Table 4 Contingency table, Chi-square tests results for clone genealogies with and without late propagation

Projects	LP-faults	LP-no faults	% of faulty LPs (%)
Druid	970	440	67
Netty	1	136	0.5
Muikku	145	157	48
Framework	3	152	2
Checkstyle	78	54	60
Gatk	134	209	39
Realm	135	186	42
Nd4j	283	325	47
Rxjava	0	103	0
K	102	167	38

Table 5 Contingency table with the Chi-square test for different late propagation types

Propagation category	LP type	Faults	No faults	p-value	OR
	No LP	42,526	48,928	<0.01	1
Propagation always occurs	LP1	244	246	< 0.01	3.953
	LP2	20	32	<0.01	0.672
	LP3	224	227	<0.01	0.922
Propagation may or may not occur	LP4	23	50	< 0.01	2.256
	LP5	68	52	<0.01	1.765
	LP6	216	161	<0.01	6.179
	LP7	803	724	<0.01	1.277
Propagation never occurs	LP8	253	437	<0.01	3.2

We conclude that there are many types that make up a small proportion of LP instances and have a very high odds ratio. Thus, when one of these LP types occurs, the risk of fault introduction is high. For example, LP6 has a high odds ratio (e.g., 6.17 in Table 5) but accounts for less than 5% of all late propagation instances in Table 2.

The two most common late propagation types in the previous research question, LP7 and LP8, in general, have low odds ratios in Table 5. This indicates that although they occur frequently, they are less fault-prone than other less common late propagation types (e.g., LP6). The result is consistent with the previous findings by Barbour et al. [1]. Overall, each type of late propagation has a different level of fault-proneness. Thus, we reject H_{02} in general.

Summary of RQ2

The most commonly occurring late propagation types (i.e., LP7 and LP8) are less fault-prone than the less commonly occurring late propagation (i.e., LP6). The result is consistent with the previous study and shows that each propagation type is different from others.

3.3 RQ3: Which Type of Late Propagation Experiences the Highest Proportion of Faults?

Motivation. In the previous research question (i.e., RQ2), we identify the fault-proneness of late propagation types as compared to the no-LP clone pairs. The results show that fault-proneness is not related to the frequency of LP type. In this research question, we want to identify which type of late propagation experiences the highest proportion of faults. In other words, we examine if, when faults occur, do they occur in large numbers?

Approach. We test the following null hypothesis H_{03}: *Different types of late propagation have the same proportion of clone pairs that experience a fault fix.* For each type of late propagation, we calculate the sum of all faults experienced by instances of that type of late propagation. We use the non-parametric Kruskal–Wallis test to investigate if the number of faults for the different types of late propagation is identical.

Results. Table 6 presents the distribution of faults for different types of late propagation. The "Total" row represents the total numbers of faults over all late propagation genealogies. To validate the results, we perform the non-parametric Kruskal–Wallis test which compares the distribution of faults between groups of different types of late propagation. The results of the Kruskal–Wallis test is statistically significant with a p-value of 2.89^{-15}. Hence, there is a statistically significant difference between the distribution of faults across all types of late propagations.

Examining the results in Table 6 for the significant cases, we see that, in general, LP7 and LP8 contribute to a large proportion of the faults. In the previous question, LP7 and LP8 have lower odds ratios. Although they are less prone to faults, when they do experience faults, the faults are likely to occur in large numbers. The change causing the inconsistency may lead to faults in the system, which may explain why the change is reverted instead of being propagated to the other clone in the clone pair. Overall, we can conclude that types LP7 and LP8 are the most dangerous. The level of fault-proneness of the other types is system-dependant. The proportion of faults for each type of late propagation is, therefore, very different. Thus, we reject H_{03}. This result is consistent with the findings of Barbour et al. [1].

Table 6 Proportion of faults for each type of late propagation

Propagation category	LP type	# of faults	% of faults (%)
Propagation always occurs	LP1	244	13.2
	LP2	20	1.1
	LP3	224	12
Propagation may or may not occur	LP4	23	1.2
	LP5	68	3.7
	LP6	216	11.7
	LP7	803	43.3
Propagation never occurs	LP8	253	13.8
	TOTAL	1851	100.00

Summary of RQ3

In terms of the proportion of faults, LP7 and LP8 are more risky and should be monitored carefully and/or refactored if possible. The risk for the other types of late propagation is system-dependant.

3.4 RQ4: Can We Predict Whether a Clone Pair Would Experience Late Propagation?

Motivation. In this research question, we use machine learning algorithms to train models that can help developers predict which clone pair will experience late propagation and have faults in the future. Using these predictions, developers would be able to refactor risky clone pair early on and/or keep them in check before the clone pair becomes inconsistent or a fault is introduced. This information about risky clone pairs will help developers in making better use of their time and resources.

Approach. For each instance in the clone pair genealogy, we calculate multiple features that may help with training the models for predicting whether a clone pair would experience late propagation or not. The features are used in a prior study by Barbour et al. [5]. Table 7 presents the description of our collected features.

We train models for two different behaviors; (1) presence of late propagation (M_{LP}) and (2) fault-prone late propagation (M_{BUG}). For every change experienced by a clone pair, we calculate 18 features as described in Table 7. We also examined the fault-proneness of the clone pairs, as described in Sect. 2.

Table 7 Description of clone genealogies features from [5] used to build the models

Metric	Description
Product metrics	
CLOC	The number of cloned lines of code
CPathDepth	The number of common folders within the project directory structure
CCurSt	The current state of the clone pair (consistent or inconsistent)
CommiterExp	The experience of committer (i.e., the number of previous commits submitted before a specific commit.)
Process metrics	
EFltDens	The number of fault fix modifications to the clone pair since it was created divided by the total number of commits that modified the clone pair
TChurn	The sum of added and the changed lines of code in the history of a clone
TPC	The total number of changes in the history of a clone
NumOfBursts	The number of change bursts on a clone. A change burst is a sequence of consecutive changes with a maximum distance of one day between the changes
SLBurst	The number of consecutive changes in the last change burst on a clone
CFltRate	The number of fault-prone modifications to the clone pair divided by the total number of commits that modified the clone pair
Genealogy metrics	
EConChg	The number of consistent changes experienced by the clone pair
EIncChg	The number of inconsistent changes experienced by the clone pair
EConStChg	The number of consistent change of state within the clone pair genealogy
EIncStChg	The number of inconsistent change of state within the clone pair genealogy
EFltConStChg	The number of re-synchronizing changes (i.e., RESYNC) that were a fault fix
EFltIncSChg	The number of diverging changes (i.e., DIV) that were a fault fix
EChgTimeInt	The time interval in days since the previous change to the clone pair

We use logistic regression, SVM classifier, Random Forrest, and XGBOOST to classify the clone pairs data. Logistic regression is a statistical model that uses a logistic function to model a binary-dependant variable. Support vector machine (SVM) is a supervised model associated with learning algorithms that analyze data for classification. Random forrest is an ensemble learning method for classification that operates by constructing several decision trees. XGBOOST [14] is an optimized gradient boosting library designed to be highly efficient and flexible. Recent studies [15, 16] have used XGBOOST for training the models for classification problems. We split the data into training (70%) and testing (30%) to train and test the models. We make sure that our data splitting is time consistent i.e., we do not use future late propagations data to predict past late propagations.

Results. Table 8 shows the results of model training using the four machine learning algorithms. We evaluate the models using three performance metrics commonly used for assessing trained machine learning models, including precision, f1-score, and AUC. Precision is the fraction of relevant instances among the retrieved instances. F1-

Table 8 Evaluation metrics for the machine learning algorithms

ML algorithm	M_{LP}			M_{BUG}		
	Precision	F1-score	AUC	Precision	F1-score	AUC
Logistic Regression	0.81	0.68	0.76	0.78	0.71	0.75
SVM Classifier	0.87	0.72	0.80	0.78	0.72	0.76
Random Forrest	0.89	**0.80**	0.85	**0.94**	**0.93**	**0.93**
XGBOOST	**0.91**	0.72	**0.87**	0.91	0.75	0.90

score is the harmonic mean between precision and recall. AUC provides an aggregate measure of performance across all possible classification thresholds. Results show that XGBOOST outperforms all the algorithms in terms of precision and AUC. However, Random Forrest achieves the highest value among the four models.

Furthermore, we analyze the most important predictors for both behaviors (i.e., late propagation occurrence and fault occurrence in late propagation). For M_{LP}, the number of consistent state changes (EConStChg) (37.5%), the number of consistent changes (EConChg) (32%), and the sum of added or changed lines (Tchurn) (23.2%) are the most significant features having more than 90% effect in the model. The number of consistent state changes (EConStChg) has a negative effect, meaning that if a genealogy experience more inconsistent changes than consistent changes, then it can be an indicator of late propagation introduction in clone genealogies. For M_{BUG}, number of fault-prone modifications in the history (CFltRate) (65%), number of previous commits by a specific developer (CommitterExp) (17%), and time interval in days since last change (EChgTime) (8%) are the most significant features having more than 90% effect in the model. The number of faulty changes divided by the number of changes (CFltRate) has a positive effect. A higher number of erroneous changes in clone genealogy history is an indicator of future fault occurrences. Experience has a negative effect, which suggests that late propagation genealogies changed by less experienced developers are more fault-prone. Developers can benefit from these results as they can leverage the trained machine learning models to assess the risks of the clone pairs.

Summary of RQ4

For M_{LP}, XGBOOST achieves the highest precision (0.91) and AUC (0.87) with consistent state changes (EConStChg) being the most significant feature. For M_{BUG}, Random Forrest achieves the highest precision (0.94) and AUC (0.93) with the number of past fault-fixing changes (CFltRate) being the most significant feature.

4 Threats to Validity

We now discuss the threats to the validity of our study. *Construct validity* threats in this study are mainly due to measurement errors possibly introduced by our chosen clone detection tool. To reduce the possibility of misclassification of code fragment as clones, we chose the best configuration for clone detection tool that has been recommended by the recent evaluation of code clone tools [7]. Another construct validity threat stems from the SZZ heuristics used to identify fault-fixing changes [11]. Although this heuristic does not achieve a 100% accuracy, it has been success-fully employed and reported to achieve good results in multiple studies [17]. *Reliability validity* threats concern the possibility of replicating this study.[4] We attempt to provide all the details needed to replicate our study. Also, the source code and git repositories of the studied systems are publicly available.

5 Conclusion

In this chapter, we replicate a previous study by Barbour et al. [1] to examine late propagation in more detail. We first confirm the conclusion from the previous study that late propagation is more risky than other clone genealogies. We then identify eight types of late propagation and study them in detail to identify which types of late propagation contribute the most to faults in the systems. Overall, we find that two types of late propagation (i.e., LP7 and LP8) are riskier than the others, in terms of their fault-proneness and the magnitude of their contribution toward faults. LP7 occurs when both clones are modified, causing a divergence and then at least one of the two clones in the pair is modified to re-synchronize the clone pair. LP8 involves no propagation at all and occurs when a clone diverges and then re-synchronizes itself without changes to the other clone in a clone pair. The contribution of other types of late propagation is found to be system-dependent. From this study, we can conclude that late propagation types are not equally risky. We train machine learning models to identify the clone genealogies with late propagation (M_{LP}) and fault-prone late propagations (M_{BUG}) early on. We use 18 different clone genealogy-related features to train four different machine learning models. For the occurrence of late propagation (M_{LP}), XGBOOST achieves the highest precision (0.91) and AUC (0.87) with consistent state changes (EConStChg) being the most significant feature. For the fault-prone late propagations (M_{BUG}), Random Forrest achieves the highest precision (0.94) and AUC (0.93) with the number of fault-prone changes (CFltRate) being the most significant feature.

---

[4] https://github.com/qecelab/latepropagation.

References

1. L. Barbour, F. Khomh, Y. Zou, Late propagation in software clones, in *2011 27th IEEE International Conference on Software Maintenance (ICSM)* (IEEE, 2011), pp. 273–282
2. M. Kim, V. Sazawal, D. Notkin, G. Murphy, An empirical study of code clone genealogies, in *Proceedings of the 10th European Software Engineering Conference Held Jointly with 13th ACM SIGSOFT International Symposium on Foundations of Software Engineering*, ser. ESEC/FSE-13 (ACM, New York, NY, USA, 2005), pp. 187–196
3. L. Aversano, L. Cerulo, M. Di Penta, How clones are maintained: an empirical study, in *11th European Conference on Software Maintenance and Reengineering* (2007), pp. 81 –90
4. S. Thummalapenta, L. Cerulo, L. Aversano, M. Di Penta, An empirical study on the maintenance of source code clones. Empir. Softw. Eng. **15**, 1–34 (2010)
5. L. Barbour, L. An, F. Khomh, Y. Zou, S. Wang, An investigation of the fault-proneness of clone evolutionary patterns. Softw. Qual. J. **26**(4), 1187–1222 (2018)
6. N. Göde, R. Koschke, Incremental clone detection, in *13th European Conference on Software Maintenance and Reengineering* (IEEE, 2009), pp. 219–228
7. J. Svajlenko, C.K. Roy, Evaluating modern clone detection tools, in *2014 IEEE International Conference on Software Maintenance and Evolution* (IEEE, 2014), pp. 321–330
8. N. Göde, Evolution of type-1 clones, in *Proceedings of the 9th International Working Conference on Source Code Analysis and Manipulation* (IEEE Computer Society, 2009), pp. 77–86
9. J. Krinke, A study of consistent and inconsistent changes to code clones, in *Working Conference on Reverse Engineering* (2007), pp. 170–178
10. C.C.S., whatthepatch—python's third party patch parsing library Online. Accessed 17 Aug 2020
11. J. Śliwerski, T. Zimmermann, A. Zeller, When do changes induce fixes? ACM Sigsoft Softw. Eng. Notes **30**(4), 1–5 (2005)
12. M. Fischer, M. Pinzger, H. Gall, Populating a release history database from version control and bug tracking systems, in *International Conference on Software Maintenance, 2003. ICSM 2003. Proceedings* (IEEE, 2003), pp. 23–32
13. D. Sheskin, *Handbook of Parametric and Nonparametric Statistical Procedures*, 4th ed. (Chapman & Hall, 2007)
14. T. Chen, C. Guestrin, Xgboost: a scalable tree boosting system, in *Proceedings of the 22nd ACM SIGKDD International Conference on Knowledge Discovery and Data Mining* (2016), pp. 785–794
15. Z. Chen, F. Jiang, Y. Cheng, X. Gu, W. Liu, J. Peng, XGBoost classifier for DDoS attack detection and analysis in SDN-based cloud, in *IEEE International Conference on Big Data and Smart Computing (bigcomp)* (IEEE, 2018), pp. 251–256
16. S.S. Dhaliwal, A.-A. Nahid, R. Abbas, Effective intrusion detection system using xgboost. Information **9**(7), 149 (2018)
17. M. Abidi, M.S. Rahman, M. Openja, F. Khomh, Are multi-language design smells fault-prone? An empirical study

A Summary on the Stability of Code Clones and Current Research Trends

Manishankar Mondal, Chanchal K. Roy, and Kevin A. Schneider

Abstract Code clones are exactly or nearly similar code pieces in the source code files of a software system. These mainly get created because of the frequent copy/paste activities of the programmers during development. Many studies have been done on realizing the impacts of code clones on software evolution and maintenance. We performed a comprehensive study on clone stability in order to understand whether clone or non-clone code in a software system is more change-prone. Intuitively, code pieces with higher change-proneness (lower stability) will require higher maintenance effort and cost during software evolution. According to our study, code clones are more change-prone than non-clone code in general and thus, code clones are likely to require a higher maintenance effort and cost. We suggest that code clones should be managed with proper tool support so that we can get rid of their negative impacts and can get benefited from their positive impacts. This document provides a brief summary of our study on clone stability. It also discusses the studies that were done mostly after the publication of our study. Finally, it mentions some possible future works on the basis of the findings of the existing studies.

1 Summary of Our Study

Although code cloning (copy/pasting code fragments) seems to be a useful software engineering practice which is often employed by the programmers during programming, such a practice has mixed impacts on software maintenance according to the existing studies [8, 22, 28, 29, 34, 36, 38, 43, 44, 50, 51, 55]. Code cloning creates exactly or nearly similar code pieces known as code clones [71, 73] in the code-

M. Mondal (✉)
Khulna University, Khulna, Bangladesh
e-mail: mshankar@cseku.ac.bd

C. K. Roy · K. A. Schneider
University of Saskatchewan, Saskatoon, Canada
e-mail: chanchal.roy@usask.ca

K. A. Schneider
e-mail: kevin.schneider@usask.ca

base. While some of the studies [22, 28, 36, 38] found code clones to have positive impacts (such as faster development, reducing development cost, and code comprehension) on software development, there is strong empirical evidence [8, 29, 34, 43, 44, 50, 51, 55] of their negative impacts (such as higher instability, bug-proneness, and late-propagation tendency) too. Such a controversy among the existing studies is expected, because different studies investigated the impacts of code clones in different ways, on different experimental setups, and using different clone detection tools. In order to resolve the controversy among the existing studies, we perform a large-scale empirical study on the comparative stability of clone and non-clone code.

Stability has been defined by different studies [22, 28, 38, 44] in different ways. It generally measures the extent to which clone or non-clone code remains stable (unchanged) during evolution. The underlying idea behind our study [49] is that if clone code appears to be more stable than non-clone code during software evolution, code clones should be considered more beneficial because they introduce less changes as well as less maintenance effort than non-clone code. In our study, we divide the code-base of each of our subject systems into two parts. One part contains the clone code fragments and the other part contains the non-clone code fragments. We then determine the stability of these two parts of code fragments using different stability measuring metrics that were proposed and used by the existing studies. We implement all the metrics on the same experimental setup using two different clone detection tools: CCFinder [35] and NiCad [17]. We perform our investigations on thousands of revisions of 12 subject systems written in three different programming languages: Java, C, and C#. The systems are of diverse variety in terms of their application domains, sizes, and revision history lengths.

We found that seven of the existing studies on code clones have investigated clone stability. These studies have proposed and used eight stability measuring metrics. We list the studies and the corresponding metrics in Table 1. While these metrics were implemented and analyzed on different experimental setups in different studies, we implement all these metrics on the same experimental setup. The reason why we targeted the stability-related metrics is that these metrics can effectively capture the change-proneness of code fragments from different perspectives. In general, the more a code fragment gets changed, the higher is the maintenance effort it requires during evolution. After implementing the eight stability measuring metrics on the same experimental setup, we compare the stability of clone and non-clone code of the 12 subject systems. We perform our comparison by analyzing through four dimensions: (1) clone-type-centric analysis, (2) clone detection tool-centric analysis, (3) system-centric analysis, and (4) programming language-centric analysis.

In clone-type-centric analysis, we analyzed which type(s) of code clones appear to be more unstable during evolution. In clone detection tool-centric analysis, we investigated whether the clones detected by each of the clone detection tools (CCFinder and NiCad) exhibit a higher instability than non-clone code. In system-centric analysis, we wanted to see whether the code clones in each of our subject systems are more unstable than the corresponding non-clone code. Finally, in programming language-centric analysis, we analyzed whether each of our investigated programming languages (Java, C, and C#) individually suggests code clones to be more unstable than

Table 1 Studies on clone stability and the related metrics

Study	Investigated metrics
[28]	The metric called *Modification Frequency* was proposed by Hotta et al. [28] to see how many times the clone and non-clone regions get changed during evolution
[22]	The metric named *Modification Probability* was proposed by Göde and Harder [22] to quantify how many tokens are likely to get modified in clone and non-clone code regions
[40]	The metric *Average Last Change Date* of clone and non-clone code was proposed by Krinke [40]
[54]	Mondal et al. [54] proposed *Average Age* of clone and non-clone code to determine how long a fragment in a particular code region remains alive during evolution
[44]	Two metrics, *Impact* and *Likelihood*, of changes in clone and non-clone code were proposed by Lozano and Wermelinger [44]
[45]	The metric called *Average instability per cloned method due to clone and non-clone code* was proposed by Lozano and Wermelinger [45]
[56]	The metric *Dispersion of changes in clone and non-clone code* was proposed by Mondal et al. [56] to determine changes in which code region (clone or non-clone) is more scattered

non-clone code and code clones in which language(s) appear to be more unstable. According to our study [49], we have the following findings:

- Clone code generally appears to be more unstable than non-clone code during software evolution.
- Type 1 (exact clones) and Type 3 (gapped clones) clones exhibit higher instability than Type 2 clones (exact clones with renamed variables and changed data types).
- Code clones in the subject systems written in two of our investigated programming languages (Java and C) are more change-prone compared to the code clones in the subject systems implemented in C#.

As code clones generally appear to be more unstable than non-clone code during software evolution, proper tool support for managing code clones is important so that we can minimize their negative impacts and, at the same time, get benefited from their positive impacts. As Type 1 and Type 3 clones exhibit a higher instability than Type 2 clones, we should prioritize those two clone types (Types 1 and 3) when making clone management decisions.

2 Research Activities Done After the Publication of Our Study

Over the past few decades, the area of clone research has attracted a lot of investigations and studies. While some of these studies were done on clone detection techniques and tools [9, 13, 23, 35, 41, 42, 72], many of the remaining studies were done on analyzing the impacts of code clones [4–8, 25, 27, 36, 38, 39, 44] on software maintenance and evolution. The impact analysis studies were done in different directions. While a number of studies found code clones to be beneficial for software development and program comprehension, other studies discovered serious negative impacts of code clones on software evolution. As different studies obtained controversial outcomes regarding the impacts of code clones, we performed a comprehensive study on the comparative stability of clone and non-clone code. We found code clones to be more unstable than non-clone code during software evolution and maintenance. Thus, clone code requires more maintenance effort and cost in general.

After the publication of our study [49], a number of studies [30, 31, 50, 51, 63] have shown empirical evidence of negative impacts of code clones such as bug replication through code cloning, higher bug-proneness of code clones than non-clone code, context adaptation bugs in code clones, bug-propagation through code cloning, and late propagation tendencies of code clones and the related bugs. Mainly considering the harmful impacts of code clones, clone researchers now suggest to manage code clones through some clone maintenance activities such as clone refactoring [82, 89] and tracking [19, 33].

Clone refactoring is the task of removing code clones from the code-base through merging. A lot of studies [4, 5, 16, 25, 26, 74, 85, 86, 91] have been done on clone refactoring. Some of these studies [12, 89, 90] investigated scheduling the task of clone refactoring in order to optimize the refactoring gain. Some studies [26, 81] suggested different patterns for refactoring clones. A number of studies [57, 58] have also investigated finding code clones that are important for refactoring and identifying useful clone refactoring patterns through mining clone evolutionary history. Some of the studies [46, 82] have also investigated automatic and semi-automatic refactoring of code clones and developed promising tools on the basis of the investigations. Clone refactoring using lambda expressions [83] has also been recently investigated.

Clone tracking means remembering code clones in the clone classes through evolution. In the presence of a clone tracker, whenever a programmer attempts to make some changes to a clone fragment, the other fragments in the same clone class will be notified to the programmer. The programmer then decides whether these other clone fragments in the same clone class also need to be modified similarly. Clone tracking has also been investigated by a number of studies [19–21, 33, 80] resulting in a number of clone trackers such as Clone Notifier [80], CCSync [15], JSync [67], gCad [75], and Clone-Tracker [20]. These clone trackers are capable of tracking clone genealogies and can work on different clone types. One study [57] has also investigated identifying code clones that can be considered important for tracking on the basis of clone evolutionary history.

Researchers have also investigated devising history-based change suggestion techniques [37, 60, 68, 69] on the basis of code clones. A change that previously occurred in a particular code fragment might be necessary for a similar code fragment in the recent revision of the code-base. Some existing studies [68, 69] have investigated providing change suggestions considering fragment-level code similarity. One study

[60] has also explored the possibility of providing method-level change suggestions by considering method-level clones detected by the NiCad [17] clone detector.

Currently, researchers are also investigating how to use code clones for improving association rule mining-based co-change suggestion techniques [1, 14, 52]. A recent study [66] has investigated a number of clone detectors in order to identify which detectors are the most efficient ones for suggesting cloned co-change candidates.

A number of studies [77, 88] have been done on detecting semantic clones and cross-language clones [2]. A recent study [3] has also established a benchmark dataset for evaluating semantic clone detectors. Semantic clone detection techniques are still at a very early stage. Currently, researchers are conducting studies and proposing different techniques for detecting semantic clones.

A number of studies [32, 76] have been done on devising clone detectors that can run on big-code (very large code-base). A very big dataset called BigCloneBench [78] has been established for evaluating clone detectors. A mutation and injection framework for evaluating clone detectors has been developed [79]. Researchers have investigated how to use machine learning techniques for designing cloud-based automatic clone validation tools [64, 65].

Researchers have also investigated the importance of micro-clones [10, 61, 84] during software evolution. Micro-clones are similar code fragments that are smaller than the minimum size of the regular code clones. Existing studies [30, 53, 61] have investigated micro-clones of at most four lines of code. It has been shown that the number of micro-clones is much higher than regular code clones in software systems [61]. Also, micro-clones are often more bug-prone than regular clones [30]. The recent studies [53, 61] have discovered that micro-clones require consistent updates like the regular clones during evolution. Thus, the necessity of managing micro-clones has been established.

Researchers have also studied inconsistent changes in code clones [11, 38, 62]. After experiencing inconsistent changes, the code clones can undergo mutation and migration [87]. Studies [11, 62] show that the inconsistent changes in code clones can lead to bugs and inconsistencies in software systems. Inconsistent changes in Type 3 clones have the highest possibility of introducing bugs in the code-base compared to Type 1 and Type 2 clones [62].

Some studies [47, 48] have investigated clone visualization techniques. Clone visualization can be useful for making clone management decisions. The existing techniques [24, 47, 48, 70] can help us visualize the genealogies of clone fragments in a code-base, locate areas in the code-base that have code clones with a high density, identify which changes in code clones introduced bugs in the code-base, and analyze how to resolve clone-related bugs. Some of the studies have also investigated clone differentiation mechanisms to assist in clone refactoring.

The following section mentions a number of future research directions on the basis of the existing studies.

3 Future Research Directions

3.1 Investigation on Refactoring and Tracking of Micro-clones

As we have already discussed, micro-clones have been recently investigated by a number of studies [10, 61, 84]. Micro-clones also need to be managed like the regular code clones during software evolution. A number of refactoring techniques for refactoring regular code clones exist. However, refactoring of micro-clones has not yet been explored. Investigation in this direction can add value to the existing knowledge on clone refactoring. Generally, there can be a large number of micro-clones in a software system. Thus, identifying micro-clones that should be considered important for refactoring is a promising future work as well.

Tracking of micro-clones has also not been investigated yet by the existing studies. A number of tracking techniques for tracking regular clones currently exists. It is important to investigate whether these existing techniques are also suitable for tracking micro-clones. Clone tracking requires detecting clone genealogies. As there are too many micro-clones in a software system, the existing genealogy detection techniques might not be feasible for micro-clones. Thus, investigation toward detecting genealogies of micro-clones can also be an important future work.

3.2 Identifying Bugs and Devising Fix Patterns for both Regular- and Micro-clones

Many existing studies [18, 29, 43, 59] have discovered bugs related to regular code clones. However, bugs in micro-clones have not been explored that much. It is important to investigate whether micro-clones also take part in replicating and propagating bugs. We still do not know whether micro-clones can contain context adaptation bugs like the regular clones. An investigation in this direction can add value to the existing research on code clones. It is also important to explore possibilities for automatically fixing clone-related bugs. Investigation on identifying patterns for fixing particular bugs related to clones can be a promising direction of research.

3.3 Comparative Stability of Regular- and Micro-clones

Existing studies [22, 28, 55] have compared the stability of clone and non-clone code. However, there is no study comparing the stability of regular- and micro-clones. Such a study can discover which clone type (regular- or micro-clones) is more change-prone during evolution and, as a result, requires more maintenance effort and cost. That particular clone type can be managed with a higher priority.

3.4   Industrialization of Clone Management Techniques

Although there are a lot of studies on clone detection and management (refactoring and tracking), the detection and management techniques have not yet been industrialized that much. Future studies on industrializing clone techniques can be very important for the clone research community. Studies can be done on realizing the opinions of the professional developers regarding code clones and their management. Some studies can be done to demonstrate to the developers how the consideration of code clones and related techniques can be useful during software development.

3.5   Minimizing Testing Effort After Clone Refactoring

After clone refactoring, the refactored code needs to be checked to see if the code is giving the expected output. If testing the refactored code requires a huge amount of time and effort, the task of refactoring might not appear to be useful to the programmers. Thus, devising automated tests for the refactored code on the basis of the existing tests can be an important direction of research. The possibility of automatic tests after clone refactoring can make refactoring promising to the programmers. Moreover, it would be very interesting if the benefits of refactoring can be quantified after implementing a clone refactoring task.

3.6   Investigating Programmer Sensitivity of Cloned Co-change Candidates

An existing study [66] reports that the precision and recall in suggesting cloned co-change candidates are generally very low. Toward improving the detection accuracy of cloned co-change candidates, it is important to investigate whether such candidates are sensitive to programmers. In other words, it would be interesting to see if a programmer generally wants to make changes only to those clone fragments that are created by himself. If a project is being developed by two or more programmers, it can be a general tendency that each programmer will take care of the code written by that programmer. An investigation in this direction can be useful in suggesting cloned co-change candidates.

4　Conclusion

This document contains a summary of our study [49] on clone stability and a brief history of research activities that were conducted in the area of code clones mostly after our study. We see that a great many studies have been done on clone detection, analysis, and management (such as clone refactoring and tracking). We also mention a number of future research directions on the basis of our study findings and believe that investigations in these directions can enrich the existing knowledge on the impacts of code clones and their management.

References

1. R. Agrawal, T. Imieliski, A. Swami, Mining association rules between sets of items in large databases, in *ACM SIGMOD International Conference on Management of Data (ACM SIGMOD'93)*, vol. 22, issue 2 (1993), pp 207–216
2. F. Al-omari, I. Keivanloo, C.K. Roy, J. Rilling, Detecting clones across microsoft .net programming languages, in *Proceedings of the International Working Conference on Reverse Engineering (WCRE'12)* (2012), pp. 405–414
3. F. Al-Omari, C.K. Roy, T. Chen. Semanticclonebench: a semantic code clone benchmark using crowd-source knowledge, in *IWSC* (2020), pp. 57–63
4. M. Balazinska, E. Merlo, M. Dagenais, K. Kontogiannis, Advanced clone-analysis to support object-oriented system refactoring, in *Proceedings of the 7th Working Conference on Reverse Engineering (WCRE'00)* (2000), pp. 98–107
5. M. Balazinska, E. Merlo, M. Dagenais, B. Lagüe, K. Kontogiannis, Measuring clone based reengineering opportunities, in *Proceedings of the 6th International Symposium on Software Metrics (METRICS'99)* (1999), pp. 292–303
6. M. Balazinska, E. Merlo, M. Dagenais, B. Lagüe, K. Kontogiannis, Partial redesign of Java software systems based on clone analysis, in *Proceedings of the 6th Working Conference on Reverse Engineering (WCRE'99)* (1999), pp. 326–336
7. L. Barbour, F. Khomh, Y. Zou, Late propagation in software clones, in *Proceedings of the 27th IEEE International Conference on Software Maintenance (ICSM'11)* (2011), pp. 273–282
8. L. Barbour, F. Khomh, Y. Zou, An empirical study of faults in late propagation clone genealogies. J. Softw.: Evol. Process. **25**(11), 1139–1165 (2013)
9. I. Baxter, A. Yahin, L. Moura, M. Sant'Anna, L. Bier, Clone detection using abstract syntax trees, in *Proceedings of the International Conference on Software Maintenance (ICSM'98)* (1998), pp. 368–378
10. M. Beller, A. Zaidman, A. Karpov, The last line effect, in *ICPC* (2015), pp. 240–243
11. N. Bettenburg, W. Shang, W. Ibrahim, B. Adams, Y. Zou, A.E. Hassan, An empirical study on inconsistent changes to code clones at release level, in *WCRE* (2009), pp. 85–94
12. S. Bouktif, G. Antoniol, M. Neteler, E. Merlo, A novel approach to optimize clone refactoring activity, in *Proceedings of the 8th Annual Conference on Genetic and Evolutionary Computation (GECCO'06)* (2006), pp. 1885–1892
13. C. Brown, S. Thompson, Clone detection and elimination for Haskell, in *Proceedings of the 2010 ACM SIGPLAN workshop on Partial Evaluation and Program Manipulation (PEPM'10)* (2010), pp. 111–120
14. G. Canfora, M. Ceccarelli, L. Cerulo, M.D. Penta, Using multivariate time series and association rules to detect logical change coupling: an empirical study, in *Proceedings of the IEEE International Conference on Software Maintenance (ICSM'10)* (2010), pp. 1–10

15. X. Cheng, H. Zhong, Y. Chen, Z. Hu, J. Zhao, Rule-directed code clone synchronization, in *ICPC* (2016), pp. 1–10
16. E. Choi, N. Yoshida, T. Ishio, K. Inoue, T. Sano, Extracting code clones for refactoring using combinations of clone metrics, in *Proceedings of the 5th International Workshop on Software Clones (IWSC'11)* (2011), pp. 7–13
17. J.R. Cordy, C.K. Roy, The NiCad clone detector, in *Proceedings of the 2011 IEEE 19th International Conference on Program Comprehension (ICPC' 11)* (2011), pp. 219–220
18. N. Göde, D. Steidl, Feature-based detection of bugs in clones, in *Proceedings of the 7th International Workshop on Software Clones (IWSC'13)* (2013), pp. 76–82
19. E. Duala-Ekoko, M.P. Robillard, Tracking code clones in evolving software, in *Proceedings of the 29th International Conference on Software Engineering (ICSE'07)* (2007), pp. 158–167
20. E. Duala-Ekoko, M.P. Robillard, Clonetracker: tool support for code clone management, in *Proceedings of the 30th International Conference on Software Engineering (ICSE'08)* (2008), pp. 843–846
21. E. Duala-Ekoko, M.P. Robillard, Clone region descriptors: representing and tracking duplication in source code. ACM Trans. Softw. Eng. Methodol. **20**(1), 1–31 (2010)
22. N. Göde, J. Harder, Clone stability, in *Proceedings of the 15th European Conference on Software Maintenance and Reengineering (CSMR'11)* (2011), pp. 65–74
23. N. Göde, R. Koschke, Incremental clone detection, in *Proceedings of the 13th European Conference on Software Maintenance and Reengineering (CSMR'09)* (2009), pp. 219–228
24. J. Harder, N. Göde, Efficiently handling clone data: RCF and cyclone, in *Proceedings of the 5th International Workshop on Software Clones (IWSC'11)* (2011), pp. 81–82
25. Y. Higo, T. Kamiya, S. Kusumoto, K. Inoue, Refactoring support based on code clone analysis. Prod. Focus. Softw. Process. Improv. (LNCS 3009):220–233 (2004)
26. Y. Higo, T. Kamiya, S. Kusumoto, K. Inoue, ARIES: refactoring support tool for code clone, in *Proceedings of the 3rd Workshop on Software Quality (3-WoSQ'05)* (2005) pp. 1–4
27. Y. Higo, S. Kusumoto, K. Inoue, A metric-based approach to identifying refactoring opportunities for merging code clones in a Java software system. J. Softw. Maint. Evol.: Res. Pract. **20**, 435–461 (2008)
28. K. Hotta, Y. Sano, Y. Higo, S. Kusumoto, Is duplicate code more frequently modified than non-duplicate code in software evolution?: an empirical study on open source software, in *Proceedings of the International Workshop on Principles of Software Evolution (IWPSE'10)* (2010), pp. 73–82
29. J.F. Islam, M. Mondal, C.K. Roy, Bug replication in code clones: an empirical study, in *Proceedings of the 23rd IEEE International Conference on Software Analysis, Evolution, and Reengineering (SANER'16)* (2016), pp. 68–78
30. J.F. Islam, M. Mondal, C.K. Roy, A comparative study of software bugs in micro-clones and regular code clones, in *SANER* (2019), pp. 73–83
31. J.F. Islam, M. Mondal, C.K. Roy, K. Schneider, Comparing bug replication in regular and micro code clones, in *ICPC* (2019), pp. 81–92
32. C.K. Roy, J. Svajlenko, Fast and flexible large-scale clone detection with cloneworks, in *ICSE-C* (2017), pp. 27–30
33. P. Jablonski, D. Hou, CReN: a tool for tracking copy-and-paste code clones and renaming identifiers consistently in the ide, in *Proceedings of the 2007 OOPSLA Workshop on Eclipse Technology Exchange (OOPSLA'07)* (2007), pp. 16–20
34. L. Jiang, Z. Su, E. Chiu, Context-based detection of clone-related bugs, in *Proceedings of the 6th Joint Meeting of the European Software Engineering Conference and the ACM SIGSOFT Symposium on the Foundations of Software Engineering (ESEC-FSE'07)* (2007), pp. 55–64
35. T. Kamiya, S. Kusumoto, K. Inoue, CCFinder: a multilinguistic token-based code clone detection system for large scale source code. IEEE Trans. Softw. Eng. **28**(7), 654–670 (2002)
36. C. Kapser, M.W. Godfrey, Cloning considered harmful considered harmful: patterns of cloning in software. Empir. Softw. Eng. J. **13**(6), 645–692 (2008)
37. D. Kim, J. Nam, J. Song, S. Kim, Automatic patch generation learned from human-written patches, in *ICSE* (2013), pp. 802–811

38. J. Krinke, A study of consistent and inconsistent changes to code clones, in *Proceedings of the 14th Working Conference on Reverse Engineering (WCRE'07)* (2007), pp. 170–178

39. J. Krinke, Is cloned code more stable than non-cloned code?, in *Proceedings of the 8th IEEE International Working Conference on Source Code Analysis and Manipulation (SCAM'08)* (2008), pp. 57–66

40. J. Krinke. Is cloned code older than non-cloned code?, in *Proceedings of the 5th International Workshop on Software Clones (IWSC'11)* (2011), pp. 28–33

41. H. Li, S. Thompson, Clone detection and removal for Erlang/OTP within a refactoring environment, in *Proceedings of the 2009 ACM SIGPLAN Workshop on Partial Evaluation and Program Manipulation (PEPM'09)* (2009), pp. 169–177

42. H. Li, S. Thompson, Incremental clone detection and elimination for Erlang programs, in *Proceedings of the 14th International Conference on Fundamental Approaches to Software Engineering (FASE'11)* (2011), pp. 356–370

43. J. Li, M.D. Ernst, CBCD: cloned buggy code detector, in *Proceedings of the 34th International Conference on Software Engineering (ICSE'12)* (2012), pp. 310–320

44. A. Lozano, M. Wermelinger, Assessing the effect of clones on changeability, in *Proceedings of the IEEE International Conference on Software Maintenance (ICSM'08)* (2008), pp. 227–236

45. A. Lozano, M. Wermelinger, Tracking clones' imprint, in *Proceedings of the 4th International Workshop on Software Clones (IWSC'10)* (2010), pp. 65–72

46. N. Meng, L. Hua, M. Kim, K.S. McKinley, Does automated refactoring obviate systematic editing?, in *Proceedings of the 37th International Conference on Software Engineering (ICSE'15)* (2015), pp. 392–402

47. D. Mondal, M. Mondal, C.K. Roy, K.A. Schneider, S. Wang, Y. Li, Clone-world: a visual analytic system for large scale software clones, in *PacificVAST* (2019), pp. 1–11

48. D. Mondal, M. Mondal, C.K. Roy, K.A. Schneider, S. Wang, Y. Li, Towards visualizing large scale evolving clones, in *ICSE Poster Track* (2019), pp. 1–4

49. M. Mondal, M.S. Rahman, C.K. Roy, K.A. Schneider, Is cloned code really stable? Empir. Softw. Eng. **23**(2), 693–770 (2018)

50. M. Mondal, B. Roy, C.K. Roy, K.A. Schneider, An empirical study on bug propagation through code cloning. J. Syst. Softw. (2019)

51. M. Mondal, B. Roy, C.K. Roy, K.A. Schneider, Investigating context adaptation bugs in code clones, in *ICSME* (2019), pp. 157–168

52. M. Mondal, B. Roy, C.K. Roy, K.A. Schneider, Associating code clones with association rules for change impact analysis, in *SANER* (2020), pp. 93–103

53. M. Mondal, B. Roy, C.K. Roy, K.A. Schneider, Investigating near-miss micro-clones in evolving software, in *ICPC* (2020), p. 11

54. M. Mondal, C.K. Roy, M.S. Rahman, R.K. Saha, J. Krinke, K.A. Schneider, Comparative stability of cloned and non-cloned code: an empirical study, in *Proceedings of the 27th Annual ACM Symposium on Applied Computing (SAC'12)* (2012), pp. 1227–1234

55. M. Mondal, C.K. Roy, K.A. Schneider, An empirical study on clone stability. ACM SIGAPP Appl. Comput. Rev. **12**(3), 20–36 (2012)

56. M. Mondal, C.K. Roy, K.A. Schneider, Dispersion of changes in cloned and non-cloned code, in *IWSC* (2012), pp. 29–35

57. M. Mondal, C.K. Roy, K.A. Schneider, Automatic identification of important clones for refactoring and tracking, in *Proceedings of the IEEE 14th International Working Conference on Source Code Analysis and Manipulation (SCAM'14)* (2014), pp. 11–20

58. M. Mondal, C.K. Roy, K.A. Schneider, Automatic ranking of clones for refactoring through mining association rules, in *Proceedings of the IEEE Conference on Software Maintenance, Reengineering and Reverse Engineering (CSMR-WCRE'14), Software Evolution Week* (2014), pp. 114–123

59. M. Mondal, C.K. Roy, K.A. Schneider, A comparative study on the bug-proneness of different types of code clones, in *Proceedings of the 31st IEEE International Conference on Software Maintenance and Evolution (ICSME'15)* (2015), pp. 91–100

60. M. Mondal, C.K. Roy, K.A. Schneider, An exploratory study on change suggestions for methods using clone detection, in *CASCON* (2016), pp. 85–95
61. M. Mondal, C.K. Roy, K.A. Schneider, Micro-clones in evolving software, in *SANER* (2018), pp. 50–60
62. M. Mondal, C.K. Roy, K.A. Schneider, A fine-grained analysis on the inconsistent changes in code clones, in *ICSME* (2020), pp. 220–231
63. Manishankar Mondal, Chanchal K. Roy, Kevin A. Schneider, Bug-proneness and late propagation tendency of code clones: a comparative study on different clone types. J. Syst. Softw. **144**, 41–59 (2018)
64. G. Mostaeen, J. Svajlenko, B. Roy, C.K. Roy, K.A. Schneider, On the use of machine learning techniques towards the design of cloud based automatic code clone validation tools, in *SCAM* (2018), pp. 155–164
65. G. Mostaeen, J. Svajlenko, B. Roy, C.K. Roy, K.A. Schneider, Clonecognition: machine learning based code clone validation tool, in *FSE* (2019), pp. 1105–1109
66. M. Nadim, M. Mondal, C.K. Roy, Evaluating performance of clone detection tools in detecting cloned co-change candidates, in *IWSC* (2020), pp. 15–21
67. H. Nguyen, T. Nguyen, N. Pham, J. Al-Kofahi, T. Nguyen, Clone management for evolving software. IEEE Trans. Softw. Eng. **38**(5), 1008–1026 (2011)
68. H.A. Nguyen, A.T. Nguyen, T.T. Nguyen, T.N. Nguyen, H. Rajan, A study of repetitiveness of code changes in software evolution, in *ASE* (2013), pp. 180–190
69. B. Ray, M. Nagappan, C. Bird, N. Nagappan, T. Zimmermann, The uniqueness of changes: characteristics and applications, in *Microsoft Research Technical Report* (2014), pp. 1–10
70. D. Reniers, L. Voinea, O. Ersoy, A. Telea, A visual analytics toolset for program structure, metrics, and evolution comprehension, in *International, Workshop on Advanced/Academic Software Development Tools and Techniques* (2010)
71. C.K. Roy, Detection and analysis of near-miss software clones, in *Proceedings of the Doctoral Symposium Track of the 25th IEEE International Conference on Software Maintenance (ICSM'09)* (2009), pp. 447–450
72. C.K. Roy, J.R. Cordy, NICAD: accurate detection of near-miss intentional clones using flexible pretty-printing and code normalization, in *Proceedings of the 16th IEEE International Conference on Program Comprehension (ICPC'08)* (2008), pp. 172–181
73. C.K. Roy, M.F. Zibran, R. Koschke, The vision of software clone management: past, present, and future (keynote paper), in *Proceedings of the IEEE Conference on Software Maintenance, Reengineering and Reverse Engineering (CSMR-WCRE'14), Software Evolution Week* (2014), pp. 18–33
74. V. Rysselberghe, S. Demeyer, Evaluating clone detection techniques from a refactoring perspective, in *Proceedings of the 19th IEEE International Conference on Automated Software Engineering (ASE'04)* (2004), pp. 336–339
75. R.K. Saha, C.K. Roy, K.A. Schneider, An automatic framework for extracting and classifying near-miss clone genealogies, in *Proceedings of the 27th IEEE International Conference on Software Maintenance (ICSM'11)* (2011), pp. 293–302
76. H. Sajnani, V. Saini, J. Svajlenko, C.K. Roy, C.V. Lopes, SourcererCC: scaling code clone detection to big-code, in *Proceedings of the 38th International Conference on Software Engineering (ICSE'16)* (2016), pp. 1157–1168
77. A. Sheneamer, J. Kalita, Semantic clone detection using machine learning, in *ICMLA* (2016), pp. 1024–1028
78. J. Svajlenko, C.K. Roy, Evaluating clone detection tools with bigclonebench, in *Proceedings of the 31st International Conference on Software Maintenance and Evolution (ICSME'15)* (2015), pp. 131–140
79. J. Svajlenko, C.K. Roy, The mutation and injection framework: evaluating clone detection tools with mutation analysis. IEEE Trans. Softw. Eng. 1 (2019)
80. S. Tokui, N. Yoshida, E. Choi, K. Inoue, Clone notifier: developing and improving the system to notify changes of code clones, in *SANER* (2020), pp. 642–646

81. M. Tokunaga, N. Yoshida, K. Yoshioka, M. Matsushita, K. Inoue, Towards a collection of refactoring patterns based on code clone categorization, in *Proceedings of the 2nd Asian Conference on Pattern Languages of Programs (AsianPLoP'11)* (2011), pp. 1–6

82. N. Tsantalis, D. Mazinanian, G.P. Krishnan, Assessing the refactorability of software clones. IEEE Trans. Softw. Eng. **41**(11), 1055–1090 (2015)

83. N. Tsantalis, D. Mazinanian, S. Rostami, Clone refactoring with lambda expressions, in *ICSE* (2017), pp. 60–70

84. R. van Tonder, C. Le Goues, Defending against the attack of the micro-clones, in *ICPC* (2016), pp. 1–4

85. W. Wang, M.W. Godfrey, Investigating intentional clone refactoring. Electron. Commun. EASST **63**, 1–7 (2014)

86. W. Wang, M.W. Godfrey, Recommending clones for refactoring using design, context, and history, in *Proceedings of the 2014 IEEE International Conference on Software Maintenance and Evolution (ICSME'14)* (2014), pp. 331–340

87. S. Xie, F. Khomh, Y. Zou, An empirical study of the fault-proneness of clone mutation and clone migration, in *Proceedings of the 10th Working Conference on Mining Software Repositories (MSR'13)* (2013), pp. 149–158

88. H. Yu, W. Lam, L. Chen, G. Li, T. Xie, Q. Wang, Neural detection of semantic code clones via tree-based convolution, in *ICPC* (2019), pp. 1–11

89. M.F. Zibran, C.K. Roy, Conflict-aware optimal scheduling of code clone refactoring: a constraint programming approach, in *Proceedings of the 19th IEEE International Conference on Program Comprehension (ICPC'11)* (IEEE, 2011), pp. 266–269

90. M.F. Zibran, C.K. Roy, Conflict-aware optimal scheduling of prioritised code clone refactoring. IET Softw. **7**(3), 167–186 (2013)

91. M.F. Zibran, R.K. Saha, C.K. Roy, K.A. Schneider, Genealogical insights into the facts and fictions of clone removal. Appl. Comput. Rev. **13**(4), 30–42 (2013)

Applying Clone Technology in Practice

Identifying Refactoring-Oriented Clones and Inferring How They Can Be Merged

Yoshiki Higo

Abstract Our research group has been working on code clones for more than 20 years. In this chapter, I review our work on merging clones published in 2008 (Higo et al. in J Soft Mainten Evolut 20:435–461, 2008 [3]), introduce two subsequent studies, and discuss prospects for future research.

1 Introduction

First of all, I would like to thank Prof. Katsuro Inoue at Osaka University and Prof. Chanchal Roy at the University of Saskatchewan for giving me the opportunity to reflect on the research in literature [3]. The literature is about identifying refactoring-oriented clones and inferring how they can be merged, which was my first research project. The results were finally accepted for publication in the Journal of Software Maintenance and Evolution: Research and Practice[1] in 2008 [3]. It is hard to believe that it has already been 12 years since literature [3] was published.

I began my research on merging clones in 2002 when I was a first-year master's student. At that time, the research group I belonged to had a tool called CCFinder [5], which enabled us to detect clones in a short time even from large-scale software. Our research group applied CCFinder to a variety of software and found that all of the software contained clones, and in some cases, more than half of the code was cloned. Also, at the time, the existence of all clones was thought to be evil. However, since CCFiner detected matching token sequences in the source code as clones, it was difficult to merge many of the detected clones into one. Therefore, we had started a research project to provide merging assistance to the clones found by CCFinder. The final results of this research are literature [3].

---

[1]The journal changed its name in 2012 and is now called the Journal of Software: Evolution and Process.

Y. Higo (✉)
Osaka University, 1-5, Yamadaoka, Suita, Osaka 565-0871, Japan
e-mail: higo@ist.osaka-u.ac.jp

In this chapter, we describe the merging assistance for clones that we proposed in literature [3] and present two subsequent research studies conducted by our research group. We also conclude with future perspectives on merging clones.

2 Assisting Developers in Merging Clones

In literature [3], we proposed a technique to assist developers in merging clones in Java source code. The technique includes the following three steps, and it tells developers which clones and how they can be merged.

STEP-1   it detects clones in a given target system.
STEP-2   it extracts mergeable parts in general clones.
STEP-3   it characterizes mergeable parts with quantitative metrics.

The remainder of this section explains each of the steps in detail.

2.1   Detecting General Clones

In this step, this technique detects clones using an existing clone detection technique. It is advisable to use a detection tool that can detect at least Type-2 clones because developers often introduce small changes to copied code fragments after they perform copying and pasting operations. We intended to support to merge clones that are made by copying and pasting operations. In our implementation of this technique, we used **CCFinder** [5]. In literature [3], we called clones detected by clone detection techniques *general clones*.

2.2   Extracting Mergeable Parts in Clones

In this step, this technique extracts cohesive structural parts included in general clones. The extracted parts are easier to merge than general clones themselves because they are structural units of programming language. Since the system that we developed based on the technique is arranged for Java language, the following structural cohesive parts included in general clones are extracted.

Declaration   class, interface
Function   method, constructor, static initializer
Block   do, for, if, switch, synchronized, try, while.

In literature [3], we called extracted parts *refactoring-oriented clones*. Figure 1 shows that refactoring-oriented clones are more suitable to be merged than general clones. This figure shows general clones detected by **CCFinder**. The try-catch blocks in the

```
        throw new BuildException(msg);                          searchForThis = DEFAULT_BUILD_FILENAME;
    }                                                       }
} else if (arg.equals("-listener")) {                   } else if (arg.startsWith("-propertyfile")) {
    try {                                                   try {
        listeners.addElement(args[i + 1]);                      propertyFiles.addElement(args[i + 1]);
        i++;                                                    i++;
    } catch (ArrayIndexOutOfBoundsException aioobe) {       } catch (ArrayIndexOutOfBoundsException aioobe) {
        String msg = "You must specify a classname when "       String msg = "You must specify a property filename when "
                + "using the -listener argument";                        + "using the -propertyfile argument";
        throw new BuildException(msg);                          throw new BuildException(msg);
    }                                                       }
} else if (arg.startsWith("-D")) {                      } else if (arg.equals("-k") || arg.equals("-keep-going")) {
/* Interestingly enough, we get to here when a user         keepGoingMode = true;
```

(a) General clones

```
        throw new BuildException(msg);                          searchForThis = DEFAULT_BUILD_FILENAME;
    }                                                       }
} else if (arg.equals("-listener")) {                   } else if (arg.startsWith("-propertyfile")) {
    try {                                                   try {
        listeners.addElement(args[i + 1]);                      propertyFiles.addElement(args[i + 1]);
        i++;                                                    i++;
    } catch (ArrayIndexOutOfBoundsException aioobe) {       } catch (ArrayIndexOutOfBoundsException aioobe) {
        String msg = "You must specify a classname when "       String msg = "You must specify a property filename when "
                + "using the -listener argument";                        + "using the -propertyfile argument";
        throw new BuildException(msg);                          throw new BuildException(msg);
    }                                                       }
} else if (arg.startsWith("-D")) {                      } else if (arg.equals("-k") || arg.equals("-keep-going")) {
/* Interestingly enough, we get to here when a user         keepGoingMode = true;
```

(b) Refactoring-oriented clones

Fig. 1 General clones and refactoring-oriented clones

clones include common instructions, while the clones also include a few extra instructions before and after the try-catch blocks. The presence of such extra statements in the clones makes it difficult to merge the clones into a new single method.

At present (at the time when I'm writing this chapter), there are many tools that detect clones at method-level or block level. If we use such tools instead of CCFinder, general clones are the same as refactoring-oriented clones, which means we can omit this step.

2.3 Characterizing Mergeable Parts

In this step, this technique characterizes refactoring-oriented clones with two viewpoints.

First viewpoint: position relationship in the class hierarchy

Java is an object-oriented programming language, which means the distance between clones in class hierarchy strongly affects how they can be merged. Figure 2 illustrates three examples.

Case 1 if clones exists in a single class, they can be merged as a new method in the same class (see Fig. 2a).

Case 2 if clones exist in different classes that are derived from the same class, they can be pulled up to the common base class (see Fig. 2b).

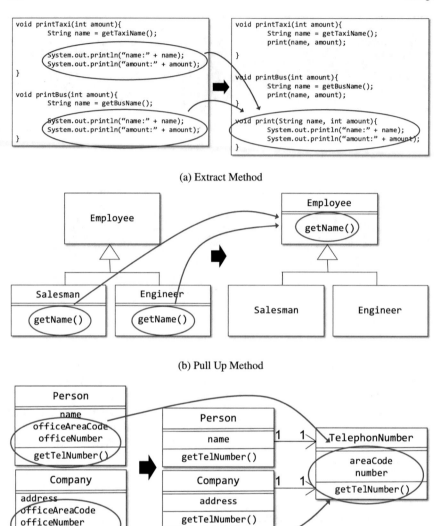

(a) Extract Method

(b) Pull Up Method

(c) Extract Class

Fig. 2 Examples of merging clones

Case 3   if clones are scattered across multiple classes, creating a new class is a way to merge the clones (see Fig. 2c). In Fig. 2c, new class *TelephonNumber* is created, and then the duplicated function in *getTelNumber* is delegated to the new method in the new class. A new class can be created as a common base class of the classes including the clones, unless the classes are already inherited from another class.

This technique utilizes the position relationship of given clones in the class hierarchy to automatically infer how they can be merged. We designed a new metric $DCH(C)^2$ for a given clone class C as follows to represent their position relationship quantitatively. Herein, we assume that clone class C includes code fragments $f_1, f_2, \ldots, f_n$ and class c_i includes code fragment f_i.

- If all of $c_1, c_2, \ldots, c_n$ represent the same class (in Case 1), $DCH(C)$ becomes 0.
- If classes $c_1, c_2, \ldots, c_n$ represent different classes but all of them are derived from common base class c_p (in Case 2), $DCH(C)$ becomes the maximum number of hops from $c_i (1 \leq i \leq n)$ to c_p in the class hierarchy.
- If classes $c_1, c_2, \ldots, c_n$ do not share a common base class, $DCH(C)$ becomes ∞.

The formula for metric $DCH(C)$ are represented as follows:

$$DCH(C) = \begin{cases} 0 & (in\ Case\ 1) \\ max\{D(c_1, c_p), D(c_2, c_p), \cdots, d(c_n, c_p)\} & (in\ Case\ 2) \\ \infty & (in\ Case\ 3), \end{cases} \quad (1)$$

where $D(c_i, c_p)$ represents the number of hops from $c_i (1 \leq i \leq n)$ to c_p in the class hierarchy. If c_i is the same as c_p, $D(c_i, c_p)$ is set as 0.

$DCH(C)$ becomes large as the degree of the dispersion of C becomes extended. If all code fragments in C exist in a single class, $DCH(C)$ is set as 0. If all code fragments in C are in a class and its direct child classes, $DCH(C)$ is set to 1. This metric is measured for only the class hierarchy of the target project because it is unrealistic to pull up application code to libraries such as JDK.

Second viewpoint: coupling between a clone and its surrounding code
As mentioned before, the basic strategy for merging clones is migrating clones to another place in the source code. To migrate a code fragment to another place, it is desirable that the code fragment has low coupling with its surrounding code.

Herein we assume that *Extract Method* refactoring is to be performed. To apply this refactoring pattern, the smaller the number of externally defined variables that are used (referenced and assigned) in the code fragment, the easier it is to migrate the code fragment to another place. If externally defined variables are used in the target code fragment, it is necessary to provide the variables as parameters to the newly extracted method. To automatically infer the ease of code migration, the degree of

---

[2] DCH means Dispersion in the Class Hierarchy.

coupling is presented as two quantitative metrics *the Number of Referenced Variables* ($NRV(C)$) and *the Number of Assigned Variables* ($NAV(C)$).

Herein, we assume that clone class C includes code fragments $f_1, f_2, \ldots, f_n$. Code fragment f_i references s_i number of variables that are defined outside the code fragment, and it assigns to t_i number of variables defined outside the code fragment. Two metrics $NRV(C)$ and $NAV(C)$ are represented as follows.

$$NRV(C) = \frac{1}{n}\sum_{i=1}^{n} s_i, \qquad NAV(C) = \frac{1}{n}\sum_{i=1}^{n} t_i. \qquad (2)$$

$NRV(C)$ represents the average of externally defined variables referenced in the code fragments that belong to clone class C. In the same way, $NAV(C)$ represents the average of externally defined variables assigned in the code fragments.

If refactoring-oriented clones described in Sect. 2.2 are Type-1 or Type-2 clones, both s_i and $t_i (1 \leq i \leq n)$ are always identical among the clones in the same clone class. In such a case, those metrics can be represented as follows:

$$NRV(C) = s_1 = s_2 = \cdots = s_n, \qquad NAV(C) = t_1 = t_2 = \cdots = t_n. \qquad (3)$$

If the refactoring-oriented clones are Type-3 clones, s_i/t_i can be different from $s_j/t_j (1 \leq i, j \leq n, i \neq j)$. In such a case, the definitions of Formula 2 must be used.

2.4 Examples of Merging Code Clones

Herein we show two examples of identifying clones to be refactored with this technique. The first example is merging clones with *Extract Method*, and the second one is with *Pull Up Method*.

Merging clones with *Extract Method*

A typical set of conditions could be as follows in a case that *Extract Method* refactoring is used to merge clones.

EC1 (Extract Method Condition 1)   The target granularities are blocks;
EC2 (Extract Method Condition 2) $DCH(S)$ is 0;
EC3 (Extract Method Condition 3) $NAV(S)$ is 1 or less.

EC1 is necessary because *Extract Method* is performed for a part of an existing method. If all clones are in a single class, it is easy to merge them as a new method in the same class, which is the reason why EC2 is used. The reason for EC3 is that, some values are assigned to two or more variables that are outside the clones, it is necessary to create a new class for such variables because Java methods can return only a single value.

Table 1 Classifying code clones satisfying (EC1) to (EC3)

	EXTRACT	PARAMETER	RETURN	OTHER
EG1	Required	–	–	–
EG2	Required	Required	–	–
EG3	Required	–	Required	–
EG4	Required	Required	Required	–
EG5	Required	Do no care	Do no care	Required

The primary operations for *Extract Method* are as follows:

EXTRACT   A set of operations for simply extracting a code fragment as a new method is required: (1) cutting the target code fragment, (2) pasting the code fragment outside the method, (3) adding a simple signature (a method name with no parameter) to the code fragment.

PARAMETER   A set of operations for removing the direct access to the externally defined variables in the extracted method are required: (1) adding parameters to the signature, and (2) replacing the references to the externally defined variables with references to the parameters.

RETURN   A set of operations for adding a return-statement to the extracted method is required: (1) defining a new local variable, (2) replacing the assignment to the externally defined variable with an assignment to the local variable, (3) adding a return-statement for passing the value of the local variable.

OTHER   Other operations than the above ones for extracting code fragments as new methods are sometimes required. For example, if a clone includes a return-statement, it is not desirable to simply perform a RETURN operation.

EXTRACT operations are required by any clones in performing *Extract Method*, whereas PARAMETER, RETURN, and OTHER operations depend on the internal logic of clones. If a clone class satisfies all the conditions EC1 to EC3, the clone class is categorized into either of five groups, EG1 to EG5 in Table 1.

EG1 (Extract Method Group 1)   Clone classes in this group can be merged by just extracting the clones as a new method in the same class. That is, the clones use no externally defined variables. Clone classes in this group require only the EXTRACT operation.

EG2 (Extract Method Group 2)   Clone classes in this group can be merged by extracting the clones as a new method by adding parameters for the externally defined variables. That is, the clones reference one or more externally defined variables. Clone classes in this group require the EXTRACT and PARAMETER operations.

EG3 (Extract Method Group 3)   Clone classes in this group can be merged by extracting the clones as a new method by adding a return-statement. That is, the clones assign to an externally defined variable. Clone classes in this group require the EXTRACT and RETURN operations.

EG4 (Extract Method Group 4)   Clone classes in this group can be merged by extracting the clones as a new method by adding parameters and a return-statement. That is, the clones reference one or more externally defined variables and assign a value to an externally defined variable. Clone classes in this group require the EXTRACT, PARAMETER, and RETURN operations.

EG5 (Extract Method Group 5)   Clone classes in this group could potentially be merged but require too much effort. Clone classes in this group, by definition, require the OTHER operations. In this group, it is irrelevant whether clone classes require the PARAMETER and RETURN operations or not. Thus, the corresponding cells in Table 1 are "do no care".

Merging clones with *Pull Up Method*

If a user wants to merge clones by performing the *Pull Up Method*, the following conditions should be reasonable:

PC1 (Pull Up Method Condition 1)   The target granularities are methods;
PC2 (Pull Up Method Condition 2) $DCH(S)$ is 1 or more (not ∞);
PC3 (Pull Up Method Condition 3) $NAV(S)$ is 0.

Pull Up Method refactoring is performed on existing methods, which is the reason for PC1. PC2 requires all classes including clones (duplicated methods) to extend a common base class. PC3 is required because it is difficult to add a new return-statement for handling an externally defined variable to methods if they already include return statements.

The primary operations for *Pull Up Method* are as follows:

MOVE   A set of operations for simply moving a code fragment to another place, for example, (1) cutting the target method from the original place, and (2) pasting it in the common base class.

PARAMETER   A set of operations for removing direct accesses to variables that cannot be used in the common base class and, instead, passing them as input parameters, for example, (1) adding parameters to the signature, and (2) replacing the references to the unavailable variables with references to the parameters.

OTHER   Other operations than the above ones. As was seen in the case of *Extract Method* pattern, not all clones satisfying PC1 to PC3 can be removed using the above two operations, EXTRACT and PARAMETER. Some clones may require more effort to remove, or it may be impossible to remove them. As a matter of convenience, such clones are defined to require OTHER operations.

MOVE operations are required by any of the code clones in performing the *Pull Up Method*, whereas the requirements of the PARAMETER and OTHER operations depend on the internal logic of the code clones. If the condition of PC3 is "$NAV(S)$ *is one or less*", one more primary set of operations, RETURN, should be added.

RETURN   A set of operations for adding a return-statement to the moved method to reflect the result of the assignment in it to the caller place.

Table 2 Classifying code clones satisfying PC1 to PC3

	MOVE	PARAMETER	OTHER
PG1	Required	–	–
PG2	Required	Required	–
PG3	Required	Do no care	Required

When $NAV(S)$ is 1, there is an assignment to an externally defined variable. Such assignments have to be changed to local variable assignments, and a return-statement has to be added for reflecting the assignment result to the caller place.

MOVE operations are required by any of the code clones in performing the *Pull Up Method*, whereas the requirements of PARAMETER and OTHER operations depend on the internal logic of the clones. If a clone class satisfies all the conditions PC1 to PC3, the clone class is categorized into one of the following groups, PG1 to PG3. Table 2 shows the relationships between classified groups and their required operations.

PG1 (Pull Up Method Group 1)   Clone classes that can be merged by just moving the clones to the common base class, that is, the clones use no externally defined variables. This group requires only MOVE operations.

PG2 (Pull Up Method Group 2)   Clone classes that can be merged by moving the clones to the common base class by adding parameters for referencing externally defined variables, that is, the clones reference one or more externally defined variables. This group requires MOVE and PARAMETER operations.

We can choose either to delete existing methods including the clones or change them to call using the new method from the inside. If the existing methods are deleted, it is necessary to change all of the caller places because the signature was changed.

PG3 (Pull Up Method Group 3)   Clone classes that require ingenuity in merging them, that is, this group requires OTHER operations. As for *Extract Method* pattern, it is irrelevant whether clone classes in PG3 require the PARAMETER operations or not, so that the corresponding cell of Table 2 is "do no care".

3 Our Research Following Literature [3]

Fortunately, literature [3] has more than 100 citations as of the end of 2020. We are very happy that this research is helping other research. Our research group has also conducted research following literature [3]. In this section, we will briefly introduce the two studies.

3.1 Refactoring Assistance for Type-3 Clones

The technique that we developed in literature [3] was intended to assist refactoring for Type-1 and Type-2 clones. In other words, the technique is not suitable for Type-3 clones, which include non-duplicated instructions. In literature [4], we have developed another technique to assist refactoring for Type-3 clones. In literature [4], clones are detected by program dependence graph, and they are checked whether they can be merged with *Form Template Method* refactoring pattern.

Form Template Method is one of the refactoring patterns proposed by Fowler et al. [1]. *Form Template Method* uses *TemplateMethod* that is one of the design patterns proposed by Gamma et al. [2]. In *Template Method*, developers write an outline of the process into a base class and implement the details of the process in its derived classes. In order to apply this pattern to similar methods that have a common base class, duplicated instructions between the methods are pulled up to the base class, and non-duplicated instructions remain in its derived classes. As a result, clones in similar methods are merged into the base class.

Figure 3 shows an example of application of *Form Template Method*. There are two classes that share the common base class, Site, and those two classes include similar methods, getBillableAmount. By applying *Form Template Method* to those methods, the common processing flow in the methods is pulled up to the base class, and the unique instructions in the two methods are extracted as new methods, getBaseAmountandgetTaxAmount. Herein, the new method written in the base class is called *Template Method*. By applying this code transformation, clones in the methods are merged into the base class, and the unique instructions in those methods are handled well by creating new methods in the original classes.

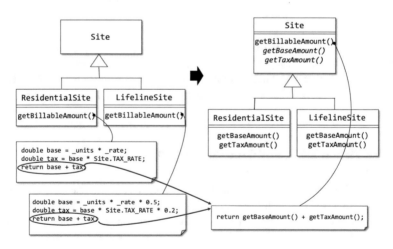

Fig. 3 Example of *Form Template Method*

The technique proposed in literature [4] is suitable to handle differences between target methods comparing to other clone removal techniques. By comparing target methods with their program dependence graphs, the technique can assist developers in merging Type-3 clones even if clones include the following differences.

- Clones include the duplicated instruction in a different order.
- Clones include the same processing with different implementation styles (such as for-loop and while-loop).

Our technique automatically identifies clones that can be refactored with *Form Template Method* and show developers how individual clone classes can be merged with the refactoring pattern.

3.2 Merging Clones in a Fully Automated Manner

In recent years, merging clones has become known as a form of refactoring. Merging clones makes it easier to keep consistencies in the source code because developers do not have to put the same changes on clones in multiple different places. However, there is a possibility that merging clones itself introduces new bugs in the source code. Consequently, merging all clones without any special reason is not realistic: a reasonable indicator is required whether or not given clones should be merged.

In literature [6], we proposed a technique to automatically measure the effect of refactoring on clones by considering the number of lines reduced by merging clones as the effect of such refactoring. In other words, in literature [6], we proposed a technique to automatically merge as many clones as possible from the target system.

The technique repeats (1) detecting clones, (2) editing source files, (3) compiling, and (4) testing. This technique enables developers to obtain actual lines of code that can be reduced by merging clones, not just estimating it.

Figure 4 shows an overview of the proposed technique. The input of the technique is a set of source files. The output is a set of source files in which clones have been merged as much as possible and their reducible lines of code. This technique does not merge clones if merging them does not reduce the lines of code of the source files. The whole of this technique is performed in a fully automated manner. In the proposed technique, a new class is generated, and the new class is used as a utility class for placing merged clones. More concretely, each merged clone is declared as a static method in the class. We have applied the proposed technique to seven Java open-source projects. Table 3 shows the target projects and the experimental results on them. As a result, the proposed technique succeeded in merging 489 clone classes in total.

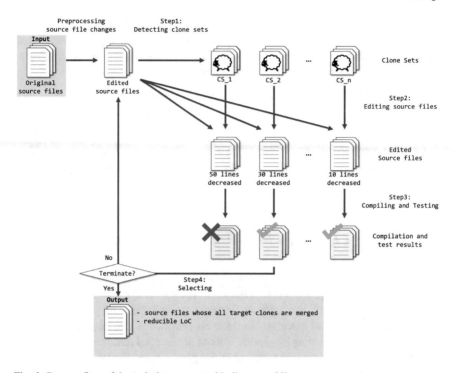

Fig. 4 Process flow of the technique proposed in literature [6]

Table 3 Target projects and experimental results

Project	Size (KLoC)	# Detected CC[a]	# Merged CC[a]	Execution time
jEdit 5.40	163	423	57	40 min
JFreeChart 1.0.19	236	848	145	2 h 48 min
JRuby 1.7.27	334	858	236	6 h 4 min
Ant 1.10.1	231	635	7	20 min
JMeter 3.2	79	114	5	3 min
Closure compiler 20190618	250	286	27	3 h 13 min
Joda-Time 2.10.3	74	89	9	7 m

[a]Clone class

4 Directions of Future Research Related to Merging Clones

Herein, we discuss the prospects for future research on merging clones.

4.1 Revealing the Purpose of Merging Clones

The first research direction is to investigate what the purpose of merging clone is. As mentioned above, merging clones allows for more efficient changes to be made to the code in the future because there are no concerns about missing changes. Reducing the size of the system (number of lines of code) is one reason to merge clones. But is there any other reason to merge clones? If we can understand the reasons for merging clones in actual software development and the frequency of merging clones for each reason, it may serve as a guidepost for future research on merging clones. For example, it would be necessary to detect cases of merging clones for open-source software managed on GitHub and to investigate the motivation for each case.

4.2 More Advanced Automatic Refactoring of Clones

In the research presented in Sect. 3.2, we have succeeded in merging clones in a fully automated manner. However, this fully automatic refactoring involves the following two issues.

- Only size reduction is considered as the effect of merging clones.
- Only extracting clones as a new method in a utility class is the way to merge clones.

One of the purposes of merging clones is to reduce the number of lines, but there are other purposes as well. As mentioned in Sect. 4.1, merging clones can prevent omissions of changes when changes are required to the code in the future. Thus, if the goal of preventing omissions of changes is a priority, merging clones may be useful even if the number of code lines increases. Therefore, it is necessary to use a multi-objective fitness function instead of a single-objective one for more practical automatic refactoring.

As shown in Fig. 2, there are various ways for merging clones, and how clones should be merged depends on the characteristics of the clones. The technique in literature [6], which is only extracting the clones into a utility class, is not sufficient. It is necessary to automatically merge clones in an appropriate way according to their characteristics and to make the quality of the code after automatic refactoring acceptable to the developers.

References

1. M. Fowler, K. Beck, J. Brant, W. Opdyke, D. Roberts, *Refactoring: Improving the Design of Existing Code* (Addison-Wesley Longman Publishing Co., Inc., USA, 1999)
2. E. Gamma, R. Helm, R. Johnson, J. Vlissides, *Design Patterns: Elements of Reusable Object-Oriented Software* (Addison-Wesley Longman Publishing Co., Inc., USA, 1994)

3. Y. Higo, S. Kusumoto, K. Inoue, A metric-based approach to identifying refactoring opportunities for merging code clones in a Java software system. J. Soft. Mainten. Evolut. **20**(6), 435–461 (2008)
4. K. Hotta, Y. Higo, S. Kusumoto, Identifying, tailoring, and suggesting form template method refactoring opportunities with program dependence graph, in *Proceedings of the 2012 16th European Conference on Software Maintenance and Reengineering* (2012), pp. 53–62
5. T. Kamiya, S. Kusumoto, K. Inoue, CCFinder: a multilinguistic token-based code clone detection system for large scale source code. IEEE Trans. Soft. Eng. **28**(7), 654–670 (2002)
6. T. Nakagawa, Y. Higo, J. Matsumoto, S. Kusumoto, How compact will my system be? A fully-automated way to calculate Loc reduced by clone refactoring, in *Proceedings of the 26th Asia-Pacific Software Engineering Conference* (2019), pp. 284–291

Clone Evolution and Management

Norihiro Yoshida and Eunjong Choi

Abstract Programmers tend to write code clones unintentionally, which can be easily avoided. Clone change management is a crucial issue in open-source software (OSS) and industrial software development (e.g., development of social infrastructure, financial systems, and medical equipment). When industrial software developers have to fix a defect, they must find the code clones corresponding to the code fragment, including it. To date, several studies have been conducted on the analysis of clone evolution using OSS. However, only a few studies have reported on the application of a clone change notification system to the industrial software development process of our knowledge. In this chapter, first, we introduce a system that notifies about the creation of code clones. Then, we report on our experience with the system after a 40-day long application of it in a corporation's software development process. In the industrial application, a developer successfully identified ten unintentionally created clones that should be merged. Moreover, we introduce the improvements that were made since we released the initial version of the notification system. Besides, we demonstrate a usage scenario of the current version. The current version of Clone Notifier and its video are available at: https://github.com/s-tokui/CloneNotifier.

1 Introduction

Good programming practice requires programmers to avoid unnecessary duplication in source code because it increases maintenance costs. For instance, once programmers fix a bug in a portion of the source code, they inspect duplicates of that portion [23]. However, they tend to create unintended code clones, especially in large-scale source codes.

N. Yoshida (✉)
Nagoya University, Furo-cho, Chikusa-ku, Nagoya, Aichi, Japan
e-mail: yoshida@ertl.jp

E. Choi
Kyoto Institute of Technology, Matsugasaki Hashikamicho, Sakyo-ku, Kyoto, Japan
e-mail: echoi@kit.ac.jp

© The Author(s), under exclusive license to Springer Nature Singapore Pte Ltd. 2021   197
K. Inoue and C. K. Roy (eds.), *Code Clone Analysis*,
https://doi.org/10.1007/978-981-16-1927-4_14

Kamiya et al. developed a tool known as CCFinder [11] for detecting code clones automatically by identifying identical token sequences from the source code. Several members of the division of software engineering in a corporation have worked to promote the use of CCFinder in their corporation. According to the feedback from the CCFinder users in the corporation, we found that developers were not motivated to merge trusted code clones after a large-scale testing process owing to the cost of re-performing the testing process. The feedback also indicated that a system is required to regularly inform the developers of newly introduced code clones so that they can notice those code clones before the large-scale testing process.

Therefore, we developed a Clone Notifier [19, 20] that performs a daily checkup of newly introduced code clones in source code (see Fig. 1). To determine the usefulness of Clone Notifier, we applied it in the actual development process in the corporation and received daily feedback that included newly introduced code clones and data on whether those code clones were merged.

In this chapter, Sect. 2 introduces the initial version of Clone Notifier. Subsequently, we report the experience with its application in the actual development process in the corporation along with the feedback from the development project in Sect. 3. Next, Sect. 4 introduces the improvements that were made since we released the initial version, and we thereafter demonstrate a usage scenario of the current version of Clone Notifier. Related works are presented in Sect. 5. Finally, we conclude our discussion in Sect. 6.

The current version of Clone Notifier and its video are available at: https://github. com/s-tokui/CloneNotifier.

2   Clone Notifier

Figure 1 illustrates the implementation of Clone Notifier. It assumes the use of a version control system such as Git. It extracts code clones that were newly introduced on the previous day, at midnight, by comparing the versions at the end of the previous day and the day before that. Thereafter, it informs of the code clones via an e-mail. We also provide a web-based code clone viewer for developers who receive an e-mail.

2.1   Extraction of Newly Introduced Code Clones

Figure 2 illustrates an overview of the extraction of newly introduced code clones by Clone Notifier. The extraction is performed by a code clone detection tool CCFinder and GNU Diff. First, CCFinder detects all the code clones from each of the two versions. Thereafter, mappings of code fragments between the two versions are identified using GNU Diff. Finally, Clone Notifier extracts the newly introduced code clones by identifying code clones that were both (i) present in the version by the end of the previous day; (ii) have no mapping to the version at the end of the day before the previous.

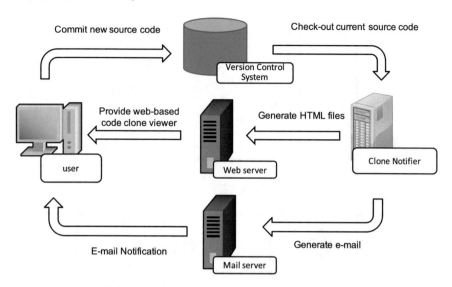

Fig. 1 Implementation of Clone Notifier

2.2 E-mail Notification

Once Clone Notifier finishes the extraction described in the previous section, it notifies of the newly introduced code clones via an e-mail. This e-mail notification aims to send an initial report of new code clones. The first part of this e-mail includes the number of newly introduced code clones, and the location information represents where each of the code clones is present. The second part comprises actual code fragments of the code clones.

2.3 Web-Based Code Clone Viewer

Figure 3 is a screenshot of a web-based code clone viewer. This viewer supports developers who receive a notification e-mail and would like to understand the details of extracted newly introduced code clones. Once a developer selects one of the newly introduced code clones, this viewer shows the source code and highlights the code clones.

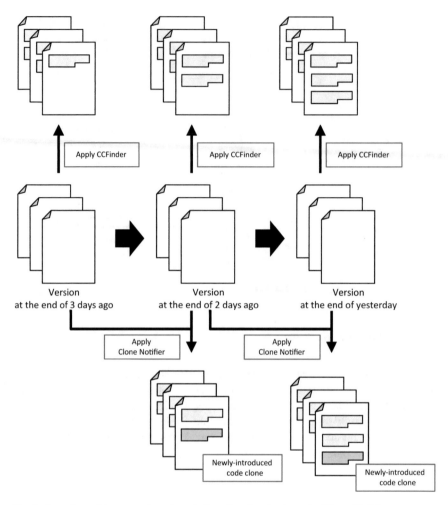

Fig. 2 Overview of the extraction of newly introduced code clones by Clone Notifier

3 Industrial Application

In our work [20], we reported the result of applying Clone Notifier in an industrial development process. In this section, we briefly introduce it. For further detail, please refer to [20].

The goal of the application is to confirm that Clone Notifier can inform code clones that should be merged. We asked a project manager to evaluate whether or not each of the extracted newly introduced code clones should be merged. The project manager is responsible for deciding on managing code clones and requesting programmers to merge them when necessary.

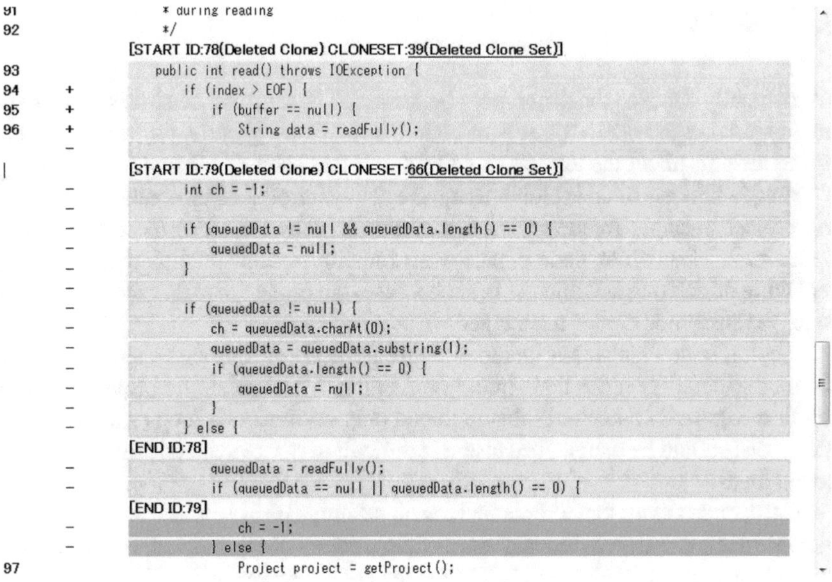

```
91                      * during reading
92                      */
            [START ID:78(Deleted Clone) CLONESET:39(Deleted Clone Set)]
93                      public int read() throws IOException {
94      +                   if (index > EOF) {
95      +                       if (buffer == null) {
96      +                           String data = readFully();
        -
 |          [START ID:79(Deleted Clone) CLONESET:66(Deleted Clone Set)]
        -                   int ch = -1;
        -
        -                   if (queuedData != null && queuedData.length() == 0) {
        -                       queuedData = null;
        -                   }
        -
        -                   if (queuedData != null) {
        -                       ch = queuedData.charAt(0);
        -                       queuedData = queuedData.substring(1);
        -                       if (queuedData.length() == 0) {
        -                           queuedData = null;
        -                       }
        -                   } else {
            [END ID:78]
        -                       queuedData = readFully();
        -                       if (queuedData == null || queuedData.length() == 0) {
            [END ID:79]
        -                           ch = -1;
        -                       } else {
97                      Project project = getProject();
```

Fig. 3 Screenshot of web-based code clone viewer

The target is a maintenance project for a web-based system. The system consists of approximately 350 files and 12 KLOC written in Java. The duration of the application is 40 days.

3.1 Results

During the 40 days of application, 119 sets of newly introduced code clones were extracted. The project manager recognized ten of them as sets of code clones that should be merged. Two of the ten sets were merged into a code fragment during the 40 days. The other eight sets were designated as candidates that will be merged during the next maintenance project.

We interviewed the project manager, and he acknowledged the usefulness of **Clone Notifier**. He was satisfied that ten sets of code clones were recognized as candidates that should be merged, and two of the ten sets were merged during the 40 days.

He also requested us to implement the feature to present numerical criteria for selecting code clones, such as the length of a code clone and number of elements in a clone set (i.e., a set of code clones identical or similar to each other) in the future. He suggested that numerical criteria help a user understand the benefit of merging each code clone set.

3.2 Findings

We manually checked the differences between the 10 sets of code clones that should be merged and the other 109 sets of code clones. Consequently, we acquired interesting insights about the ten sets of code clones that should be merged.

First, in the case of code clones that were newly introduced by adding a new code, the project manager frequently recognized those code clones as those that should be merged. Meanwhile, code clones were sometimes accidentally created by only replacing or deleting statements. In such a case, the project manager mostly decided to leave those code clones unchanged.

Second, code clones that included entire portions of loop or branch statements were considered as those that should be merged. Meanwhile, the project manager rarely recognized code clones that included only portions of a loop or branch statements that should be merged because it is difficult to merge syntactically incomplete code clones.

Third, code clones that did not include consecutive if-else blocks and consecutive variable declarations were considered as those that should be merged. However, such code clones are unavoidable owing to the lack of expressiveness of Java.

3.3 Discussion

According to the project manager's interview, we believe that this industrial application was a success.

The main remaining problem is that **Clone Notifier** extracted useful sets of code clones as well as useless sets of code clones. The ratio of the useful code clones to useless code clones is 8.4%. We are not satisfied with the ratio. One promising solution is presenting numerical criteria to characterize a clone set, as mentioned by the project manager. Criteria such as the length of a code clone and the number of elements in a clone set are expected to support the understanding of each clone set's benefit. Another promising solution is opting out of code clones that are unnecessary. Syntax-based filtering is expected to identify code clones that include syntactically incomplete sentences, consecutive if-else blocks, and consecutive variable declarations.

4 Improvements of Clone Notifier

After releasing the initial version of **Clone Notifier**, we have continued to improve it. In our recent tool demo paper [19], we introduced the current version of **Clone Notifier**. Hereafter, we describe the details of the main improvements.

4.1 Support for Type-3 Clone Detection Tools

The current version of Clone Notifier supports Type-3 clone detection tools (i.e., SourcererCC [18], CCVolti [21]). The clone relation of Type-2 clone detection tool is an equivalent relation. Meanwhile, the clone relation in the Type-3 clone detection tool is not equivalent because it is not transitive. Therefore, it is necessary to change the approach for constructing clone sets from clone pairs. The current version of Clone Notifier constructs sets of clones from clone pairs of JGraphT[1] for solving the maximal clique problem. A clique is a subset of vertices of an undirected graph, such that edges are present between two different vertices in the clique. A maximal clique is a clique that is not exclusively present within the vertex set of a larger clique. For instance, there are four code fragments c_1, c_2, c_3, and c_4. When detecting the four clone pairs (c_1, c_2), (c_2, c_3), (c_3, c_1), and (c_3, c_4), Clone Notifier detects (c_1, c_2, c_3) and (c_3, c_4) as the sets of code clones. As the sets of code clones are maximal cliques of the JGraphT, they can be included in code clones that may need simultaneous modification without a surplus or deficiency.

4.2 Notification of Inconsistent Changes of Clones

Along with refactoring [5], an essential motivation for code clone detection is to determine inconsistent changes to code clones [8–10]. As one of the improvements, we have incorporated the idea of inconsistency detection proposed by Kim et al. [12] into Clone Notifier so that it can notify the inconsistent changes of code clones.

4.3 Usage Scenario

We demonstrate a usage instance of Clone Notifier to detect the inconsistent change clone sets. Moreover, we examine the results to uncover the code clones that should be fixed.

First, the developer sets the configurations of the Clone Notifier. After downloading Clone Notifier, the developer executes setting.jar and writes (e.g., the code clone detection tool, two versions of the directory path, email address, and configuration file name) to generate the configuration file. Next, the developer executes Clone Notifier with the configuration file as an argument. Finally, after completing the execution, the developer receives an email from Clone Notifier with a summary of the results. In this use case, one inconsistent changed clone set is detected. To investigate the presence of any defect in the code clone, the developer accesses the URL provided in the email and checks the results.

---

[1] https://jgrapht.org/.

Stable Code Clone	Modified Code Clone
File: src/backend/executor/execMain.c	File: src/backend/executor/execMain.c

2097 {	1852 {	
2098 TupleDesc old_tupdesc = RelationGetDescr(rel);	1853 + TupleDesc old_tupdesc;	
2099 AttrNumber *map;	- TupleDesc old_tupdesc = RelationGetDescr(rel);	
2100	1854 AttrNumber *map;	
2101 rel = resultRelInfo->ri_PartitionRoot;	1855	
2102 tupdesc = RelationGetDescr(rel);	1856 + root_relid = RelationGetRelid(resultRelInfo->ri_PartitionRoot);	
2103 /* a reverse map */	1857 + tupdesc = RelationGetDescr(resultRelInfo->ri_PartitionRoot);	
2104 map = convert_tuples_by_name_map_if_req(old_tupdesc,	1858 +	
2105 tupdesc,	1859 + old_tupdesc = RelationGetDescr(resultRelInfo->ri_RelationDesc);	
2106 gettext_noop("could not convert row type"));	- rel = resultRelInfo->ri_PartitionRoot;	
2107	- tupdesc = RelationGetDescr(rel);	
2108 /*	1860 /* a reverse map */	
2109 * Partition-specific slot's tupdesc can't be changed, so allocate a	1861 map = convert_tuples_by_name_map_if_req(old_tupdesc, tupdesc,	
2110 * new one.	1862 gettext_noop("could not convert row type"));	
2111 */	1863	
2112 if (map != NULL)	1864 /*	
2113 slot = execute_attr_map_slot(map, slot,	1865 * Partition-specific slot's tupdesc can't be changed, so allocate a	
2114 MakeTupleTableSlot(tupdesc, &TTSOpsVirtual));	1866 * new one.	
2115	1867 */	
	1868 if (map != NULL)	
	1869 slot = execute_attr_map_slot(map, slot,	
	1870 MakeTupleTableSlot(tupdesc, &TTSOpsVirtual));	
	1871 }	

Fig. 4 Inconsistent change (previous commit ID: f7ea1a4233, current commit ID: e8b0e6b82d)

When accessing the URL, the home page is displayed. If the developer clicks a category name of a clone set, they can check the detailed information about that category. On the clone set page, the developer can confirm the change information of the code clone for each clone set. The information includes whether the code clone has been modified, contains a file, and the line location of the source code. When the developer clicks the code clone ID, they can access more detailed information about changes. In the source code page, as shown in Figs. 4, 5, and 6, the code clone in the source code is displayed. If changes have been made, the changes are colored.

4.4 Findings

This section illustrates three instances of inconsistent changes detected by the Clone Notifier.

The first instance of inconsistent change on 29 December 2018 is the clone set of three code fragments, as shown in Fig. 4. These code fragments are in the same file. Although it was necessary to refactor the other two similar code clones, the modified code clone was refactored. The commit message includes that *the modified coding is excessively convoluted and hard to follow*. Approximately 2 weeks before the receipt of this commit message, the committer discussed with PostgreSQL developers and improved the readability of this code via e-mail.[2] When a code clone in a clone set was very convoluted, the other code clones are also convoluted. Thus, they should be identified as refactoring candidates.

---

[2] https://www.postgresql.org/message-id/20181206222221.g5witbsklvqthjll@alvherre.pgsql.

Stable Code Clone	Modified Code Clone
File: src/backend/utils/cache/lsyscache.c	File: src/backend/utils/cache/lsyscache.c

```
775    get_attgenerated(Oid relid, AttrNumber attnum)
776    {
777        HeapTuple    tp;
778
779        tp = SearchSysCache2(ATTNUM,
780                ObjectIdGetDatum(relid), Int16GetDatum(attnum));
781        if (HeapTupleIsValid(tp))
782        {
783            Form_pg_attribute att_tup = (Form_pg_attribute) GETSTRUCT(tp);
784            char    *result;
785
786            result = pstrdup(NameStr(att_tup->attname));
787            ReleaseSysCache(tp);
788            return result;
789        }
790
791        if (!missing_ok)
792            elog(ERROR, "cache lookup failed for attribute %d of relation %u",
793                    attnum, relid);
794        return NULL;
795    }
```

```
836     get_attgenerated(Oid relid, AttrNumber attnum)
837     {
838         HeapTuple    tp;
839 +       Form_pg_attribute att_tup;
840 +       char    result;
841
842         tp = SearchSysCache2(ATTNUM,
843                 ObjectIdGetDatum(relid),
844                 nt16GetDatum(attnum));
845 +       if (!HeapTupleIsValid(tp))
  -         if (HeapTupleIsValid(tp))
  -         {
  -             Form_pg_attribute att_tup = (Form_pg_attribute) GETSTRUCT(tp);
  -             char    result;
  -
  -             result = att_tup->attgenerated;
  -             ReleaseSysCache(tp);
  -             return result;
  -         }
  -         else
846             elog(ERROR, "cache lookup failed for attribute %d of relation %u",
847                     attnum, relid);
848 +       att_tup = (Form_pg_attribute) GETSTRUCT(tp);
849 +       result = att_tup->attgenerated;
850 +       ReleaseSysCache(tp);
851 +       return result;
852     }
```

Fig. 5 Inconsistent change (previous commit ID: 82150a05be, current commit ID: edda32ee25)

Stable Code Clone	Modified Code Clone
File: src/backend/utils/adt/pgstatfuncs.c	File: src/backend/utils/adt/pgstatfuncs.c

```
1365    pg_stat_get_db_checksum_last_failure(PG_FUNCTION_ARGS)
1366    {
1367        Oid    dbid = PG_GETARG_OID(0);
1368        TimestampTz result;
1369        PgStat_StatDBEntry *dbentry;
1370
1371        if ((dbentry = pgstat_fetch_stat_dbentry(dbid)) == NULL)
1372            result = 0;
1373        else
1374            result = dbentry->last_checksum_failure;
1375
1376        if (result == 0)
1377            PG_RETURN_NULL();
1378        else
1379            PG_RETURN_TIMESTAMPTZ(result);
1380    }
```

```
1542    pg_stat_get_db_checksum_last_failure(PG_FUNCTION_ARGS)
1543    {
1544        Oid    dbid = PG_GETARG_OID(0);
1545        TimestampTz result;
1546        PgStat_StatDBEntry *dbentry;
1547 +
1548 +      if (!DataChecksumsEnabled())
1549 +          PG_RETURN_NULL();
1550
1551        if ((dbentry = pgstat_fetch_stat_dbentry(dbid)) == NULL)
1552            result = 0;
1553        else
1554            result = dbentry->last_checksum_failure;
1555
1556        if (result == 0)
1557            PG_RETURN_NULL();
1558        else
1559            PG_RETURN_TIMESTAMPTZ(result);
1560    }
```

Fig. 6 Inconsistent change (previous commit ID: 9010156445, current commit ID: 252b707bc4)

The second inconsistent change on 5 April 2019 is the clone set of three code fragments, as shown in Fig. 5. These code fragments are in the same file. Although it was necessary to refactor the other two similar code clones, the modified code clone of these code fragments was refactored, such that the condition statement changes to the condition negative form. The commit message indicates that *"the developer rewrites get_attgenerated( ) to avoid compiler warning if the compiler does not recognize that error log does not return"*. Therefore, to avoid the compiler warning with the other code clones in the clone set, these code clones should be modified with the same change. If Clone Notifier is constantly used, the developer can consistently refactor.

The third inconsistent change on 17 April 2019 is the clone set of two code fragments, as shown in Fig. 6. These code fragments are in the same file. One of these code fragments was refactored, such that it added a NULL return if *DataChecksumsEnabled* is false. It was necessary to refactor the other code clone in the same way as the refactored code fragment. The commit message includes that *"returning 0 could falsely indicate that there is no problem, but returning NULL correctly indicates that there is no information about potential problems"*.

5 Related Work

Several studies have been conducted to investigate and support clone evolution [16].

Kim et al. studied genealogies of code clone [12]. They defined a model of clone genealogy to study the evolution of code clones across multiple versions of source code. Other clone evolution models have been proposed and discussed [1, 2, 6, 13]. Duala-Ekoko et al. presented *Clone Region Descriptors* to track code clones moved to other locations in source code [3, 4].

Nguyen et al. developed a clone management tool *JSync* to notify developers of the changes and the inconsistencies of code clones in source files [15]. Additionally, Jiang et al. [9] and Li et al. [14] proposed the detection of code clones from a single version of source code.

Recently, Honda et al. developed CCEvovis [7], which is a system that visualizes the evolution of code clones [20]. It highlights and visualizes the clone change for developers to understand. Saha et al. described the design and implementation of a near-miss clone genealogy extractor, gCad [17], which can extract and classify both exact and near-miss clone genealogies.

Additionally, Yoshida et al. proposed a proactive clone recommendation system for "Extract Method" refactoring [22]. The proposed system that was implemented as Eclipse plug-in monitors code modifications on the fly. Once the proposed system detects an "Extract Method" refactoring instance based on code modifications, it recommends code clones of the refactored code as refactoring candidates.

6 Summary

We reported an industrial experience with **Clone Notifier** that performs daily checkup of newly introduced code clones in source code. **Clone Notifier** successfully suggested that the code clones should be merged. Through further analysis of the result, we acquired interesting insights for improving **Clone Notifier**. Moreover, we introduced the improvements we have made since we released the initial version. Thereafter, we demonstrated a usage scenario of the current version of **Clone Notifier**.

Acknowledgements We would like to thank Ms. Fusako Mitsuhashi and Mr. Shin'ichi Iwasaki of NEC Corporation for data collection. We also thank Yuki Yamanaka, Shogo Tokui, Mananu Sano, Seiya Numata, Kazuki Yokoi, and Katsuro Inoue of Osaka University for their contribution to Clone Notifier. This work was supported by JSPS KAKENHI Grant Numbers JP18H04094, JP19K20240, JP20K11745.

References

1. L. Aversano, L. Cerulo, M. Di Penta, How clones are maintained: an empirical study, in *11th European Conference on Software Maintenance and Reengineering (CSMR'07)* (2007), pp. 81–90. https://doi.org/10.1109/CSMR.2007.26
2. T. Bakota, R. Ferenc, T. Gyimothy, Clone smells in software evolution, in *2007 IEEE International Conference on Software Maintenance* (2007), pp. 24–33. https://doi.org/10.1109/ICSM.2007.4362615
3. E. Duala-Ekoko, M.P. Robillard, Tracking code clones in evolving software, in *Proceedings of the 29th International Conference on Software Engineering, ICSE '07* (IEEE Computer Society, USA, 2007), pp. 158–167. https://doi.org/10.1109/ICSE.2007.90
4. E. Duala-Ekoko, M.P. Robillard, Clone region descriptors: representing and tracking duplication in source code. ACM Trans. Softw. Eng. Methodol. **20**(1) (2010). https://doi.org/10.1145/1767751.1767754
5. M. Fowler, *Refactoring: Improving the Design of Existing Code* (Addison-Wesley, Boston, MA, USA, 1999)
6. J. Harder, N. Gode, Modeling clone evolution, in *Proceeding of the 3rd International Workshop on Software Clones*, pp. 17–21 (2009)
7. Honda, H., Tokui, S., Yokoi, K., Choi, E., Yoshida, N., Inoue, K.: CCEvovis: a clone evolution visualization system for software maintenance, in *2019 IEEE/ACM 27th International Conference on Program Comprehension (ICPC)* (2019), pp. 122–125. https://doi.org/10.1109/ICPC.2019.00026
8. K. Inoue, Y. Higo, N. Yoshida, E. Choi, S. Kusumoto, K. Kim, W. Park, E. Lee, Experience of finding inconsistently-changed bugs in code clones of mobile software, in *2012 6th International Workshop on Software Clones (IWSC)* (2012), pp. 94–95. https://doi.org/10.1109/IWSC.2012.6227882
9. L. Jiang, Z. Su, E. Chiu, Context-based detection of clone-related bugs, in *Proceedings of the the 6th Joint Meeting of the European Software Engineering Conference and the ACM SIGSOFT Symposium on The Foundations of Software Engineering, ESEC-FSE '07* (Association for Computing Machinery, New York, NY, USA, 2007), pp. 55–64. https://doi.org/10.1145/1287624.1287634
10. E. Juergens, F. Deissenboeck, B. Hummel, S. Wagner, Do code clones matter?, in *Proceedings of the 31st International Conference on Software Engineering, ICSE '09* (IEEE Computer Society, USA, 2009), pp. 485–495. https://doi.org/10.1109/ICSE.2009.5070547
11. T. Kamiya, S. Kusumoto, K. Inoue, CCFinder: a multilinguistic token-based code clone detection system for large scale source code. IEEE Trans. Softw. Eng. **28**(7), 654–670 (2002). https://doi.org/10.1109/TSE.2002.1019480
12. M. Kim, V. Sazawal, D. Notkin, G. Murphy, An empirical study of code clone genealogies (Association for Computing Machinery, New York, NY, USA, 2005), pp. 187–196. https://doi.org/10.1145/1095430.1081737
13. J. Krinke, A study of consistent and inconsistent changes to code clones, in *14th Working Conference on Reverse Engineering (WCRE 2007)* (2007), pp. 170–178. https://doi.org/10.1109/WCRE.2007.7
14. Z. Li, S. Lu, S. Myagmar, Y. Zhou, CP-Miner: finding copy-paste and related bugs in large-scale software code. IEEE Trans. Softw. Eng. **32**(3), 176–192 (2006). https://doi.org/10.1109/TSE.2006.28

15. H.A. Nguyen, T.T. Nguyen, N.H. Pham, J. Al-Kofahi, T.N. Nguyen, Clone management for evolving software. IEEE Trans. Softw. Eng. **38**(5), 1008–1026 (2012). https://doi.org/10.1109/TSE.2011.90

16. J.R. Pate, R. Tairas, N.A. Kraft, Clone evolution: a systematic review. J. Softw. Evol. Process **25**(3), 261–283 (2013)

17. R.K. Saha, C.K. Roy, K.A. Schneider, gCad: a near-miss clone genealogy extractor to support clone evolution analysis, in *2013 IEEE International Conference on Software Maintenance* (2013), pp. 488–491. https://doi.org/10.1109/ICSM.2013.79

18. H. Sajnani, V. Saini, J. Svajlenko, C.K. Roy, C.V. Lopes, SourcererCC: scaling code clone detection to big-code, in *2016 IEEE/ACM 38th International Conference on Software Engineering (ICSE)* (2016), pp. 1157–1168. https://doi.org/10.1145/2884781.2884877

19. S. Tokui, N. Yoshida, E. Choi, K. Inoue, Clone notifier: developing and improving the system to notify changes of code clones, in *2020 IEEE 27th International Conference on Software Analysis, Evolution and Reengineering (SANER)* (2020), pp. 642–646. https://doi.org/10.1109/SANER48275.2020.9054793

20. Y. Yamanaka, E. Choi, N. Yoshida, K. Inoue, T. Sano, Applying clone change notification system into an industrial development process, in *2013 21st International Conference on Program Comprehension (ICPC)* (2013), pp. 199–206. https://doi.org/10.1109/ICPC.2013.6613848

21. K. Yokoi, E. Choi, N. Yoshida, K. Inoue, Investigating vector-based detection of code clones using BigCloneBench, in *2018 25th Asia-Pacific Software Engineering Conference (APSEC)* (2018), pp. 699–700. https://doi.org/10.1109/APSEC.2018.00095

22. N. Yoshida, S. Numata, E. Choiz, K. Inoue, Proactive clone recommendation system for extract method refactoring, in *2019 IEEE/ACM 3rd International Workshop on Refactoring (IWoR)* (2019), pp. 67–70. https://doi.org/10.1109/IWoR.2019.00020

23. A. Zeller, *Why Programs Fail: A Guide to Systematic Debugging*, 2nd edn. (Morgan Kaufmann Publishers Inc., San Francisco, CA, USA, 2009)

Sometimes, Cloning Is a Sound Design Decision!

Michael W. Godfrey and Cory J. Kapser

Abstract The practice of *copy-paste-edit*—also known as *code cloning*—has always been popular with software developers; however, evidence suggests that code cloning also carried risks: code bloat, creeping system fragility and design drift, increased bugginess, and inconsistent maintenance are all possible side effects of code cloning. Early research into this practice often tacitly assumed that it was always problematic, and sought to identify instances of it ("clone detection") for later elimination. However, our studies of how cloning has been practised in the development of several large open-source systems suggested a more nuanced view might be appropriate: we found that code cloning seems to be practised for a variety of reasons, and sometimes with principled engineering goals in mind. That is, the idea that "code cloning is uniformly harmful to software system quality" is itself harmful. We argue instead that code clone instances should be evaluated along a number of criteria—such as developer intent, likely risk, and mitigation strategies—before any refactoring action is taken. Also, after some years of reflection on our original studies, we further suggest that instead of concentrating only on source code and other technical artifacts, there is much to be gained by shifting our focus to studying how developers perceive and practice code cloning.

1 Introduction: A Problem Reconsidered

In much of the early literature on the topic [1, 2, 14], the practice of code cloning is assumed to be detrimental to software system quality. For example, we know that code clones can cause additional maintenance effort; changes to one segment of code may need to be propagated to several others, incurring unnecessary maintenance costs compared to forming one reusable abstraction at a single place in the code base [11].

M. W. Godfrey (✉)
Cheriton School of Computer Science, University of Waterloo, Waterloo, Canada
e-mail: migod@uwaterloo.ca

C. J. Kapser
ZoeInsights, Calgary, AB, Canada
e-mail: cjkapser@coryk.afraid.org

© The Author(s), under exclusive license to Springer Nature Singapore Pte Ltd. 2021
K. Inoue and C. K. Roy (eds.), *Code Clone Analysis*,
https://doi.org/10.1007/978-981-16-1927-4_15

Also, locating and maintaining these clones pose additional problems if they do not evolve synchronously. With this in mind, methods for automatic refactoring have been suggested [2], and tools specifically to aid developers in the documenting [8] and manual refactoring of clones [13] have also been developed, but these techniques have not seen widespread industrial adoption.

With this evidence in mind, it seems fairly safe to assert that code cloning is *sometimes* an indication of sloppy design, and in such cases should be considered to be a kind of development "bad smell" [9]. However, in our studies we have found that there are many instances of cloning that seem, at worst, harmless and may even be beneficial to the system's overall long-term health. For example, cloning may be used to introduce experimental strategies to core subsystems without negatively affecting the stability of the main code branch; also, sometimes programming languages lack abstraction features such as genericity, which can lead to functions that look very similar to each other but cannot be further unified. Thus, we argue that a variety of concerns—such as stability, code ownership, and design clarity—need to be considered before any refactoring is attempted; a developer or manager should try to understand the reasoning behind the intentional duplication before deciding what action, if any, to take.

This chapter describes eight cloning patterns that we uncovered during case studies we performed on large software systems [17, 18]. These patterns present both good and bad motivations for cloning, and we discuss both the advantages and disadvantages of these patterns of cloning in terms of development and maintenance. Our goal is not to categorize clones for purposes of refactoring but to document the types of cloning that occur in software to aid the general understanding of how cloning is used in practice. In some cases, we identify patterns of cloning that we believe are beneficial to the quality of the system.

To support our basic argument—that code cloning can sometimes be a beneficial design practice—we studied several widely used open-source software systems, including the *Linux* kernel, the *PostgreSQL* relational database management system, the *Apache httpd* web server and the *Gnumeric* spreadsheet application. In this work, we explored the observed uses of code cloning by the developers, the apparent rationale behind the uses, and the relative frequency of "good" versus "bad" clones.

We also show how high-level cloning patterns can be organized in a fashion similar to the cataloging of design patterns [10]. There are several benefits that can be gained from this characterization of cloning. First, it provides a flexible framework on top of which we can document our knowledge about how and why cloning occurs in software. This documentation can further help to crystallize a vocabulary that researchers and practitioners can use to communicate about cloning. Second, our categorization is a step towards formally defining these patterns to aid in automated detection and classification of the practice of code cloning. These classifications can further be used to define metrics concerning code quality and maintenance efforts. Automatic classifications provide us with better measures of code cloning in software systems and the severity of the problem in general. For example, a software system that contains many clones that are intended to evolve separately, such as experimental variation clones described in Sect. 3, will require different maintenance strategies and tools compared to a software system containing many clones that need to be maintained synchronously, such as those clones introduced because of language limitations.

2 Finding Code Cloning Patterns

Our broad research goal in performing these studies was to better understand the rationales behind why developers apparently often chose to engage in *copy-paste-edit*, as well as to investigate likely risk factors and mitigation strategies. In particular, we wished to answer the general question of how code clones are used and what types of code are cloned. The study subjects of these initial investigations were the *Linux* kernel and *PostgreSQL* [17], and it is from this pilot study that we devised our set of cloning patterns as well as the pattern catalogue template. While this initial investigation was not explicitly intended to examine patterns of cloning, during our analysis we uncovered several recurring ways in which developers duplicated behaviour. These patterns are defined by what is duplicated and why, and to some extent how the duplication is done. More specifically, the patterns we observed concern both cloning of large architectural artifacts, such as files or subsystems, and finer-grained cloning, such as functions or code snippets. The apparent reasons why developers use these patterns range from difficulty in abstracting the code to minimizing the risk of breaking a working software system. In some cases, documentation explicitly states the reasons for code cloning. While this is a subjective assessment, both authors are experienced developers and have a strong understanding of software design and maintainability. When we discuss how the duplication is performed, we describe what the new artifacts will be rather than the tools that are used to perform the duplication.

To describe and categorize our patterns, we created the following template, based on experiences from our pilot study [17]:

Pattern name—Describes the pattern in a few words.
Motivation—Discusses why developers might use this cloning pattern rather than an appropriate abstraction.
Advantages—Describes the benefits of this pattern of cloning compared to other methods of reusing behaviour.
Disadvantages—Describes the negative impacts of this pattern of cloning.
Management advice—Presents ideas on how this type of cloning can be managed in the long term.
Long-term issues—Discusses issues to be aware of when deciding to use a cloning pattern as a long-term solution.
Structural manifestations—Discusses how this type of cloning pattern occurs in the system. This section describes the scope and type of code copied, as well as the types of changes that are expected to be made.

Examples—Provides examples of the pattern from real systems, drawn from the *Linux* kernel (various versions), *PostgreSQL* version 8.0.1, *Apache httpd* version 2.0.49, and *Gnumeric* version 1.2.12.

We have categorized the eight patterns into three related meta-groups: *Forking*, *Templating*, and *Customization*; this partitioning is based on the presumed high-level motivation for the cloning pattern. Below, we give a description of the meta-categories as well as the individual patterns we found in our second study, using *Apache httpd* and *Gnumeric* as the example systems. Space does not permit a detailed exposition of the patterns using this template in this chapter, so instead we briefly describe each and give a short overview of an observed real-world example; full details of the study can be found elsewhere [18].

2.1 Forking

Forking is cloning used to bootstrap development of similar solutions within a new context, with the expectation that the clones will likely evolve independently, at least in the short term. A major motivation for forking is to protect stability of the main codebase, by allowing for experimentation to occur away from the core system. In these types of clones, the original code is copied to new source files and then independently developed. Forking helps to do this by pushing points of variation out to the fringes. In so doing, hardware or platform variants can interact with the rest of the core system through a kind of virtualization layer; also, experimental new designs or features can be tested with relatively little risk to the core system. Short-term forking can lead to careful evaluation of new ideas, with the goal of later integrating them into to main code base or abandoning them if they prove to be undesirable. In the longer term, forking can be an effective strategy when variants need to continue to evolve independently but in parallel with each other and at least informally aware of the each others' existence.

Forking differs significantly from the other two categories in that the granularity of copying is often coarse, at the file or directory level; by comparison, the granularity of templating and customizing tends to be at the level of whole functions or contiguous code snippets.

We observed three patterns of cloning that fit into the category of *Forking*.

2.1.1 Hardware Variation

Hardware variation can occur when a new piece of hardware is released that is highly similar to previous hardware, yet different enough that some special handling is required. For example, we observed a common implementation and management strategy for device drivers within the *Linux* kernel: If the new and old devices were highly similar, often the existing device driver was adapted to handle both devices;

however, if the differences were more fundamental, then the code from the old driver was copied into a new space and edited as needed. With this latter strategy, the existing working driver is left untouched, thus posing no risk to users of the older device. However, the development of the new driver can use the existing driver code as a starting point. The old and new drivers are then maintained independently, implying that if bugs are found, developers of related drivers must notify each other.

The *Linux* SCSI driver subsystem has several examples of this pattern of cloning [25]. In one example, the file NCR5380.c was copied to the file atari_NCR5380.c and adapted for the Atari hardware device. This new file was then cloned as sun3_NCR5380.c to be adapted to the Sun-3 platform. Another example of driver cloning is the file esp.c which has been duplicated and modified in NCR53C9x.c. What is interesting in the *Linux* SCSI drivers is that the authors duplicating the new file explicitly reference the file they have duplicated, making the chains of replication easy to verify.

2.1.2 Platform Variation

When porting software to new platforms, low-level functionality responsible for interaction with the platform will often need to change. Rather than writing portable code such as a virtualization layer, it is sometimes easier, faster, and safer to clone the code and make a small number of platform-specific changes. In addition, the complexity of the possibly interleaved platform-specific code may be much higher than several versions of the cloned code, making code cloning a better choice for maintenance. In the case of source code within virtualization layers themselves, avoiding this complexity is often a reason to clone code. This pattern differs from hardware variation in that the drivers are often comprised of lower level source code, possibly with embedded assembly language.

However, the differences in the type of source code in these artifacts raise different types of maintenance concerns. The code will evolve along two dimensions: the requirements of the software and the support of the platform. Bug fixes may be difficult to propagate as it may not be clear how or if the bugs are present in each version of the code. Changes to the interface of the platform-specific code become more problematic because these changes will need to be performed across several versions of the library. As groups of platform-specific code clones grow, the common interface that they support will become more brittle and difficult to change because of the number of places where lower level changes will need to be made. In order to guarantee consistent behaviour on supported platforms it will be vital to ensure that visible behaviour from each of the clones remains consistent.

As an example, platform variation is apparent in several subsystems within *Apache*'s portable library, the *Apache Portable Runtime* (APR) contained within the *httpd* webserver. This subsystem is a portable implementation of functionality that is typically platform dependent, such as file and network access. In the version of *Apache httpd* that we examined, we found two examples of this type of cloning: the fileio and threadproc subsystems. In these two subsystems, there are four directories: `netware`, `os2`, `unix`, and `win32`. `threadproc` has an additional subsystem `beos`. In each case, the subsystems performed their tasks slightly differently, depending on the target operating system. In these cases, the differences are typically insertions of additional error checking or application program interface (API) calls.

2.1.3 Experimental Variation

Developers may wish to optimize or extend pre-existing code but be reluctant to risk system stability. By forking the existing code into a new branch, users can have the choice to experiment with new features and designs, or to use the performant, trusted stable code. Many modern systems use this approach: developers create a "safe sandbox" for experimentation by cloning the existing codebase—a practice known as *branching*—and can then try out new ideas. Designs or features that seem advantageous can then be backported into the main codebase, while less desirable or problematic features can simply be abandoned. Alternatively, the whole system variant can be explicitly merged back into the main codebase.

An example of experimental variation can be found in the *Apache httpd* web server. In the multi-process management subsystem, the subsystem `worker` was cloned multiple times as `threadpool` and `leader` [17]. The cloned subsystems are experimental variations on `worker` that are designed to provide better performance. Because they are separated from `worker`, the webserver remained stable while optimizations were being developed.

2.2 Templating

Templating is used as a method to directly copy behaviour of existing code when appropriate programming language abstraction mechanisms, such as inheritance or generics, are unavailable. Templating is used when there is a common set of requirements shared by the clones, such as behaviour requirements or the use of a particular library. When these requirements change, all clones must be maintained together. Often, template clones differ from each other in minor but important ways; they appear to be *almost* unifiable into a single parameterized solution, but for various technical reasons, this is not practical. For example, consider the following code written in the C programming language, taken from *Gnumeric*:

```
gnumeric_oct2bin (FunctionEvalInfo *ei, GnmValue const * const *argv) {
    return val_to_base (ei, argv[0], argv[1],
        8, 2,
        0, GNM_const(7777777777.0),
        V2B_STRINGS_MAXLEN | V2B_STRINGS_BLANK_ZERO);
}
gnumeric_hex2bin (FunctionEvalInfo *ei, GnmValue const * const *argv) {
```

```
return val_to_base (ei, argv[0], argv[1],
    16, 2,
    0, GNM_const(9999999999.0),
    V2B_STRINGS_MAXLEN | V2B_STRINGS_BLANK_ZERO);
}
```

These two functions are part of a whole family of routines for converting data to and from various numeric formats (hexadecimal, octal, binary, etc.). Since C does not support generics, one must create a different function for each supported numeric type, despite the function implementations differing only in explicit constant values. Templated clones often maintain their close similarity over time compared to forking clones, where explicit semantic divergence may be a goal.

2.2.1 Parameterized Code

This pattern represents cases where there is a simple and precise mapping between variants, but the programming language does not provide enough support to be able to unify them into one function. The *Gnumeric* functions above are a good example of parameterized code. In this case, it is likely that the cloning will be well known to the system's developers; the clones may occur together as a group in the same file and are likely to be carefully maintained in parallel as the system evolves. Parameterized code clones are, in essence, a side-effect of the inexpressiveness of the underlying programming language and are likely to be unavoidable.

2.2.2 Boilerplating

This pattern is a generalization of the parameterized code pattern, in which there may not be a simple and precise mapping between the clones. Like templated code, boiler-plating is largely a side-effect of the choice of implementation language; it is particularly common in systems written in older procedural languages such as FORTRAN and COBOL. The lack of language-level support for user-defined abstractions— commonly found in more modern languages—may mean that solutions to relatively straightforward tasks can be unusually lengthy, awkward, and complicated. Consequently, developers have a strong incentive to seek out and adapt existing solutions for their needs; working solutions to common problems are seen as design assets to be exploited again and again [5].

2.2.3 API Protocols

This pattern can be seen as a looser version of boilerplating, albeit for different reasons. When a developer uses a complex library or framework, there is often a required protocol for use; documentation "cookbooks" often provide code exemplars of how to use a given API, which developers are encouraged to *copy-paste-edit* to adapt for their specific needs. For example, when creating a GUI button using the Java SWING API, the usual steps are (a) instantiate the appropriate button class, (b) add the button to a container, and (c) assign action listeners to the button. Repetitive formulas like this may be very common within a system that makes extensive use of a given API; however, detailed inspection of the code often reveals that the variants are different enough that it is hard to form a single unified abstraction, say, for all of the different buttons in a GUI.

2.2.4   Programming Idioms

This pattern models the case where a development team may have language- or project-specific conventions to perform certain kinds of low-level tasks. For example, a common idiom in *Apache httpd* is how a pointer to a platform-specific data structure is set in the memory pool; we found 15 occurrences of this idiom in the APR subsystem. Different platforms may require special handling, yet these variants may appear throughout the system's source code since the low-level tasks recur over and over.

2.3   *Customization*

Customization occurs when existing code is found that solves a problem that is similar to the task at hand, but different enough that a common abstraction is impractical; the existing code is cloned into a new programmatic context and tailored to solve this new problem. In some cases, such as concerns about system stability or code ownership, existing code cannot be modified "in place" to encompass the additional behaviour.

Customization patterns differ from templating in that customization requires more than simple parametric changes to the copied code, such as when significant functionality must be added to or removed from the clone. Also, while templating and forking typically have the goal of maintaining high-level consistent behaviour between clones, customization does not. Customization is opportunistic and unconstrained reuse of existing code to solve today's problems right now. The ad hoc changes that occur in customization clones set them apart from other clones in important ways: their differences can be harder to spot, the effects of the changes on behaviour may be harder to understand, and the code clones may be harder to detect.

In this section we describe two customization patterns.

2.3.1 Bug Workarounds

Due to code ownership issues or unacceptable exposure to risk, it may be difficult to fix a bug at the source, so workarounds may be necessary. Copying the buggy code to a new file, and then fixing the bug there may be the best short-term option. In other situations, it may be possible to guard the points where buggy code is called; this guard can then be copied as part of the usage of the procedure.

For example, one of the authors built an application around the internals of Sun's `javac` compiler. On finding a small bug in the `javac` source code, he cloned the offending code into a descendant class of the original within his application and fixed the bug there. Because he did not have commit permission to the `javac` source code repository, he could not fix the bug directly; instead he applied this fix and submitted a bug report.

2.3.2 Replicate and Specialize

Replicate and specialize are simply customization clones that are not bug workarounds. As developers implement solutions, they may find code in the software system that solves a similar problem to the one they are solving. However, this code may not be the exact solution, and modifications may be required. While the developer could decide to generalize the original code, this may have a high cost in testing and refactoring in the short term. Code cloning may appear to be a more attractive alternative and is commonly used in practice to minimize costs associated with risk [5]. Replicate and specialize clones can be small and specialized or broad and wide ranging. For example, LaToza et al. noted a practice within Microsoft of "clone and own": when a product group wanted to specialize existing functionality belonging to another product group, they had the option of creating a clone of the original, with the understanding that they would be responsible for any ongoing maintenance of the specialized library version.

3 Case Study

To better understand the phenomenon of code cloning as practised in large industrial projects as well as to explore the utility of our cloning categorization, we performed a manual study on two large open-source systems: *Apache httpd* version 2.2.4 and *Gnumeric* version 1.6.3; both of these systems comprised more that 300,000 lines of code [18].

We created a clone detection and analysis tool called *CLICS* (CLoning Interpretation and Categorization System) [17], whose detection algorithm was largely modelled on that of *CCFinder* [15]. We looked for "type 2" clones according to Bellon's taxonomy [3]; that is, we ignored differences in identifier names and explicit string or numeric constant values. We required code regions to match at least 60 consecutive tokens to be considered a clone; within the research community, this is a fairly high threshold, which helps to eliminate false positives from the result set.

Using these settings, CLICS identified 21,270 clones instances across 1580 groups for *Apache httpd* and 11,400 clones instances across 3437 groups for *Gnumeric*. We then took a random sampling of 100 clone groups from each system for manual examination. We discarded groups that we considered to be false positives, leaving us with 93 clone groups for *Apache httpd* and 71 clone groups for *Gnumeric*. Finally, we picked representative clone specimens from each group and did a manual examination of each, categorizing across two dimensions: (1) which of our proposed categories was the best fit for this clone, and (2) was the use of cloning beneficial to the system design or harmful or was the cloning simply unavoidable. The results are summarized in the table below.

Group	Pattern	Apache httpd			Gnumeric		
		Good	Unavoidable	Harmful	Good	Unavoidable	Harmful
Forking	Hardware variation	0	0	0	0	0	0
Forking	Platform variation	10	0	0	0	0	0
Forking	Experimental variation	4	0	0	0	0	0
Templating	Boilerplating	5	0	0	6	0	1
Templating	API protocols	0	17	0	0	8	1
Templating	Programming idioms	0	0	12	1	0	1
Templating	Parameterized code	5	1	12	10	0	24
Customizing	Bug workarounds	0	0	0	0	0	0
Customizing	Replicate +specialize	12	0	4	15	0	1
Other		3	0	8	1	0	3
Total		39	18	36	33	8	30

Overall, we judged about 35–40% of the clones to be "good", a little fewer to be "bad" or harmful to the design, and about 15–20% to be unavoidable. In all, we felt this was strong evidence that code cloning was often practised not simply out of laziness, but as an engineering tool to improve the health of the software system.

4 Recent Work

We now briefly discuss some research on code cloning that we have done since the original studies. This work builds on the premise that code cloning can be a positive design decision. There are three major components: a case study of cloning in a large open-source system, an exploration of how the process of compilation affects cloning, and the construction of a classifier to predict which code clones are the best candidates for refactoring.

4.1 Cloning Within Linux SCSI Drivers

At the time of this work, much of the existing research on software code cloning had concentrated on detection and analysis techniques and their evaluation and most empirical studies of cloning have investigated cloning within single system versions. We decided to perform a longitudinal evolutionary study of cloning within a well-known industrial software system: the SCSI driver subsystem of the *Linux* kernel [25]. We chose the SCSI driver subsystem as a test subject as it is known that cloning has been embraced by some of these developers as a design practice: when a new SCSI card was introduced into the marketplace that was similar to an old one, but different enough to warrant its own implementation in a separate file, a new driver might be cloned from an existing one [12].

Our study consisted of three main parts. In the first, we performed an high-level design analysis of the *Linux* SCSI subsystem; we found that there were three architectural layers, with the top two levels providing driver-independent infrastructure and the lowest level consisting of a large collection of hardware-specific low-level drivers that implement the same basic functionality. We note that a single driver file might provide support for several related SCSI cards, with IFDEFs separating out the implementation differences. Cloning was common between these IFDEF code fragments, but we also found a lot of cloning between individual driver files as well. We examined how cloning was practised in each of the levels, and we found that both the absolute number and *clone coverage rate*—that is, the percentage of the source code that is part of a clone—among low-level drivers were significantly higher than among files in the upper two levels.

In the second part, we examined how cloned drivers evolve between versions and over time. Similar to other studies [4, 20, 21], we found that clones were much more likely to be changed inconsistently than consistently. We also observed several spikes in clones being deleted. Manual analysis suggests that these were mostly due to support for older SCSI cards being deprecated and implementation details being removed from the driver files; in each case, we found that there was also a spike in new clones being created, suggested that a lot of refactoring was occurring as well.

In the third part, we explored if the presence of cloning could be used as an effective predictor of hardware similarity. We decided to concentrate on the bus architecture of the cards because this information could be automatically extracted from the KConfig files, which contain configuration information used by the *Linux* build process; that is, we could establish a clear "ground truth" for the vast majority of the drivers. We then randomly picked 100 pairs of drivers and compared their bus type similarity. We found that if two drivers had a clone relationship between them that there was over an 80% likelihood that their bus types were compatible. This was a much stronger predictor of compatibility than the other two models we created: having the same manufacturer led to a 65% chance that the bus types were compatible, and a randomized model found only 24% were compatible. This suggests that within our study cloning may be strongly driven by similar hardware features; that is, the presence of cloning can provide useful information about the problem domain.

4.2   Cloning in Source Code and in Binaries

In this work, we sought to explore the relationship between cloned source code and compiled code [19]. While most research into code clone detection has focused on source code, sometimes we would like to investigate the provenance of a system for which we have access only to compiled code. For example, we might suspect that a given binary contains code released under the GPL but has not been attributed as such. Prima facie, the relationship between similarities at the source code level and similarities within a binary file is unclear. While others have performed clone detection tools to binaries previously, to the best of our knowledge no one had performed an analysis of how compilation affects source code clones. Source code clones may indeed be compiled into binaries that also resemble each other in the corresponding places, but this relationship has not yet been carefully studied and will likely vary considerably by compiler.

Consider a pair of clones in the source code base of a system: While a compiler will preserve the semantics when transforming the source code to an executable, the corresponding binary segments may differ significantly in their structure due to additional context, the possible addition and deletion of entities in the source model (e.g., inner classes in Java), and optimizations which may radically change the structure of the compiled code. That is, compilation may transform source code clones into very different entities within the binary. At the same time, compilation can also acts as a kind of source code normalization, transforming syntactically different but semantically similar source code segments into the same binary-level representation.

In this exploratory work, we used the tool CCFinderX [13] to find clones in both source code and the corresponding bytecode of four large Java open-source systems; CCFinderX performs clone detection on arbitrary token streams, and so was a good fit for our purposes.

Our study yielded three major observations. First, we found that applying a token-based clone detection tool on both source code and the resulting bytecode produced significantly different result sets. Across the four systems—`netbeans-javadoc`, `eclipse-ant`, `eclipse-jdtcore`, and `javax-swing`—we found a similar number of clones in the source code (1845) and bytecode (1985). However, when we mapped the clones from source to byte code, we found that only 488 of them—about 25% of the total—occurred in both result sets.

Second, we found that there are kinds of clones that can be detected only within the source code and will not be apparent in the bytecode. This is because the compiler may shorten code sequences, create extra `.class` files, and may generate different opcodes instead of operands.

Third, we found that there are kinds of clones that can be detected only at the bytecode level and will not have corresponding clones in the source code. This is because the compiler may elongate the code sequences and normalize control flows.

4.3 Recommending Clones for Refactoring

While our main work described above advocates for a nuanced view of the practice of code cloning—and in particular that sometimes cloning can be beneficial to the long-term health of a software system—we also recognize that sometimes clones are created out of expediency to meet a project deadline. In principle, these clones should be viewed as a kind of short-term "technical debt" that, in principle, should eventually be refactored when the project schedule permits. But simply running a clone detection tool over the codebase of a large software system often results in a very large result set of candidate clones, and it is unclear if it is worth developer time and effort to sort through to identify which clones should high-priority candidates for refactoring. "Fixing" a code clone involves an invasive redesign of the system, and not all clones may be worth the risk to system stability to fix.

In this work, we used machine learning to explore the landscape of source code clones and refactoring prioritization [26]. That is, assuming we have the results of a clone detection analysis on a software system, we seek to build a recommendation engine to suggest clones that are most appropriate for refactoring in terms of the likely benefits, costs, and risks. In particular, we created a decision tree-based classifier incorporating features of the clones, such as the design of the source code, the programmatic context, and properties of the cloning relationship.

We ran a clone detector over the source code of three medium- to large-sized open-source software systems: *ArgoUML*, *Apache Ant*, and *Lucene*. We then labelled each clone as being *refactored* or *unrefactored* by checking if the clone was present in subsequent versions of the system. For the training data, we selected an equal number of *refactored* and *unrefactored* clones—323 instances of each—and used tenfold cross validation, creating a classifier for each of the three projects. Our within-project models achieved a precision of between 77 and 88%; we found that cross-project precision was also strong, between 73 and 89%.

This work illustrates the promise of automated help in managing code clones within a large software system. By recommending which clones are the most promising candidates for refactoring, our work supports better resource allocation for refactoring, more effective maintenance practices, and improved software quality in the long term.

5 Summary

Early research into the practice of code cloning tacitly assumed that it was a bad practice, usually done in haste or out of laziness. In his chapter on bad smells in Fowler's well-known book *Refactoring*, Kent Beck referred to duplicated code as "number one in the stink parade" [9]. However, Cordy and others suggested that in some contexts, code cloning was a sound engineering decision and could improve overall system quality [5]. Our work in creating a qualitative catalogue of how and why cloning is practised, together with our case studies on two large open-source systems, supports this view. We feel that it is important for developers to understand context behind the decision to clone code before attempting invasive removal; automated tools such as a refactoring recommendation system can help.

What is the future of research in code cloning? Since the publication of our original study, the number of research papers published on clone detection, analysis, and management has grown substantially. More detection techniques have been proposed and evaluated [23], many case studies of code cloning and its effects on software quality have been performed [22, 24], and there been many applications of clone detection techniques to other problem areas [6]. However, we still feel that there is room for more exploration of the developer rationale behind cloning. We suggest that instead of concentrating only on source code and other technical artifacts, there is much to be gained by shifting our focus to studying how developers perceive and practice code cloning through qualitative studies.

Finally, we note that the title of our original paper was "'Cloning considered harmful' considered harmful" [16]. Of course, we realize that we could have been phrased the basic idea more simply, such as "Sometimes, cloning is a sound design decision!". However, to do so—that is, to refactor the title to remove the cloning— would have lost the meta-reference to Dijkstra's famous meme [7]. The prose cloning in the title seems to have made it more memorable; with more than 10 years of hindsight, we believe that the decision to clone was, in this case, a sound one.

References

1. B. Baker, On finding duplication and near-duplication in large software systems, in *Proceedings of the 2nd Working Conference on Reverse Engineering (WCRE)* (1995)
2. I.D. Baxter, A. Yahin, L. Moura, M. Sant'Anna, L. Bier, Clone detection using abstract syntax trees, in *Proceedings of the 14th International Conference on Software Maintenance (ICSM)* (1998)
3. S. Bellon, R. Koschke, G. Antoniol, J. Krinke, E. Merlo, Comparison and evaluation of clone detection tools. IEEE Trans. Softw. Eng. **33**(9), 577–591 (2007)
4. N. Bettenburg, W. Shang, W. Ibrahim, B. Adams, Y. Zou, A.E. Hassan, An empirical study on inconsistent changes to code clones at release level, in *Proceedings of the 16th Working Conference on Reverse Engineering (WCRE)* (2009)
5. J.R. Cordy, Comprehending reality: practical barriers to industrial adoption of software maintenance automation, in *Proceedings of the 11th IEEE Workshop on Program Comprehension (IWPC)* (2003)
6. Y. Dang, D. Zhang, S. Ge, C. Chu, Y. Qiu, T.X. Xiao, Tuning code clones at hands of engineers in practice, in *Proceedings of the 28th Annual Computer Security Applications Conference (ACSAC)* (2012)
7. E.W. Dijkstra, Letters to the editor: go to statement considered harmful. Commun. ACM **11**(3), 147–148 (1968)
8. E. Duala-Ekoko, M. Robillard, Tracking code clones in evolving software, in *Proceedings of the 29th ACM/IEEE International Conference on Software Engineering (ICSE)* (2007)
9. M. Fowler, K. Beck, J. Brant, W. Opdyke, D. Roberts, *Refactoring: Improving The Design of Existing Code* (1999)

10. E. Gamma, R. Helm, R. Johnson, J. Vlissides, *Design Patterns: Elements of Reusable Object-Oriented Software* (1995)
11. R. Geiger, B. Fluri, H.C. Gall, M. Pinzger, Relation of code clones and change couplings, in *Proceedings of the 9th Internatoinal Conference of Fundamental Approaches to Software Engineering (FASE)* (2006)
12. M.W. Godfrey, D. Svetinovic, Q. Tu, Evolution, growth, and cloning in Linux: a case study, in *Proceedings of the CASCON Workshop on Detecting Duplicated and Near Duplicated Structures in Large Software Systems: Methods and Applications* (2000)
13. Y. Higo, T. Kamiya, S. Kusumoto, K. Inoue, Aries: refactoring support environment based on code clone analysis, in *Proceedings of the 8th IASTED International Conference on Software Engineering and Applications (SEA)* (2004)
14. H. Johnson, Substring matching for clone detection and change tracking, in *Proceedings of the 10th International Conference on Software Maintenance (ICSM)* (1994)
15. T. Kamiya, S. Kusumoto, K. Inoue, CCFinder: a multilinguistic token-based code clone detection system for large-scale source code. IEEE Trans. Softw. Eng. **28**(7), 654–670 (2002)
16. C. Kapser, M.W. Godfrey, "Cloning considered harmful" considered harmful, in *Proceedings of the 13th Working Conference on Reverse Engineering (WCRE)* (2006)
17. C.J. Kapser, M.W. Godfrey, Supporting the analysis of clones in software systems. J. Softw. Maint. Evol. Res. Pract. **18**(2), 61–82 (2006)
18. C.J. Kapser, M.W. Godfrey, 'Cloning considered harmful' considered harmful: patterns of cloning in software. Empir. Softw. Eng. **13**(6), 645–692 (2008)
19. O. Kononenko, C. Zhang, M.W. Godfrey, Compiling clones: what happens? in *Proceedings of the 30th IEEE International Conference on Software Maintenance and Evolution (ICSME-14), Early Research Achievements (ERA) Track* (2014)
20. J. Krinke, A study of consistent and inconsistent changes to code clones, in *Proceedings of the 14th Working Conference on Reverse Engineering (WCRE)* (2007)
21. Z. Li, S. Lu, S. Myagmar, Y. Zhou, CP-Miner: finding copy-paste and related bugs in large-scale software code. IEEE Trans. Softw. Eng. **32**(3), 176–192 (2006)
22. F. Rahman, C. Bird, P. Devanbu, Clones: what is that smell? in *Proceedings of the 7th IEEE Working Conference on Mining Software Repositories (MSR)* (2010)
23. C. Roy, J. Cordy, Nicad: accurate detection of near-miss intentional clones using flexible pretty-printing and code normalization, in *Proceedings of the 16th IEEE International Conference on Program Comprehension (ICPC)* (2008)
24. G.M. Selim, L. Barbour, W. Shang, B. Adams, A.E. Hassan, Y. Zou, Studying the impact of clones on software defects, in *Proceedings of the 17th Working Conference on Reverse Engineering (WCRE)* (2010)
25. W. Wang, M.W. Godfrey, A study of cloning in the Linux SCSI drivers, in *Proceedings of the 11th IEEE International Working Conference on Source Code Analysis and Manipulation (SCAM)* (2011)
26. W. Wang, M.W. Godfrey, Recommending clones for refactoring using design, context, and history, in *Proceedings of the 30th IEEE International Conference on Software Maintenance and Evolution (ICSME)* (2014)

IWSC(D): From Research to Practice: A Personal Historical Retelling

Rainer Koschke and Stefan Bellon

Abstract The two authors of this chapter were among the founding participants of the *First International Workshop on Software Clone Detection (IWSCD)*—nowadays known as the *International Workshop on Software Clones (IWSC)*. This chapter briefly summarizes the history of this community-building workshop from its early days until today. IWSC(D) has had not only an impact on research but also in practice. Indeed the authors have also developed clone detection tools—among other static program analyses to assess the internal quality of programs—used in the software industry by thousands of developers. The foundations of these tools were laid in software clone research, which highlights both the relevance of this topic for industry and what impact research may be capable to achieve. This historical retelling will not only be a summary of almost 20 years of the history of our primary community event—trying to be as accurate and complete as possible—but also provide the personal perspectives of the two authors along with some anecdotes.

1 Introduction

We were among the participants of the first *Workshop on Software Clone Detection (IWSCD)* that is now known as the *International Workshop on Software Clones (IWSC)*—our primary scientific meeting solely devoted to software clones. IWSC has not only been a major factor in shaping our research community, in general but has also made a considerable impact on our professional and personal life. As often in history, all that has started more or less coincidentally, just out of curiosity and with no intent or foresight what would arise from it.

As a matter of fact, we were not only participants but we were even the organizers of the first IWSDC. Since then we have devoted a large part of our research on this

R. Koschke (✉)
University of Bremen, Bremen, Germany
e-mail: koschke@uni-bremen.de

S. Bellon
Axivon GmbH, Stuttgart, Germany
e-mail: bellon@axivion.com

© The Author(s), under exclusive license to Springer Nature Singapore Pte Ltd. 2021
K. Inoue and C. K. Roy (eds.), *Code Clone Analysis*,
https://doi.org/10.1007/978-981-16-1927-4_16
225

subject and kept being involved in organizing IWSC and other kinds of scientific meetings on software clones. In these roles, we have been witnesses to the history of IWSC since its early days. Yet, we want to point out here that the possessive determiner *its* relates to IWSC only and not to software clone research in general. We actually arrived late to the game, other researchers have worked in this field for about a decade already.

In this chapter, we want to tell the story of IWSC, how it came about and how it developed further. In addition, we also reflect on how it influenced our professional life—an academic life and a life as a professional tool developer. This part of the story gives an example of the sometimes meandering ways on how research can achieve a real impact in the industry.

2 The Birth of IWSCD

In the early years of the new millennium, the first author was a postdoc at the University of Stuttgart in Germany where he designed a new course on software reengineering. One of its topics was detecting software clones. There was a large variety of techniques ranging from textual and lexical over syntactic approaches to techniques based on program dependency graphs. At the end of this section on software clones, he always felt somewhat discontented that he could not present any comparative study on the relative strengths and weaknesses of those existing techniques. For this reason, he figured it would be worthwhile to conduct a study comparing those techniques in terms of recall, precision, and computational costs. Luckily, he found a very capable student—who happened to become the second author of this book chapter many years later—willing to do this study as his Master's thesis. As a matter of fact, it was not a Master's thesis but the German counterpart of that, called *Diploma thesis*—which, however, has a misleading connotation when verbally translated into English. Although the Bologna declaration was just stated in the European Union in 1999, it would take a couple of years until the various higher education qualifications were finally unified into Bachelor and Master degrees in the EU.

For our comparative study, we invited leading current researchers in clone detection at that time to participate in the study. These were Baker (token-based) [1], Merlo and Antoniol (token-based and metric-based) [2], Krinke (data-flow-based) [3], Rieger (token-based) [4], Baxter (syntax-based) [5], and Kamiya (token-based) [6]. The researchers on this who-is-who list of clone detection scientists applied their tools to a set of C and Java programs the second author of this chapter provided. The second author also judged the submitted clone candidates blindly. The resulting dataset has been named the *Bellon benchmark* and was later re-used by diverse researchers. Other researchers have challenged the design of the study [7–9] or proposed alternative approaches to compare the results of clone detectors [10–13].

The results of the comparative study were initially documented in the Master thesis by Bellon [14] written in German. The idea was to publish the outcomes later in an English publication, but it took almost 5 years until that actually happened

[15]. In hindsight, writing the Master thesis in German was a mistake, but at the time of writing we did not anticipate the impact this work would have and how long it would take to publish it in a journal. As a consequence, this thesis may have become the German Master thesis most frequently cited by international authors in software engineering despite it was written in German.

In the evaluation of our study, we classified the clones submitted by the participants into the three classic categories [14, 15]:

- **Type 1** is an exact copy without modifications (except for whitespace and comments).
- **Type 2** is a syntactically identical copy; only variable, type, or function identifiers were changed.
- **Type 3** is a copy with further modifications; statements were changed, added, or removed.

Our paper [15] is often cited for this classification. In recent years, scientists seem to prefer to cite Roy and Cordy's comprehensive survey on software clones [16] instead, which is citing our paper for this classification, and thus constitutes only an indirect citation. Yet, our paper is neither the appropriate original reference for this classification. We do not precisely remember where this classification came from exactly. Someone in our study—either one of our participants or we—must have been aware of it and proposed it as a foundation for our intended study to which all participants agreed. It is very unfortunate that we seem to have taken it for granted and did not cite its original source—a mistake that we want to repair now. Quite likely, the first authors proposing this classic classification are actually Carter et al. [17]. Their definition is as follows:

- **Type 1**—An exactly identical source code clone, i.e., no changes at all.
- **Type 2**—An exactly identical source code clone, but with indentation, comments, or identifier (name) changes.
- **Type 3**—A clone with very similar source code, but with small changes made to the code to tailor it to some new function.
- **Type 4**—A functionally identical clone, possibly with the originator unaware that there is a function already available that accomplishes essentially the same function.

We note that their and our definitions are slightly different regarding whitespace, which is disregarded for our type-1 clones, but explicitly ignored only for their type-2 clones. Other authors have later rephrased those classifications, however, sometimes also introducing similar subtle differences. In particular, the distinction between type-3 and type-4 clones is often blurred, as some authors think of type-4 clones as only some minor syntactic transformations between code fragments, such as replacing while loops by for loops, whereas the original definition by Carter et al. would allow a completely different solution to a similar problem; thus, BubbleSort and QuickSort would be type-4 clones of each other.

As another aside, we find it interesting that Carter et al. used neural networks to detect clones already in 1993, which is a current trend these days. Many papers are being published on using artificial intelligence techniques to detect similar code fragments. Quite likely the authors of those papers should take a look at the paper of Carter et al. not only because of the original clone-type classification.

In the year of 2002, when Bellon finished his research, the time of such comparative studies seems to have come. Independently from our study, Bailey and Bird have conducted a similar study [18]. Since then a number of works have been published on comparing clone detectors and creating benchmarks to do so, which is a good indicator of the maturity of this field—although thorough comparisons relative to tasks at hand is still an ongoing research topic in itself.

After the study was done, we wanted to meet with the participants of our experiment to discuss the results. The earliest opportunity was the *International Conference on Software Maintenance (ICSM)* at Montreal in 2002. Ettore Merlo, who was the General Chair of ICSM 2002 and also participant of our study, kindly offered us a meeting room for an informal meeting parallel to the conference program. Yet, there was one participant who intended to come to our meeting only. He did not have a paper at ICSME or one of its co-located events and would not get travel funding for only an informal meeting. For this reason, we turned our meeting initially planned to be informal into an official workshop and gave it the name *First International Workshop on Software Clone Detection (IWSCD)*. We were about 15 people at this meeting. Interestingly, IWSCD drew the attention not only of the participants of the experiment even though we did not advertise this workshop. Neither the participant who is the reason for our informal meeting to become an official workshop nor ourselves would have expected that this would be the start of a long series of an ever-growing established workshop.

3   Progression and Broadening

Already 7 months later, we organized another working session on benchmarking for clone detectors at the *International Workshop on Program Comprehension (IWPC)* 2003 [19]. Two of the three organizers of this working session, namely, Andrew Walenstein and Arun Lakhotia, were no participants of the original study discussed at the first IWSCD. Obviously, the subject of comparing clone detectors has quickly caught the interest of other researchers, even from other fields.

As a consequence of the increasing interest in the community, the second IWSCD was then held in 2003 in Victoria, Canada, as a satellite workshop of the *Working Conference on Reverse Engineering (WCRE)*. The organizers were again Andrew Walenstein, Arun Lakhotia, and the first author of this chapter. This workshop drew about 35–40 participants and resulted in a summary published in ACM Software Engineering Notes [20].

The next major milestone was a Dagstuhl seminar in 2005 named "Duplication, Redundancy, and Similarity in Software," where Ettore Merlo joined the team of the organizers of previous IWSCD instances. This seminar, which was by invitation only, was solely devoted to this ever-increasing research topic. It drew more than 40 international experts in the field to meet for several days, and rekindled interest in both the techniques and the applications of the area. It included long debates on the definition of clones—a question for which we still have not reached a consensus. It was there where Ira Baxter stated his frequently cited provocative recursive definition of clones: "Clones are segments of code that are similar according to some definition of similarity." And there are still many different definitions of similarity as of today.

Following an informal ad hoc meeting of about 20 members of the community at ICSM 2008 in Beijing, the third *International Workshop on Software Clones (IWSC)* was organized and held in Kaiserslautern, Germany, as part of the *Conference on Software Maintenance and Reengineering (CSMR)* 2009, organized by a a new team consisting of Stanislaw Jarzabek, James Cordy, Katsuro Inoue, and the first author of this chapter. The latter three would serve as the steering committee of IWSC for many years. About 30 researchers gathered to present and discuss their new results. It was the occasion where the "Detection" in the workshop's original name was dropped. The focus of the workshop was no longer the narrow topic of just finding clones but also the empirical impact of clones, reasons for clones, and their evolution—basically all aspects of cloning. It is interesting to note that all but one scientific meeting IWSCD was co-located with have changed their names after the renaming of IWSCD: CSMR and WCRE merged into SANER, ICSM migrated to ICSME, and IWPC became ICPC. Only ICSE is still ICSE and the *International Conference on Software Engineering (ICSE)* was the next event IWSC co-located with. IWSC joined ICSE 2010 in Cape Town, South Africa, where it had one of the highest attendance levels of any ICSE workshop, with 31 registered participants and about 10 drop-in observers. The fifth IWSC associated again with ICSE 2011, this time in Honolulu, Hawaii, hit also a big success among many ICSE workshops, with 39 registered participants.

A second Dagstuhl seminar took place in 2012 with the title "Software Clone Management Towards Industrial Application," where three of the five organizers were from industry. Unlike previous similar events, this Dagstuhl seminar put a particular emphasis on the industrial application of software clone management methods and tools and aimed at gathering concrete usage scenarios of clone management in industry, which was intended to help to identify new industrially relevant aspects in order to shape future research. Research in software clones is very close to industrial applications. Among other things, we focused on issues of industrial adoption of our methods and tools, which was made possible also by our strong industrial participation. We managed to reach a percentage of about 30% participants from the industry.

The partnership with ICSE continued for another 2 years until 2013. IWSC then departed from ICSE in 2014 and co-located with the first and last joint event of CSMR and WCRE in Antwerp, Belgium, where both conferences decided to merge into a new *IEEE International Conference on Software Analysis, Evolution and Reengineering (SANER)*. The reason to no longer co-locate with ICSE was simply because of ICSE's policy for workshops, which would not allow key role holders of a workshop to submit to their own workshop, which the steering committee of IWSC felt to be counterproductive for a small workshop with a clearly focused topic where strong contributors of the community often serve also in key roles of organizing scientific events around this topic.

The co-location with SANER was running successfully for several years, but it became increasingly difficult for our Japanese members to come to SANER because the time when SANER usually takes place collides with the annual time in which many Japanese universities have their final defenses of Bachelor and Master students, making it extremely difficult for both Japanese faculty and students to travel. Because the community of IWSC has a very strong base in Japan, the steering committee decided to co-locate with ICSME in the future. How this will work out, we will see very soon in the near future.

4   From Academia to Practice

After his graduation, the second author of this chapter became a Ph.D. student in the research group where the first author worked as a postdoc. Naturally, his intent was to continue with his work on clone detection. The head of the research group of the two authors of this chapter, however, considered clone detection to be a dead field and argued him out of pursuing research in this area. In hindsight, given the hundreds of publications that came after from a very large number of researchers around the globe, that was a capital misjudgment.

Working on static program analysis to detect structural flaws—known as bad smells or software erosion—and seeing an increasing interest in industry for such analyses, we decided to create a spin-off, which eventually became the company Axivion, officially founded in 2006 and now one of the leading companies on static analysis for stopping software erosion. Clone detection is just one kind of software erosion that can be detected by the tools provided by Axivion. The tool suite includes checkers for dead code, coding style violations, cyclic dependencies, architecture violations, metric outliers, and defects. Typically, companies will offer a large variety of such analyses, where clone detection is only one of them. There were other companies focusing on only clones, but they have not lasted long.

The focus of Axivion is not just detecting such flaws or technical debts, but really to manage them. In particular, for clones that means that clones will be tracked over time and if they are changed or even deleted, all developers ever having dealt with those clones—which can be retrieved from change history recorded in the version control system—will be informed. This way inconsistent changes may be avoided. This approach is parallel to what we have seen in research, where the focuses have shifted from pure clone detection to clone management.

4.1   Clone Detectors of Axivion and How They Came About

The tool suite of Axivion includes different clone detectors and those clone detectors have changed over time. There is a token-based clone detector for a large variety of languages including C, C++, C#, Java, and Ada, and a syntax-based clone detector for C, C++, and C#. Both have their roots in research.

The syntax-based clone detector follows the ideas by Baxter et al. [5], that is, hashing and comparing syntax trees. The program is represented by its syntax tree, then subtrees of this syntax tree are hashed into buckets, and finally, pairs of subtrees in the same bucket are compared to each other structurally. There is obviously more to that simplified summary, for instance, to deal with subtrees representing sequences, to filter subtrees considered clones subsumed by other subtrees also considered clones, and to detect subtrees forming type-3 clones. Those details can be found in the original paper [5].

There are a few differences between Axivion's syntax-based clone detector and the original approach outlined by Baxter et al. such as handling sequences and foremost that Axivion's syntax-based clone detector is based on a unified abstract syntax tree capturing all languages of interest (C, C++, and C#) together, which offers a way to add new languages without the need to change anything in the clone detector. As already shown in our comparative study that formed the starting point of our involvement in clone research in the first place [14, 15], syntax-based clone detection offers higher precision than other approaches—because all of its clones are guaranteed to be syntactic units—at, however, higher costs. The cost for the syntactic analysis, however, can be neglected here because the code needs to be parsed anyway to enable all other analyses offered by the Axivion tool suite. And the available syntactic information can be leveraged. As a more substantial enhancement, thus, Axivion's syntax-based clone detector offers preprocessing and postprocessing steps to transform the input and filter unwanted clones. These processing steps take advantage of the available information about the syntax and are, hence, more powerful than those suggested by Kamiya et al. [6] at the token level. The preprocessing steps of Axivion's syntax-based tool, for instance, allow one to exclude enum declarations in C which are very regular and thus re-occurring syntactic patterns due to the rigid C grammar for these; they can easily be falsely proposed as type-2 clones by token-based tools. These patterns can even be specified by the user.

The token-based clone detector of Axivion used today has its roots also in research, although it has gone through a series of more drastic changes. It started with a re-implementation of Brenda Baker's token-based approach based on so-called p-suffix trees [1]. A suffix tree is a very compact representation of all suffixes of a program, where the program is viewed as a sequence of tokens. The compact representation is achieved by putting two suffixes with a common prefix onto the same sequence of edges from the root to the node in the suffix tree at which the two suffixes start to be different. Obviously, if there are two suffixes with a common prefix, that means that this prefix occurs at least twice in the program and, hence, is a candidate for a clone. That is, clones can be detected simply by looking for inner nodes in the suffix trees whose depth is large enough to exceed a user-defined threshold for clones to be considered too short. This data structure has been developed a very long time ago for string matching. It could be straightforwardly used for detecting type-1 clones when a program is represented as a token sequence (the string). If we want to detect type-2 clones with consistent renaming, however, we need to abstract from the textual appearances of certain tokens (such as identifiers or literals) but not from their order of occurrences. The important contribution by Baker was to adapt the construction of a suffix tree to so-called p-strings rather than bare strings. A p-string in the context of clone detection is a sequence of tokens where certain types of tokens—called parameter tokens, e.g., identifiers and literals—are replaced by an index. That index abstracts from the textual appearance of parameter tokens but not from the order in which the parameter tokens appear. Through Baker's extension, it became possible to detect consistently renamed type-2 clones.

The first author became a professor at the University of Bremen where he continued to work on clone detection and implemented Baker's token-based approach in a tool written in the programming language Ada. In Bremen, he found yet another very talented student interested in clone detection, namely, Nils Göde. The task to be solved as part of his Diploma thesis was to devise and implement an approach to detect clones incrementally [21, 22]. Göde's implementation is based on a generalized suffix tree, already a known concept at that time capable of representing not only a single string but also multiple strings. In our case, each string would represent the token sequence of another version of the same program. The generalized suffix tree can be built incrementally and is, thus, very attractive if a series of program versions is to be analyzed as it is required when the evolution of clones is to be studied.

For the implementation of this incremental approach, Göde extended our existing re-implementation of Baker's token-based approach in Ada. Because Baker's concept of p-strings could not easily be adapted to generalized suffix trees, however, our Ada implementation ended up having two separate data structures: one suffix tree for p-strings and one generalized suffix tree for multiple ordinary strings, that is, strings without Baker's replacement of parameters through indices.

After Nils Göde finished his Diploma, he re-implemented the incremental approach as part of his Ph.D. research [23] in Java without Baker's concept of p-strings. The tool was named *iClones* and has since then been used by many other researchers in their studies, in particular, on the evolution of clones. The advantage of Baker's approach was to report only consistently substituted type-2 clones. Consistent substitution must be checked in a postprocessing step in *iClones*. On the other hand, inconsistently substituted clones would not be detected by Baker's approach and they maybe particularly interesting in evolutionary studies because they uncover inconsistencies during the evolution possibly hinting at oversights.

iClones was always available for academic users and has meanwhile become publicly available as open source.[1] It has never made it into the Axivion tool suite, however. *iClones* has its use case for analyzing a large series of program versions at once, which is often conducted in the context of research studies. Axivion, however,

---

[1] https://github.com/uni-bremen-agst/iclones.

offers tools that are integrated into the daily continuous integration process of companies, where typically the program is checked out and built once every night, then all analyses including clone detection are run and their results are stored in a database. Clone detection is only a small contributor to the computational resources needed and the time between analyzing two revisions of a program is long compared to the scenario where researchers analyze all revisions at once in a batch computation. In the latter case, holding the generalized suffix tree in memory makes sense, in the case of a continuous integration process that is triggered once per day, it would make less sense—in particular, because all other kinds of static analyzes are typically not incremental.

The currently used token-based clone detector in the Axivion tool suite was developed by the first author of this paper. It was a completely new development in C++ where a suffix array is used instead of a suffix tree. Suffix arrays are an alternative data structure to suffix trees with the advantage of being much more compact so that even the complete Linux kernel can be represented in memory of an ordinary computer. Other than that, it allows answering the same kind of questions as suffix arrays. The computational costs are dominated by scanning the source code from disk. The costs of the algorithm to construct the suffix array are negligible. The tool does not use Baker's concept of p-string so that inconsistently substituted type-2 clones can be detected, too.

This history of the development of clone detectors shows several interesting things. First, all those tools had their roots in research, which demonstrates that we as a research community may achieve an impact on practice. This may, however, be relativized by the fact that both authors were originally from academia (or still are) where they researched clone detectors. We do not know what effect our work has on tool developers that never show up at our scientific meetings. They may or may not read our research papers. Second, the path from an academic prototype to an industrial-strength tool may not always be straightforward. In case of the syntax-based clone detector, it was rather straightforward (although we should note that Baxter's original approach was enhanced by preprocessing and postprocessing steps to filter uninteresting clones), whereas the token-based clone detector has undergone a more substantial evolution. Third, the use cases of clone detectors in academia may not always apply to industrial applications, too. The incremental clone detection implemented in *iClones* has its strength in academic research where a large series of program versions is to be analyzed one after the other, which is rather different from an integration into a continuous integration process for a company's code on a daily basis.

4.2   Practical Experiences with Axivion's Clone Detectors

The primary tool used for clone detection in practical applications of the Axivion tool suite is the syntax-based clone detector because of its higher accuracy. A token-based detector may be used if a new programming language needs to be analyzed for which there is no abstract syntax tree and the costs for developing a parser generating such abstract syntax trees are prohibitive. A token-based detector may also be useful if the code of a potential client is analyzed in a workshop with limited time and resources to give a rough estimation on the degree of cloning quickly. Because it requires only a lexical analysis, the code can be incomplete or even be syntactically incorrect, and there is no need to integrate the tool into an often complicated existing build process as it would be required for syntactic tools.

The use of those clone detectors in practice emphasizes once more that cloning is a practically relevant issue. The clients of Axivion are aware of the problem and take it seriously. Tools that not only detect clones but also trace and manage clones over time are highly appreciated. The data gathered by the company with a syntax-based clone detector even suggests that proprietary code may have a higher clone rate than open-source programs. What was found for client code is higher than what we have found in open-source projects [24], even though the open-source study used a token-based clone detector that is known to have higher recall than the syntax-based clone detector used by Axivion [15].

The experience by Axivion indicates that the clone detectors available today seem to be "good enough" in general. They have sufficient recall and, in particular, the syntax-based clone detector provides sufficient precision, too. Yet, what constitutes a clone in a technically or formally correct sense may not always be meaningful to a user and more work needs to be done to distinguish meaningful clones from less interesting ones—a problem our research community has identified long ago and still has not solved. We have explored various kinds of filters to distinguish useful from useless clones in research, such as size, change rate, number of developers, etc. What we have not yet fully explored is additional semantic information on the clones. For instance, type-2 clones abstract from names, but maybe we should take a closer look at the categories of names. Renaming a local variable is likely more acceptable when it comes to similarity than calling different functions. Name binding, typing information, call contexts, and def-use chains have not been explored to make this distinction to the best of our knowledge. In other words, the semantics of the differences should be consulted.

5 Conclusions

In this chapter, we have retold the story of IWSC, which is the primary scientific event specifically on software clones. It somehow started on a spontaneous whim without a vision to form a community, but maybe someone else would have done something similar if we had not. The time seemed to be ripe for consolidating and foster a research community around software clones as evident by the fact that other researchers were also working on comparative studies and how sparks skipped and other people got involved so quickly.

When IWSC(D) was started, we would not have expected that software clones become such a long-lasting research topic. The contribution of IWSC to this research line is hard to assess. The problem of software clones was real (and still is) when the first publications on software clones came out—often conducted in the context of real and large software applications. IWSC started only after about one decade of prior research on clone detection, and hence we can argue that this topic would have continued to be researched without IWSC. Yet, the topic gathered momentum at the time when IWSCD started and IWSC may have served to get together the critical mass of researchers for that. Anyhow, IWSC has certainly succeeded in providing a forum to meet with other clone researchers as evident by the continuously high participation at the workshop and the joint papers and projects that came out of it as a result of researchers that had not been working together before. IWSC has definitely had a sustainable effect on our life as a researcher and tool developer and many ideas on research topics we investigated and techniques we developed in practical tools used in industry came from this community.

References

1. J. Mayrand, C. Leblanc, E.M. Merlo, Experiment on the automatic detection of function clones in a software system using metrics, in *IEEE International Conference on Software Maintenance* (1996), pp. 244–254
2. N. Göde, R. Koschke, Incremental clone detection, in *European Conference on Software Maintenance and Reengineering* (IEEE Computer Society Press, 2009), pp. 219–228
3. N. Göde, Incremental clone detection. Diploma Thesis, University of Bremen, 2008
4. T. Kamiya, S. Kusumoto, K. Inoue, CCFinder: a multi-linguistic token-based code clone detection system for large scale source code. Trans. Softw. Eng. **28**(7), 654–670 (2002)
5. I.D. Baxter, A. Yahin, L. Moura, M. Sant'Anna, L. Bier, Clone detection using abstract syntax trees, in *IEEE International Conference on Software Maintenance* (1998), pp. 368–378
6. S. Bellon, R. Koschke, G. Antoniol, J. Krinke, E. Merlo, Comparison and evaluation of clone detection tools. Trans. Softw. Eng. **33**(9), 577–591 (2007)
7. S. Carter, R.J. Frank, D.S.W. Tansley, Clone detection in telecommunications software systems: a neural net approach, in *International Workshop on Application of Neural Networks to Telecommunications* (1993), pp. 273–287
8. S. Bellon, Vergleich von Techniken zur Erkennung duplizierten Quellcodes. Master's thesis, University of Stuttgart, Germany, 2002
9. A. Charpentier, J.R. Falleri, F. Morandat, E.B.H. Yahia, L. Réveillère, Raters' reliability in clone benchmarks construction. Empir. Softw. Eng. **22**(1), 235–258 (2017)
10. C.K. Roy, J.R. Cordy, A mutation/injection-based automatic framework for evaluating code clone detection tools, in *International Conference on Software Testing, Verification, and Validation Workshops* (2009), pp. 157–166
11. C.K. Roy, J.R. Cordy, R. Koschke, Comparison and evaluation of code clone detection techniques and tools: a qualitative approach. Sci. Comput. Program. **74**(7), 470–495 (2009)
12. M. Stephan, Model clone detector evaluation using mutation analysis, in *IEEE International Conference on Software Maintenance and Evolution* (2014), pp. 633–638
13. A. Walker, T. Cerny, E. Song, Open-source tools and benchmarks for code-clone detection: past, present, and future trends. SIGAPP Appl. Comput. Rev. **19**(4), 28–39 (2020)
14. S. Ducasse, M. Rieger, S. Demeyer, A language independent approach for detecting duplicated code, in *IEEE International Conference on Software Maintenance* (1999)
15. J. Krinke, Identifying similar code with program dependence graphs, in *IEEE Working Conference On Reverse Engineering* (2001)

16. N. Göde, Clone evolution. Ph.D. Dissertation, Bremen, Germany: University of Bremen, 2011. ISBN: 978-3-8325-2920-8
17. J. Bailey, E. Burd, Evaluating clone detection tools for use during preventative maintenance, in *IEEE International Workshop on Source Code Analysis and Manipulation* (2002), pp. 36–43
18. B.S. Baker, Program for identifying duplicated code, in *Computer Science and Statistics 24: Proceedings of the 24th Symposium on the Interface* (1992), pp. 49–57
19. B.S. Baker, Finding clones with dup: analysis of an experiment. Trans. Softw. Eng. **33**(9), 608–621 (2007)
20. R. Koschke, S. Bazrafshan, Software-clone rates in open-source programs written in C or C++, in *International Workshop on Software Clones; published in Proceedings of IEEE International Conference on Software Analysis, Evolution and Reengineering*, vol. 3 (IEEE Computer Society Press, 2016), pp. 1–7
21. A. Lakhotia, J. Li, A. Walenstein, Y. Yang, Towards a clone detection benchmark suite and results archive, in *IEEE International Workshop on Program Comprehension* (2003), pp. 285–286
22. A. Walenstein, N. Jyoti, J. Li, Y. Yang, A. Lakhotia, Problems creating task-relevant clone detection reference data, in *IEEE Working Conference On Reverse Engineering* (2003), pp. 285–294
23. A. Walenstein, A. Lakhotia, R. Koschke, Second international workshop on detection of software clones: workshop report. ACM SIGSOFT Softw. Eng. Notes **29**(2), 1–5 (2004)
24. C. Roy, J.R. Cordy, A survey on software clone detection research. Technical Report No. 2007-541 (School of Computing, Queen's University at Kingston, Ontario, Canada, 2007)

Correction to: NiCad: A Modern Clone Entector

Manishankar Mondal, Chanchal K. Roy, and James R. Cordy

Correction to:
Chapter "NiCad: A Modern Clone Detector" in: K. Inoue
and C. K. Roy (eds.),
Code Clone Analysis,
https://doi.org/10.1007/978-981-16-1927-4_3

In the original version of the book, the following belated correction has been incorporated: In chapter "NiCad: A Modern Clone Detector", the author "J. R. Cordy's" affiliation has been changed from "Queen's University, Belfast, Northern Ireland" to "Queen's University, Kingston, Canada".

The correction chapter and the book have been updated with the change.

The updated version of this chapter can be found at
https://doi.org/10.1007/978-981-16-1927-4_3

Printed in the United States
by Baker & Taylor Publisher Services